And Then I Thought I Was a Fish

And Then I Thought I Was a Fish

Peter Welch

And Then I Thought I Was a Fish

Printed in the United States of America

First Printing: April 2012

ISBN: 978-0-9853181-3-0

12by3 Press
P.O. Box 110126
263 S 4th St.
Brooklyn, NY 11211-9997

www.12by3.com

For Trinity and Pocahontas

Thanks to Barb, Tom, Sam, Acadia Hospital, the guy in the restaurant, Jake, JD, Jun, Ashleigh, Norm, Dana, Jonathan, Deirdre, and Amy

Apologies to Big Drug, Earth Mother, Jake's parents, the waitresses, my employers, the Bar Harbor police department, the Southwest Harbor police department, the University of Maine, Sirius, Crow Abilities, everybody living on Maple Street, the woman Jake almost killed, the store Jake wrecked, the third floor of York Hall, the taxi driver whose car I stole, the woman whose truck I almost stole, and my parents

Introduction

Just the fact of having had a psychotic episode creates social difficulties, long after the business of actually having it is over.

The least successful year of my dating career was my stint at UMass, Amherst. This was partly because I lived in a dorm full of students from the suburbs whose life experiences differed somewhat from mine. I had a protracted conversation with my neighbors that I let unfold with sick fascination as I tried to communicate that when I wanted to borrow a bowl to smoke pot, I wasn't talking about cooking. This was the first year I let slip to a stranger that I'd been in a mental institution, and since it was one of those students, she immediately made some excuse to leave and stopped talking to me.

If she had known the whole story, she probably would have changed schools. Her initial reaction was just ignorance: plenty of people take a break in the nuthouse for minor breakdowns or other temporary and unshocking reasons. The appropriate response to "I was in a mental institution," is "Why?" Unfortunately for me, the answer to that question is "I had a full blown psychotic episode because I took too many drugs, thought I was Jesus, and stole some cars."

A decade later, I live in Brooklyn, I'm surrounded by jaded New Yorkers, and I work in IT,[1] so I have fewer professional and social worries about elaborating on this particular section of my life.

---

[1] Where an active cocaine habit isn't necessarily a deal breaker.

The summer of my twentieth year on the planet obliterated every measure of good, evil, truth, beauty, reality, and fantasy I'd had before, and makes everything that's happened since seem banal. It's the reason I will never believe in anything again, the reason I play music, and the reason the Acadia Hospital nursing staff thinks I'm a crackhead. There are probably three or four dozen people that won't talk to me to this day because of these events, and I am a local legend in Bar Harbor, Maine.

I'm writing this down for a number of reasons, first among them being that I'm sick of telling it. If I know somebody long enough, this story eventually comes up, and I have to tell it again with a varying level of detail depending on the listener's level of interest and my level of blood alcohol. The shortest, no-frills version that does it any amount of justice is upwards of half an hour. With questions it's usually a one- to two-hour conversation. Even I get bored talking exclusively about myself for more than forty-five minutes. If you have a good LSD story, it can take fifteen minutes to tell it in all its glory, and that's just an eight- to twelve-hour ride that feels a lot longer because your sense of time is on a lunch break. This story is about a 2,304-hour[2] ride, and my senses were a lot further gone than some measly industrial-grade psychedelic drugs could have taken them. It's just too long to tell.

I'm also telling it because I need to get it out of my head and I've been putting off getting it down in its entirety because it makes me feel weird thinking about it, as it is the cause of my PTSD.[3] But I think eleven years ago is long enough that I can dig through the memories without wigging out.

It's not all bad. My mind changed, chemically and psychologically, and ultimately for the better. It was also one of those crucial experiences secretly treasured by chaotic and intemperate people

---

[2] Approximated.

[3] I have a crippling fear of losing my mind, matched only by my pathological fear of death. Naturally, creative thinking lets me assuage my death fears, but also triggers the out-of-control free-associative process that triggers my PTSD and removes my ability to think or talk coherently, replacing it with shivering, anxious sweating for a few hours.

like me, in which the suffering and fallout are so monstrously disproportionate to the original sin that you are freed from judgment—internally, externally, and, at least in my case, cosmically.[4]

This is the complete, annotated, and unabridged story of how I went crazy for three months.

---

[4] Although, I'm sad to report, not legally.

Prelude 1: Why We Thought It Would Be Such a Great Idea to Drop Acid at Noon in Bar Harbor

Any good story of a stupendously bad decision should have a little preamble about how the decision, out of all decisions, was weighed and chosen.

Part of the reason I made this bad decision was because we—we being my heterosexual life-mate Jake and myself—had made nearly the same decision a month prior, and it worked out great. The fact is, acid is a blast unless it destroys your mind and life. Jake and I had just had what was possibly the perfect trip. It is the happiest I have ever been or ever will be. It was every existential dilemma not just cast aside, but thoroughly solved. All the answers of life, the universe, and everything were laid at our feet, the whole of creation stepped out from behind the curtain and said, "Yes, it's okay, this is how it works, everything is fine, and you're pretty cool."

This is how it began:

One morning, Jake said, "Fuck it, let's do some acid."

At the end of my table-waiting shift, a friend of mine walked up to me and said, "I would like to shake your hand," shook my hand, and put a ten strip of acid into it.

There's no better preparation for an acid trip.

We started at about midnight. Maybe later. Lesson 1: Midnight is a better time to start tripping than noon. You have a little time to get a handle on things before you have to deal with people. This was Jake's first trip, so we worked our way gently through the opening stages.[1] You have to bounce around with tripping. It comes in waves; at the top of each wave, reality falls apart a little more, you lose your sense of what's real, the subject/object, other/self dichotomies break apart, you're not sure why, then you come back down a bit and remember you're on drugs and everything's okay. We wandered around, getting more and more tripped out, then found ourselves on the beach, at dawn, at the exact moment we started peaking.

I don't know what this acid was. I heard George Washington print and Tim Leary print.[2] It would not have surprised me if this was the concoction that got Tim so worked up for the second half of his life.

Bar Harbor has a neat little feature, which is a sand bar that bridges a smallish island to the main-ish land (Bar Harbor is on an island to begin with) at low tide. At that moment, while we were peaking, just after dawn, the tide was as low as we'd ever seen it, leaving a vast walkway to this island, the fringes of which were covered in sparkling green sea plants and scuttling sea bugs. Directly above this bridge, the sky was split as if by a razor: to our left, black storm clouds stretching to the western horizon, to our right, crystal blue sky with the perfectly yellow sun coming over the sea. It was in the low 70s.

At this point we were already beside ourselves with joy. We headed across the bar to the island.

A dog ran up to us, which was the funniest thing ever, for some reason. If you haven't done acid, but have smoked pot, acid giggles are like pot giggles . . . well, on acid. The dog ran back to some other people, and we just kept moving, not wanting to kill our vibe by running into sober kids.[3] At some point Jake bursts out laughing and points to a kid lying comatose on the beach, wearing a Grateful

---

[1] There will be inevitable homoerotic overtones to much of this chapter.

[2] "Print" refers to a particular batch of paper acid produced, denoted by the artwork stamped on the sheet.

[3] We should have known that nobody awake at dawn in Bar Harbor is sober and we needn't have worried.

Dead tie-dye T-shirt. We laugh about it, then stop and look at each other.

"Uh. He might be dead," giggle.

"Dude."

"Let's check on him."

We wander back and notice he's severely bruised around his face and shoulders.

"Uh, dude. You okay?"

He snorts, opens his eyes and looks up at us.

"Never better," he says, then rolls over and goes back to sleep.

This is the funniest thing in the history of the universe to us, so we walk on, holding our sides laughing. We start up the winding trail that leads to the open field on the peak of the island and notice the two people attached to the dog behind us. We assume they're hippie tourists. Then we think they're following us. So we walk on.

It's extremely difficult to make progress in any specific direction while tripping. You have to keep stopping and watching the leaves wave at you, the clouds burst into fractal mosaics, the ground writhe with life, and think about how it all means stuff and you can see every tiny detail of your tripping buddy's body, mind, and soul and how it's ebbing and flowing with the energy of the sound—which you can see, by the way—and the pulse of the cosmos. At least, on this acid you could. We communicated in total nonsense language and knew exactly what was meant. So we would head up the trail at a good clip, half-believing the people behind us were stalking us, then get distracted by something that was the awesomest thing ever except for that other thing that happened what time is it oh shit they're following us again.

After an hour or so of this, we came to a bend in the trail where the roots had created a kind of stairway landing and the trees a natural gazebo roof, and I said, "Let's see who these guys are."

"Well, this is totally the place to do it."

"What's the worst that could happen?"

Reflecting on this, a lot of bad things could have happened, but we were clearly harmless, and they looked just as harmless. I have to give some back and future story to explain how ridiculous the identities of our stalkers turned out to be.

The one I'll call Pill Dude was a guy I met at a college party in Orono five months prior. We'd gotten sick of the frat kids and gone upstairs to do a fairly obscene amount of Ritalin off the washer-dryer combo, and we'd bonded over a bunch of college stories the way you do when you're getting high on prescription ampheta-mines.

I'd never met the person with him, and in fact I knew him for several months before I figured out who he was: he was the gay kid who dated an ex-girlfriend in college right after me and right before she killed herself, after which he got sent home because he lost it for a couple of months. She was the only girl he ever dated or had any interest in dating. I'd heard endless stories about him while I was still in Massachusetts. We knew all the same people. People told us we should meet. We didn't, until two years later, on an is-land, on LSD, at 8:00 A.M., six hundred miles away from where we'd previously lived two miles from each other for a year. Call him Red.

At the moment, I was more stunned to see Pill Dude.

"Pill Dude!"

"Pete!"

"We're on acid!"

"Us too!"

"The GW stuff?"

"Totally!"

"We thought you were stalking us!"

"We were!"

Then we all fell over laughing. I didn't even know the story behind Red, and this seemed like the craziest coincidence ever. It's obviously not, but if I put it in a movie, no one would believe it. After a couple of cigarettes and some catching up, we pulled our-selves together and made it to the top of the island and lay around in the grass. If anybody had happened upon us, we would have looked like your average group of tripped-out hippies, except that the only person not sitting up was Red, who, for no reason either he or Pill Dude could explain, looked like he'd just been beaten up by a bar mob. It took us a while to notice, but he was covered in blood and bruises, so what it actually looked like was three WASP kids just beat a gay kid to death.[4] We had a laugh about that, then headed out and naturally parted ways.

There are some hazy points, but I remember an animated conversation with a gas station attendant who said Jake and I were sweet kids, then we watched the storm brew until it started to rain, then we went back to my place and played with loose change and dark lights for a while. For a good hour, we were crying with joy over the perfect beauty of everything in the universe. Then we watched American Movie, as self-referential documentaries are about the best thing you can watch on acid. We giggled at the water from the storm we'd watched form over the last fourteen hours as it dripped through my ceiling. As we came down and realized how many cigarettes we'd smoked,[5] we still felt the perfect harmony of everything, and felt like better, healthier people for at least three weeks. It was the perfect weird and amazing combination of coincidence and really good drugs.

Acid is not like pot, or alcohol, or any other "mind-altering" drug. You don't know what mind-altering means unless you've been on a serious psychedelic trip.[6] It's like you suddenly realize you've been seeing the world in two dimensions and now you can see four. The rules change. People around you become perfectly comprehensible and beautiful creatures, instead of the average dicks they are most of the time. I reject completely that acid doesn't bring some insight about the universe; yes, it's all in your head, but so is the everyday, non-tripping, non-psychotic universe. You have one tool with which to experience the totality of your conscious life; if you make any deductions about the world around you with it, you have

---

[4] I also didn't know Red was gay until six months after meeting him. I swear I'm not that blind, it just never came up, and he didn't have any tells. I mean, our favorite pastime was to non-euphemistically punch each other in the parking lot. And it's not like Red's a little gay, or maybe gay; he did gay porn, and not just for the money.

[5] A lot. People who trip and smoke often refer to "The Eternal Cigarette" because it seems like your cigarette never goes out. This is only because you chain smoke and never remember lighting the one in your hand.

[6] Or lost your mind in some other fashion.

to reevaluate your deductions when you realize you can interpret the world in a completely alien way by rewiring your perceptions with a fraction of a gram of chemicals. Acid puts the whole meaning-and-being-versus-reality play you leave on the TV as background noise directly in front of you on an IMAX screen with surround sound and popcorn. Whatever experience of the universe there is to be unveiled by the modern human brain, an investment-worthy percentage of it can be seen during a good acid trip.

The moment for us, the thing that we held on to for weeks afterward, was that the universe *Is*. It just Is. Everything, in fact, Is, in pure simplicity. Despite the fact that every time I went to the bathroom in my red and black striped shirt I would look in the mirror and see a fluctuating combination of myself, my father, and Calvin from *Calvin and Hobbes*, I knew these were all forms my brain was playing with on top of my perfect Is-ness. Coming to Aldous Huxley late in life, I was struck by my experience's similarity to this passage from the Doors of Perception:

> *Istigkeit*—wasn't that the word Meister Eckhart liked to use? "Is-ness." The being of Platonic philosophy—except that Plato seems to have made the enormous, the grotesque mistake of separating Being from becoming and identifying it with the mathematical abstraction of the Idea. He could never, poor fellow, have seen a bunch of flowers shining with their own inner light and all but quivering under the pressure of the significance with which they were charged; could never have perceived that what rose and iris and carnation so intensely signified was nothing more, and nothing less, than what they were—a transience that was yet eternal life, a perpetual perishing that was at the same time pure Being, a bundle of minute, unique particulars in which, by some unspeakable and yet self-evident paradox, was to be seen the divine source of all existence.

This experience of is-ness is like seeing a thing as it is when it makes its first, jarring entrance into the mind; the way a place is surprising and wondrous the first time you see it, and completely forgettable after a week of regular visits. The experience of is-ness is like seeing everything from the perspective of a fully conscious being opening its eyes for the first time and having its first visual perception, and never letting its brain regulate any property of the objects before its eyes into assumption or memory. The categorizing of input that lets the brain regulate important and unimportant data ceases, along with the normal restraint the brain shows in not applying fun patterns to incoming sense data. Every change of shade and color takes on its own visual history, seeming to exist over a second or two, and not necessarily the same seconds as the color next to it. In this stretched and visually fragmented sense of time, each motion and surface takes on its own perspective, separate from but in harmony with the perspectives and time frames of its neighboring surfaces and motions. The patterns of the mind apply themselves to the experience of the senses and the world, and the differences between all things crumble in the ecstasy of being as music, musician, and audience, at once observing and observed, being the object and subject of consciousness.

My mind, even if I'm drunk out of it and commanding it to work better, is not capable of the happiness we achieved during those sixteen hours. Much as I love the universe, it will never be as beautiful, barring a radical shift in the nature of being human.

Why wouldn't we do it again?

Prelude 2: Why I Should Have Known Better

The first time I did acid did not go so well. I went in thinking it would be like getting extra high on good weed. I was utterly innocent of the degree to which my mind could be stretched, and I took it as a way to escape some very difficult emotional issues, so I was depressed and on edge.

It was about three years prior to the events above. I don't know how it came up, but it seemed like a good idea. The brand of acid was Purple Jesus, and was purported to be "triple-dipped," which meant nothing to me. It was two small pieces of paper. Since I had been setting a large amount of green plants on fire and inhaling them on a regular basis, I wasn't too worried. I figured it would help take my mind off things.

I dimly remember the beginning, when the lights seemed to drag a bit. A couple of hours later, my fatefully unprepared dealer and "guide" had decided I should be locked in a dorm room with a group of more experienced people, and maybe a couple of large men.

I lost all sense of time and space. The world was passing by in fractal patterns. In the rare moments I could distinguish faces, they immediately melted into red and green triangles and blended with the background, which was waving and spinning. I sat on the couch and the floor, staring at people with a giant grin on my face, totally unable to comprehend what they were saying, except for a period where I was watching three people who may or may not have been there having this conversation:

"It's like . . . déjà vu."

"Like it's . . . coming back around on itself."

"Like everything's . . . repeating."

I watched this conversation about three hundred times, in my head. I don't know if it even happened once, but I do know that while I was watching it, people's heads were swiveling toward me like owls' heads. At one point I thought I was in Vietnam, and artillery was going off while civilians were being torn apart by tigers. In the middle of it, I managed to go to the bathroom, with some guidance, and made the mistake of looking in the mirror, where I saw a deranged, demonic clown staring back at me. I have no idea what happened in what order.

At the peak, all connection to reality was gone. The sum of my consciousness floated away from me in frames forming an infinitely complex and inescapable maze that I saw from no vantage point, since my vantage points past and present were floating away from me and twisting themselves in the million-dimensional knot both in and around my head. There was nothing left of me, and it wasn't precisely fear or love or non-ego or ego or bad or good or waking or dreaming or consciousness or unconsciousness. It was the total detonation of my brain.

After that, I became obsessed with time, since the clock occasionally said 4:00, sometimes 9:00, sometimes 13:92, and got stuck switching between 5:01 and 5:02 for significantly longer than it should have. I was constantly afraid I was dying, but had no way to communicate this to anyone, and they made me feel uncomfortable and unworthy when I tried to talk to them, although I expect they were doing their best to keep me sane and intact, as tiring as it must have been.

When the trip ran its course, I was traumatized for days. I wasn't sure what was real. I went to my predominantly non-tripping friends and asked them to take care of me for a while.

I swore off acid until a couple of years later, when I met Big Drug at the University of Maine. This nickname is a little unfair, since we'd been enabling one another for the entire previous year. He got me back into acid; I got him into kiddy crack.[1] I distantly recall one session, on April 20, 2000, wherein Heineken had all the

---

[1] ADD medications used recreationally.

weed, but wanted to drink, Big Drug had all the beer, but wanted Ritalin, and I had all the Ritalin, but wanted weed. You can imagine how this played itself out. In the end, Heineken made a dash for the bathroom, and we listened to him throw up for about fifteen minutes. Finally, I got up and said, "Well, I'm calling it," and proceeded to shake uncontrollably until I snapped forward, bounced off the table, grabbed for the chair, took it down with me, and twitched on the floor until I blacked out. I came to about five seconds later, with Big Drug gaping at me.

"Dude. What the fuck?"

When he tells this story, he describes spending the next hour thinking, "What's going to happen to me?"

Big Drug and I partied extensively in our rooms because we lived directly across the dorm wing from each other, on either side of the bathroom that connected the hallways, so it was a ten-second commute. We both had two-person dorm rooms with roommates who'd been kicked out of school, and we both liked doing lots of drugs. He was the most charismatic twenty-year-old I've ever known, with big smiles and an easy, funny manner. He told some of the best stories I've ever heard. Most of the jokes I make about my present-day ego are stolen from him. His lovability made up for the fact that he'd blown out his episodic memory with copious hallucinogens: he would regularly look at me intently for several minutes, nodding while I talked, and making little "Mmhm" sounds, then suddenly stop me and say, "Sorry, dude, I was totally somewhere else. What were you talking about?" Things that stayed in his room for more than a month just became his, though he'd come round if you described exactly how it wasn't his for ten to fifteen minutes. He also blatantly stole one of my stories after convincing himself that it had happened to him, despite the fact that I could call people to verify that it had happened to me.

Prior to the adventure with Jake, I had my last mushroom trip with Big Drug. The acid trips we had together were always fun, but we had a fundamental problem with mushrooms: he peaked immediately and was on his way down after three hours, which was right when I was coming up, so we only had an hour or so overlap when we did them together. The last time we did this, right as we were nearing our overlap, the following things happened, in order:

We couldn't get the DVD player to work.

The cappuccino machine exploded, complete with sparks and smoke.

We couldn't find his cat.

Something started dying horribly in the woods, probably a porcupine.

When we went into the woods to see if the screaming involved his cat, we simultaneously started seeing giant, thirty-legged spiders in the dark, so we fled.

After finally getting the movie started, he gets a call from his girlfriend, and she asks to talk to me. This is our conversation:

"Hey, Pete. I'm mad at my boyfriend."

"Uh, hi. I'm on a whole bunch of drugs right now, so maybe you shouldn't tell me about—"

"You know what, I don't need people telling me what to say or do right now. Give the phone back to my boyfriend."

After ten minutes of what sounds like a trying conversation on the phone, Big Drug agrees to drive to where she's staying with her friend, about an hour and forty minutes from where we were. I can't even attempt to dissuade him, because by then I'd lost the ability to form coherent sentences. I would start with "I . . ." and the rest of it would just drip away in double meanings and semantic quandaries and I'd have to wait fifteen minutes to try again.

When we finally get there, I'm beginning to recover, and Big Drug's girlfriend's friend opens the door. I'm going to call her Victim, because she'd obviously just been beaten up, and I later discovered she'd been beaten up by her boyfriend and spent a fair amount of the evening trying to convince us he "wasn't that bad a guy."

Tired from our near-two-hour drive, and still tripping, we follow Victim's technicolor purple and blue bruises up the stairs and sit down to watch some documentary, or maybe MTV. Immediately, Big Drug's girlfriend stands up and says, "I'm going to have a cigarette on the porch with Peter, *not* Big Drug."

Desperate for a cigarette, I follow her out to the porch and light up.

"Hey, Peter. How are you doing?"

"Eh," I say.

"I'm having a nervous breakdown."

"Uh . . . nervous breakdowns can be kind of like dominos, so—"

"So my friend Jen[2] really misses you. She talks about you a lot and wants to see you again, and I really think you should call her because she needs someone to talk to and someone in her life right now because she's in a bad place and I think she might do something bad to herself if you don't call her."

To this day, I do not know who Jen is.

I say, "Okay," and try to finish my cigarette quietly. Big Drug and his girlfriend reach some kind of resolution, or at least stalemate, allowing us all to go to bed, where I watch the giant, hallucinatory spiders crawl around the ceiling for a few hours.

The point is, I knew by now that difficult things can happen on strong hallucinogens, and you have to pay attention to one's mindset and circumstances, or set and setting as Leary would say.

When Jake and I took our next trip, our set was unadulterated arrogance, and our setting was Bar Harbor, Maine.

---

[2] Name changed, I think.

Everything Goes Straight to Hell

Acadia National Park contains most of what I love about Maine. Rocky mountains, hidden streams and valleys, rainwater lakes, ocean views that stretch to the horizon, and hikes short enough for the average smoker to complete without too much complaint. If you wander through the park with people who know how to shut up once in a while, you can almost trick yourself into believing you've been spirited away to some forever fairy realm, never to return.

Bar Harbor, where most people sleep and eat while visiting, is a scum-laden monument to cheap excess and exploitation. Come June, in a town that spent eight months subsisting on fewer notable businesses than the fingers on a lobsterman's hands,[1] junk shops and hippy traps and overpriced restaurants pop up overnight, as their out-of-state owners return to thaw out their commercial zones and suck the tourist teat so they can cart the money back out of the state. By day the streets are lousy with Hawaiian shirts and ambling families buying moose hats and lobster ice cream. By night, the bars are packed with all the local employees pumping money into liquor and drugs with the visiting rich kids.

Since everybody works two or more service jobs, wraps up the night with a pocketful of cash, and lives in temporary housing that would make a section-8 contractor cry, the Bar Harbor summer

---

[1] For those of you who don't know any lobstermen, this is fewer than you think.

scene for a waiter is a nonstop orgy of drugs, booze, and sex.[2] I went to Simon's Rock, and Simon's Rock has nothing on a Bar Harbor summer.

Enter me, with five hits of acid, on August 13, 2000.

If you get a good acid trip going, you feel like a god. People become easy. Everything becomes easy. You can do things you can't do sober. Or at least you can do them without all the pesky practicing you have to do while sober. It seems like you can see right through people. All the tiny, subliminal signals we respond to, and that are written about in books on body language and poker tells, are right in front of your face and flashing pretty colors.

A veteran tripper knows to be careful. Even a budding pro, as I was, knows that you can lose control if you get too much confusing input, like, say, a tourist town in August. Jake didn't realize this, and he was so eager, and the last trip was so, so good, I figured we could rock the day the same way we'd rocked the night.

We did our two and a half hits around eleven in the morning. One thing I didn't find out until later was that Jake was operating on two hours of sleep, and was perhaps not in the most stable state of mind. It probably wouldn't have stopped us.

What happened next requires a map. In this case, a very small black and white map, due to cost constraints.

---

[2] Unless you have no game, like I didn't. Many of my bad decisions probably could have been avoided by getting a little action back in the day.

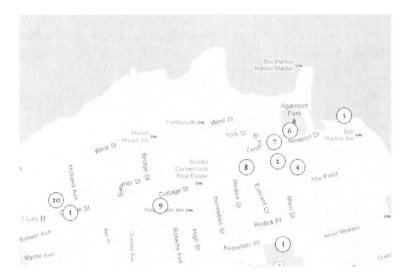

Bear in mind this whole journey is probably less than two miles, and was completed over the course of two or three hours. Here is what happened at each point on the map.

1: At the apartment

We hang out at my apartment until the acid kicks in a little bit, and head out right after the first peak. We both have backpacks filled with toys, which is indicative of one of our many mistakes: we planned too much, especially Jake, who just didn't understand the finer points of tripping yet, one of the basic rules being you can't over-prepare, because you will quickly get frustrated by your inability to achieve anything. It's like meditating: you can't order your mind to empty, or demand a revelation. You know that guy who always wants to create an intimate moment when nobody's drunk enough, and it ends up forced and awkward? Like that. The difference with acid is that the consequences of trying to make something happen that won't are infinitely worse.

No matter. I would teach my student well, and we would again ascend to Olympus.

We hit the street at noon. I would say we were the two dumb-est people in Bar Harbor that day, but that couldn't possibly be true, and Jake had no idea of the risks, whereas I did and I ignored them, so I was by far the dumber companion.

I sent a draft of this chapter to Jake, so there will be some of his commentary and corrections, but I'm leaving in what I remember, even if it's wrong in places. Here's Jake:

> We dropped the tabs then went to the grocery store, after picking up some tripping toys from the chick that lived in the upstairs apartment next to yours, and bought a bunch of food; most notably way too much dried fruit. Then we headed to the park. Also, I'm pretty sure me met up with a wait-ress (who happened to be in my class from grade school through high school and whom I'd known since I was eleven years old, and I will admit that I had a crush on her for at least a few of those years) at a local restaurant to make plans for her to later drive you to Massachusetts that night.

2: Corner of Cottage and Main

We hit an intersection. Things are starting to get a little trippy, and there are a lot of people on the street. I am not yet questioning the wisdom of our journey, but even after all my experience with acid, I'm beginning to have trouble focusing. Whatever. We head for the park.

3: The park

We take off our backpacks and sit in the park, then stare at the sky, since the visuals are really taking off. We're still happy at this point and mostly just giggling and looking at stuff.

In one of the most awesome events that has ever occurred to me in any state of mind, one of the landscapers working on the park, about fifty and heavily bearded, walks by us, leans down, and says:

"The effect's better on mushrooms."

I know I claimed many things were the funniest thing ever in the first chapter, but this was absolutely the funniest thing that has ever happened. We crack up, wave at him, and think this will be even better than the first time.

4: Cutting down to the water

This is the moment where I start to worry about Jake. He starts repeating himself. He also starts commenting on how fake everything and everybody is. And he starts mentioning, just offhand, how we can do anything we want. It is very important, when tripping, to maintain a death grip on the knowledge that you can *not* do anything you want. Physics and legal systems have a way of making themselves known when you forget this.

The repeating himself bit is also bad. Tripping is by turns neurotic and psychotic: the neurotic moments are about obsessing over some unspeakable fact of the universe that you can finally acknowledge and communicate to others in a way you simply can't when you're not tripping.[3] Then somebody makes a joke and you remember it's all a joke and the world is pretty and it's someone else's turn to talk. People spend their whole lives on acid because tripping with a few other people is just a long night of the best conversations you'll never be able to have again and the greatest jokes you've ever heard.

But Jake wasn't hearing my jokes, or my attempts to get him out of his neurotic cycle, and this is why you have guides on your first few trips, because, very occasionally, when people get like that, they don't come back. The odds aren't high, but it doesn't take a lifetime of drug abuse to wreck a mind: one bad trip will do it. Al-

---

[3] You just can't. I've tried. Many people much smarter than I am have tried. You are in the moment of knowing it or you're not. Leary was right: 4000 years of philosophy look laughably pointless after eight hours on acid.

bert Hoffman put it best, while discussing the early complacence with LSD experimentation:

> Like the other hallucinogens, however, LSD is dangerous in an entirely different sense. While the psychic and physical dangers of the addicting narcotics, the opiates, amphetamines and so forth, appear only with chronic use, the possible danger of LSD exists in every single experiment. This is because severe disoriented states appear during any LSD inebriation. It is true that through careful preparation of the experiment and the experimenter such episodes can be largely avoided, but they cannot be excluded with certainty. LSD crises resemble psychotic attacks with a manic or depressive character.

I decide we need to get away from the crowds, and make a right, toward the beach.

5: By the ocean

We sit on the rocks and check out the ocean. I decide maybe a game of Go will focus us and get back on track, so I whip out my travel board and try to get him to play. He's having none of it. He stares at the board for a few seconds, possibly attempting to play, then swats a few pieces out to sea and shouts:

"Just be! We can just BE!" in my face.

I realize this is bad, and we have to get home, immediately. I pack up what's left of the Go pieces and start strongly but carefully hinting that we should make our way back to my place. It takes about twenty minutes, or in on-acid-next-to-your-freaking-out-best-friend time, six hundred years.

Here's Jake:

> There was a good amount of time on the beach where the clouds were spelling out words, a la Yel-

low Submarine. You kept asking me what they said as I kept repeating this was so but I told you I couldn't read what words they were, just that they were words. I do distinctly remember knowing, and saying to you, that it wasn't possible for clouds to spell words but my eyes were telling me they were.

6: Turning back

After leading us across a park full of hippies, which was stupid but seemed to calm him down—and more importantly, or so I thought, calm me down, since I was now the only person capable of being responsible for us—I make the next worst decision of my life, which is to lead us back up to the main shopping drag. Considering I specifically led us away from the main drag six hundred years prior, I can only guess I was trying to find the fastest route back, assuming I could control Jake's decaying mindset. You will notice from the map that there was an obvious route back that was almost the same distance and didn't involve walking down the worst road in Bar Harbor. It can be hard to walk down it stone sober.

Acid's a powerful drug.

And it didn't matter. We didn't even make it to the main drag. Here's Jake:

> In the park I actually fall on the grass, flailing and rolling around like a cat in catnip, and only have a moment of clarity and get up to follow you when I look up at you, after you trying to coax me up and away, and you say, "Fine, I'm leaving, you can get arrested." Halfway across the park I hear a booming echo that drowns out every sound on the very busy street and if I want to my voice becomes this echo. I vaguely recall mentioning this to you but perhaps I am mistaken.

7: Coming up Main

Jake is still in we-can-do-anything mode.

"We can say whatever we want!"

"Yes, that's true, let's just head this way, okay?"

"We can do whatever we want!"

"Yes, as long as the cops don't get involved. Come on, we can do anything we want at my apartment."

"We can go anywhere! I'm going to go in here."

Poof.

Jake dives into a clothing and trinket store.

This is the exact moment that changes my life forever.

I didn't know this yet. At the time, I was peaking on two and a half hits of the best acid I'd ever had, so I sit down on a bench and start chatting up a Hawaiian T-shirt, since there's no way I'm following Jake into the store.

"How do you like Bar Harbor?"

"Uhh. Is your friend okay?"

"I have no idea. You here with family?"

"Um . . . huh . . . yes, we're just . . ."

At this point he looks inside the store. I have no idea what's happening; I'm just trying to focus and I sense I'm losing my conversation partner.

"Have you been on the whale watch tour?"

He's obviously uncomfortable, and I'm trying to soothe him.

"Where are you from?"

At this point, the conversation ends, as Jake comes flying, nearly sideways, out of the door. This is not just drugs: it's a cinematic exit. Sans backpack. It looked like he was hurled out of the store by a two-hundred-pound bouncer. He hits the bench with his leg, gives the finger to the store, and starts stalking down the street.

I turn to my new friend. "Nice to meet you, I need to check up on him."

My new friend had already fled like he'd just met two drugged-out nut cases. I hope I didn't give him a stroke. I run after Jake and try to be practical.

"Jake, what happened to your backpack?"

"We can do what we want!"

"Yeah, yeah, I know, what happened to your backpack?"

"Just be!"

Things are not going well, but I can still get him to follow me, so we continue to the corner, and start down the main drag.

Here's Jake:

> Once inside the store I sort of don't remember where I am or how I got there for a moment. An employee asks me, "Can I help you?" I look at him then turn to a stack of sweaters on a shelf and think something like, "Those would be soft," and hug them like a child, then fall backwards to the ground, pulling them with me. Then I have another moment of clarity and think, "I gotta get out of here." Apparently, I found out later, when I hit the bench outside I tore the bolt holding it down out of the concrete. It didn't even leave a bruise, though it probably should have broken my hip.

8: Across from The Thirsty Whale

Jake is shouting nonsense and flipping off strangers. Bar Harbor in the summer is not like New York City. People notice when you're nuts. The tourists are not amused. People are protecting their children and crossing the street. He knocks over one of those chalkboard restaurant advertisements and kicks it for good measure. His mood swings are astounding: He's laughing for two seconds, then crying for three, then angry for two, repeat. I'm trying to manhandle him down the street, and at some point, as I'm apologizing to strangers with hand gestures while keeping my own mind together and trying to prevent Jake from pissing anybody new off, I turn to look at him and he's as angry as a wounded wolf mother and screams:

"Juuust BE!" and smacks me across the face.

Then bursts into tears.

Then starts stalking down the street again.

I'm terrified, in a way that you can only be terrified when you've just fed your best friend hallucinogens and it looks like he might kill somebody on his way to eternal madness in the most public place in America east of Vegas. I realize I'm going to have to get physical, and I run up to him, say something I assume was brilliant, and keep a grip on his shoulder as I walk us down the street.

9: Almost home

What I didn't know at this point was that the Bar Harbor police force was already in hot pursuit. I wasn't looking behind me as I had all four eyes—plus the wacky one that comes out of your forehead when you're on great drugs—fixated on Jake's every move. It's not enough. He breaks free, laughing, and starts running down the street. I'm almost too late when I realize what he's running toward, which is a young woman helping a very old woman out of a car.

I know exactly what's going to happen, and I start running faster than any human has ever run before, since Jake's wiry, fast, and already halfway there. I get in front of him at exactly the moment he jumps up with a whoop and kicks the car door, which would have broken half the bones in this grandmother's body had I been a tenth of a second slower and not already had a grip on the door. I push Jake back and apologize profusely, and, for some reason I will never understand, the younger woman smiles at me as if it's okay. This may have been because Jake was back in sobbing mode, and stumbling away. I assume she assumed we were drunk. I'm not sure how that makes it okay, but since this situation was entirely my fault, I was taking what I could get.

Here's Jake:

> And this is, beyond any other, the reason I will never do acid again. I also have absolutely no recollection of this whatsoever.

10: Back at the apartment

I manage to get Jake home, after only one or two near deaths, and in getting him in the door I also inadvertently and unknowingly shake the impressive police force that's been chasing us.

Once I get him inside, he starts rolling on the floor moaning. It's an endless loop alternating between an unenthusiastic, "Well, we might as well" in a British accent and a much more enthusiastic, "Just be!"

Here's Jake:

> The before-mentioned waitress showed up with a friend and basically all three of you stared at me rolling on the floor mumbling until they decided to leave.[4] I also recall trying, very ineffectively, to play your bass while repeating nonsense ad nauseum.

At this point I settle in for the ride and wonder how many hours of this I have to endure.

Turns out to be one, since an hour after we get home, Jake's older brother calls me.

"Pete?"

"Dude, you will not believe the day I've had."

"Uh, yeah, I think I might. My dad's on his way to your place. With the police."

"FUCK. Thanks."

I hang up, and shout at Jake.

"Jake! Them! Here! Coming! Run!"

This breaks through Jake's loop, and we book it.

We dash out of the apartment and I take us up to the apartment next door. This was more shitty housing, occupied by up to eight temp service industry workers that I'd befriended over the summer. Improbably, nobody was there, which in retrospect is the best possible condition for the apartment to have been in. I wanted

---

[4] This explains why I didn't get my ride from her later that night.

someplace that wasn't on the cops' radio, and I wanted help. Storming into this apartment on acid with the cops on their way would not have improved my relationship with anyone in that apartment, but, since I didn't keep in touch with any of them, if I could rewrite history in a shortsighted way, I would have written in one of the more mature residents to take care of us and deal with the cops properly and accepted the fact that I'd instantly lost eight friends, as opposed to losing them the usual way. As it was, we were completely alone. Jake somehow lost a shoe, and he had to go back for it later, which must have been a conversation I'm sorry to have missed.

Jake sat down on a chair. Then he screamed.

I've heard a lot in my life. I worked in an institute for the mentally-screwed-beyond-all-hope-of-repair. I went to several liberal arts schools and almost as many state colleges. I've seen people tweak. I've seen people die, afraid, and needing help.

Nothing will match Jake's scream. Nothing will match the moment of tripping my ass off, watching one of the two friends I consider family screaming in a way that logically contradicted his being human. If you've ever heard a porcupine scream, you've felt true fear. This was worse. This was a thinking human screaming from a half a billion years ago when its crustacean ancestor was murdered by a hive of Japanese horror movie monsters. I shudder to this day at the memory of the sound.

I am paralyzed as completely as if he'd been a banshee and killed me with his cry, so I'm unprepared when he dashes down the stairs. I dash after him, and see him again as he's running into the street, waving his arms, screaming, directly into the arms of the police and his father. I run after him, screaming.

"Jake! Jake! JAAAKE!"

This is when I have my first and last out-of-body experience. Most of the out-of-body experiences I've read about are gentle things that happen near death or in dreams. Mine was more like a mallet whacking my mind out of my head where it could be dragged away from my body by rabid harpies.

As I'm screaming Jake's name, the universe stalls. My brain ceases. I am in the midst of perfect experience. My senses collapse into each other, my train of thought jumps the tracks, I pull back in a melodramatic Hollywood zoom out, to the sound of the single note of my own screaming. I see my body in front of me, surrounded by cops and my screaming friend, and the universe and all my senses and perceptions fly together into my body in front of me as I drift powerless above it, in a giant collapsing X.

To be precise, the universe was collapsing into my bowels, which may explain why I shit myself at this point.

I snapped back into the more standard, consciousness-in-my-body state, to see Jake's father trying to hold Jake's arms back.

"I don't know what the hell you're getting him into," says my best friend's father. He has nothing more to say to me. I turn my head and there's a cop six inches in front of my face.

"What's he on? We need to know!"

"Two and a half hits of acid."

"Thank you."

Jake shoves another cop away from him, and the cop says, "Whoa there, buddy." I manage to think that this is a stupid response on the cop's part. Then I realize there's shit running down my pants. I grab what I can, and run, crying, as high on acid as I've ever been, back to my apartment.

This is the beginning.

I Get the Hell Out of Kansas

One of the principles I live my life by is that I don't care what people say behind my back. If you say something nasty about me when I'm not around, my opinion is that the tree didn't make a peep. If you don't say it to my face, you either like me too much to hurt my feelings, which is fine, or you're afraid of me, which is also fine, or you're just not in a position to tell me to my face, which is perfect. People only have to like me enough to pay me, have sex with me, and serve me beer,[1] and if they have something else on their mind they're welcome to keep it to themselves or repeat it like a bad vacation story when I'm out of earshot.

This is not some enlightened realization about ego protection and emotional stability. This is something I trained myself to do out of necessity, since if I allowed myself to care about what people didn't say, I would have killed myself a decade ago.

It is very important to remain calm when peaking on acid. Crying and shaking in your apartment bathroom while shit streams down your legs is not calm. Somehow, I pulled myself together, stripped, and got into the shower. My roommate came home at that point, laughing, and said:

"Oh man, you done fucked up."

---

[1] Turns out you don't have to like someone very much to do any of these things.

Luckily for me, my roommate was about the chillest human being on Earth. I'll call him JD. He was about forty, the premiere DJ for Bar Harbor's best club,[2] and friends with the cops, despite being one of the extremely rare black people in what is a shockingly racist state. I can't remember clearly, but I think he cleaned my shit off the floor and gave me tips on how to deal with situations like this in the future.

"You need to keep some Valium on you when you trip. Chills you right out."

Take notes.

JD helps me calm down, and I pull myself together and start dealing with the facts of the situation. The facts are bad, so I give up on thinking about them and just try not to freak out. The one thing I need to sort out is that I'd already been planning to attend a hippy festival in Massachusetts and the girl who was going to give me a ride probably wasn't eager to spend six hours in a car with me after the day's events.

Eventually, I go out for a smoke and end up running into a neighbor who'd heard about everything. He invites me up to one of the more crowded apartments, full of stoned people, and that sounds just about perfect, so I go up and hang out with a remarkably sympathetic audience for the next few hours.

Inevitably, the cops show up. The stoners ask me if I want to hide out, but I'm relaxed enough to deal with it, although I'm still tripping. I head downstairs because I really don't want them to go for a warrant and find a bunch of drugs in my apartment.

"Hey. You Peter Welch?"

"Yeah, yeah, that's me. What can I do for you?"

"I assume you know why we're here."

"I can guess."

"I need to see your ID."

"Yeah, I have a passport, one second."

I go into the apartment to get my ID. The cop whips out a flashlight and seems intent on following me in, but I shut the door in his face as innocently as possible, since I'm about as fucking far

---

[2] It's okay. I wouldn't go.

from innocent as it gets, and the living room table alone could have put me and JD in jail on the spot. In my room, I see a few of Jake's things and briefly lose it, but I know I can't go off on some angsty tripped-out reflection while the cops are waiting for me. I grab my passport and take it outside.

The cop and I get into a discussion about LSD. For some reason it gets relaxed and chatty, and I end up telling him I'm still tripping. He looks up and points the light in my eyes.

"Really? I couldn't tell."

"If you can handle it, nobody really can."

This is true. In the previous year, I'd downed some acid gel tabs, not realizing exactly how long they would last, and ended up having to go to lunch with my dad and my brother while still tripping. I sucked it up and went to a Chinese restaurant. On the way there, I went off on some philosophical rant, and my dad asked me if I was stoned, and I said, "Of course not. Do you think I could be this eloquent if I was stoned?" to which he replied, "Good point." I spent the next hour making small talk while trying to ignore a demon that had appeared in my tea and spent the whole lunch shouting "Hey! Hey! I'm looking at you!" in an attempt to get my attention. I didn't even want the tea, but I drank it just to shut him up.

The cop was unimpressed.

"Your friend didn't handle it so well."

I had nothing to say to that.

He takes my information, hands me my passport, and tells me not to leave town for a while. I ask him if Jake's okay, but he has no idea. Then I tell him I'm leaving town as soon as possible for a festival, but I'll be back in a few days. He takes this well and we part amicably.

Crisis averted. This cheers me up, but I'm still worried about Jake, so I putter and mope for a while. My ride never shows up, naturally. When I relate this to JD, he mentions he's going to Massachusetts to pick up some records and can drop me in Boston, which is a short bus trip from where I need to be, which solves my second to last problem. I turn in to catch some Z's until we leave in the morning.

Turns out getting a ride was my third to last problem. I couldn't sleep. I still didn't know what happened to Jake, and there was no one to call. I definitely wasn't calling his parents. The cops didn't know. I didn't know what hospital he was in and they wouldn't have told me anything if I did. So I lay in my bed staring at the ceiling until 5:00 A.M. when JD and I packed into his van and headed for Boston.

That drive was like any wistful, angsty, I-just-screwed-up-something-brutal drive your average teenager would take, except better music. I smoked a lot and kept quiet, JD kept the mood chill, and I tried not to think about tripping. It was hard, because I still was. Anybody who's done acid will tell you that you don't really finish the trip until you sleep. Whatever sleep does to you normally, it also undoes the wackiness psychedelic drugs do to you. So the trip gets less intense, but it doesn't stop completely until you sleep.[3]

When we get to Boston, it's been twenty-four hours. I was starting to feel punchy. The single most important thing to me was still to remain calm.

I wander around a bit, look at some obscure records, then JD drops me off at the bus station. I'd already made arrangements to meet up with some of my old college buddies, so everything was going according to plan, aside from the not sleeping, friend in the hospital/jail/maybe dead, and still on drugs situations.

I hop on the bus and try to get some shuteye for the two-hour ride. No luck. I eventually get off in Amherst, MA, and I sit down to wait for my friends.

I have a young druggy purse of toys, so I pull out a fancy looking ball and start contact juggling. If you don't know what this is,

---

[3] I've been challenged on this, so it's worth debate. Not coming down until you sleep is standard trippers' lore, but there's no medical evidence for the fact. The end of a trip is not unlike staying awake for too long, and acid does keep you up, so I suspect that the lore comes from the seamless transition from tripping to sleep deprivation. However, in all trips prior to this one, there was a lingering visual and mental disturbance until I got a full night's sleep.

it's what David Bowie is doing with the fancy balls in Labyrinth.[4] This is not a skill I worked on. This was just something I could suddenly do. More about that later. The other people waiting at the bus station are a group of Tibetan monks. One of them sees me rolling my ball around, comes over, points at it, says something in what I assume was Tibetan, and smiles emphatically.

I talk a lot of smack about hippies. Specifically neo-hippies. But I was a neo-hippy for a couple of years, which is what gives me the right to talk smack, in the same way that watching *Star Trek: The Next Generation* in the background as I'm writing this gives me the right to talk smack about geeks. If you're a neo-hippy, there is not one single thing that can give you more satisfaction than a Tibetan monk giving you his approval. This is the first instance of my severely altered state of mind being validated by the people around me. In this case, by a monk. I chat with him for a minute, but the conversation is difficult because we share no common languages. I follow him back to his companions and they have an animated conversation, which involves motions towards me. I will never know what they were saying, but I felt like I'd been selected above all humans by the coolest of all monks,[5] though for all I know, they were talking about golf.

At that point, my friends arrive. We'll call them Jun, Duke, and Some Girl. Jun and Duke I knew from college, Some Girl was just that, and had dated Jun for a while and then moved on to Duke. It was none of my business, and I'm positive none of them thought I'd someday be putting their business in a book.

I related the story of the past few 24 hours to them, thinking the version they heard would be the story I told for the rest of my life, no blood, no foul.

This is hour 27. I think I'm home free, except I don't know what happened to Jake. I haven't slept, thus I still feel like I'm trip-

---

[4] The ones in his hands, not the ones revealed by the disturbingly tight spandex.

[5] Not precisely: the Benedictines gave us a lot more ways to consume alcohol, so they really get this award, but I was young and didn't have my priorities straight.

ping. I'm around friends who think my story is awesome. We have a good laugh, and we head to Great Barrington, Massachusetts.

I Party With a Bunch of
Hippies and Do More Drugs

I never, ever go a night without sleep anymore. If it's five in the morning and I'm awake, I call out of work, regardless of the circumstances. I would rather lose my job. It used to be fun to get a little high from an all-nighter. I've always had the totally unfounded theory that lack of sleep tells the body there's danger present and it puts you into a constant fight-or-flight mode. Whatever the reason, lack of sleep can cause, among other things, aching muscles, confusion, headaches, tremors, hallucinations, dehydration, increased blood pressure, and eventual psychosis followed by death. Humans tend to be incapable of staying awake long enough to die without the help of amphetamines or a rare condition called fatal familial insomnia, something so terrifying to me I can't research it properly. Suffice to say "fatal" is not an obscure Latin term.

If you don't go to dreamland, dreamland comes to you. Think about all the things you've believed, unquestioning, while dreaming. When you dream, you are InstaFanatic about whatever ludicrous set of rules you're presented with. That's not a great place to be when you're awake, unless you're looking to start a religion.

The scene in Great Barrington was much as I'd left it the prior year. The town remained a vaguely tourist nook with aspirations of being a college town. Jun and Duke and Some Girl were all staying at Jun's place for the moment. There were a couple of other kids wandering in and out whom I knew to varying degrees, plus Jun's roommates, one of whom I don't remember, and one of whom spent the next three days locked in his room taking mushrooms and acid with two girls. The relationships there were not clear. Some Girl, as mentioned before, had been dating Jun until a few weeks prior, when she spent a few days in jail with Duke after the WTO protests went south. They bonded, and Some Girl started hooking up with Duke. Jun seemed gracefully disappointed, and the tension was relatively low. I was waging emotional war on my own mind to stay calm and try not to worry about Jake or my continuing trip, so other people's problems didn't figure big.

We caught up on the ride home and chatted and hung out that evening. Video games abounded. I smoked some weed and had a couple beers and tried to relax. I felt I was doing okay.

That night, still worried about Jake, I couldn't sleep again. This may also have had something to do with trying to sleep while on a small, decaying recliner. I semi-sobered up over the course of the night and poked at the chair, thinking, thinking, thinking . . .

Eventually it was about noon. I nudged Jun awake and told him I was going to check out Berkfest for a bit on my own. He nodded and I wandered off.

I couldn't have been better dressed for the event. I had my dad's old hippy shirt, a corduroy crimson vest with billowing hemp sleeves with flowers embroidered at the cuffs.[1] My jeans were in the midst of becoming the flannel layer beneath the denim. Beads may have been involved, and I had a black pouch of goodies at my side. I felt like the Wizard of LSD, mostly because I was stoned, partly because I was still keeping my shit together.[2]

I walked down the road and ran into a couple of girls coming the other way. I asked them where Berkfest (the local festival) was and they looked at me somewhat disbelievingly, since I didn't notice but you could already hear the bands, and I looked like the last person on Earth who wouldn't know this information. I was in ultra-

---

[1] I tend to leave the details of my old wardrobe out of the conversations I have about hating neo-hippies.

[2] What was left of it. I hadn't eaten much since I lost the lion's share.

friendly mode, but when you're twenty or younger, ultra-friendly comes off as creepy.

I finally get close, walk over a hill, and see what would become my vision of Heaven for the next five years, until I discovered Brooklyn.

Start with rolling hills. Don't just write off "rolling hills" as a cliché: think hills with the sweep, dip, and rise of a wave crossing its ephemeral moment of quintessential waviness, transcribed by da Vinci's hand from the memory of seeing it during a moment of silence on a really good date.

Add a forest. Not any forest: a forest that serves both as line between civilization and the grassy valleys of the hills the trees surround, and as the mysterious depth on the far side of those valleys, promising tygers, dragons, and the infinite unknown.

Now, in the grassy valleys of these forested hills, add thousands of multicolored tents filled with nubile hippies, pretty colors, flashing lights, and the smell of five-to-ten in Texas.

I decided I wasn't quite ready to deal with it on my own, and headed back to Jun's place for more video games and movies.

At this point, in my attempt to remain calm, something was starting to switch over. I had achieved a consistent zenned-out quality. I merely acted, and allowed my mind to do whatever it wanted while I focused on keeping my pulse down. I was in a constant state of detached, semiconscious self-monitoring.

That afternoon, I get a call from Jake's brother, and finally find out that Jake is okay. I'm so relieved I almost start crying again. Jake's brother makes it clear that I probably shouldn't stop by the house for a while, but that after a few hours strapped to a hospital bed, Jake was fine, and not even in much trouble, since his family's rage was reserved exclusively for me, and the cops were understanding about him being on drugs, but otherwise a good kid. I told him that worked for me, and I'd see him in six months.

Free of the worries that had been haunting me for the past sixty or so hours, I celebrated by smoking a cigarette and telling all my friends, then we all celebrated by smoking about two metric shitloads of weed and playing more video games. I tried to enjoy the day, and looked forward to the coming restful night when I could sleep and finally stop tripping.

A few weird things happened that evening. I played a game of Go against Great Barrington's best player. I'm partly responsible for the Go craze that swept Great Barrington, having introduced Jun to it the previous summer. The local toy shop repeatedly stocked Go boards on his or my request, and they were wiped out within a week each time. Despite this, I'm not an especially skilled player, and Jun and his friends rapidly outpaced me. I'd barely played in the intervening year, so even if the town wasn't the source of the world's finest Go masters, I expected to have my ass handed back to me after a thorough rape and some token whippings. I ended up fighting him to a standstill. The room hushed and watched us play. I wish someone had taken a picture of the game, because it was a solid mass of pieces, without a single capture, migrating out from the center of the board. After three or four hours, my opponent and I agreed the tension was just too much, neither of us wanted to have to figure out how we would calculate the score once we got to the edges of the board, and we called it a draw.

The next thing that happened was I picked up a video game about some space warrior who got stuck alone in the middle of no-where and decided to piss off all the alien species he could find. Jun recommended it, saying it was fun but kind of hard. I got through two thirds of the game without dying once. Jun piped up at one point with, "How are you doing this?"

I remember saying, "Oh it's easy. You just have to read the algo-rithms." In a Matrixy way, it really seemed like I could see the equa-tions powering the angry aliens, and I could just figure them out and be in the right place at all times. Eventually this fell apart when one of the bosses was a giant spider, and we started passing the con-troller around, joking about how my arachnophobia was killing my flow. Eventually I beat it, and cruised through the rest of the game perfectly. Perfectly. I didn't miss a shot. I didn't take a hit. On my first try. I outperformed a roomful of near-professional gamers on the most difficult game in the room, one I'd never heard of, on my first try.

Here's the problem: since the moment of my out-of-body experience, I was surrounded by near-constant validation. My roommate laughed it all off. My neighbors were sympathetic. The monks were fascinated by me. My friends were glad to see me, and said I looked fine. I performed feats I'd never before achieved, and haven't been able to since. The universe itself was complimenting my new-found state of mind. Everything was implicitly validating my coping mechanism, and the humility I gained through messing up in the near worst way possible was telling me to accept everything around me, including whatever lessons could be learned, and to ascend to some higher state of mind. I do believe, and this may be the only thing I believe with any amount of certainty or faith, that I was tapping into some hidden potential of my mind. There's no way to describe this, but it involves all the usual things people say when they try: my mind and body became one because I realized they were never separate. I could feel the ebb and flow of all my senses and the world around me, the vibration of existence, the most delicate transactions of energy that constitute the changing universe. At some point on this arc, I achieved enlightenment. Not the enlightenment you get from realizing it's all bullshit. I achieved the total destruction of all symbolism, experienced pure experience and thought as a single unmoving moment. Do you know what it's like to transcend the illusion of time? It's fucking awesome. Not to mention a little hard to describe, since there's the assumption that transcending this illusion should somehow make time stop, or at least allow you to travel around in it. Since I'm here, writing this, that obviously didn't happen. It's like having consciousness expand to wrap around the experience of the mind as a whole, instead of the few seconds of short-term memory with which it normally contents itself. The past and present lose their distinctions, and the notions of passing and past become an experience of the changing totality of the mind, and the possibility of investigating each moment changes from attempting to gather and assimilate sense data to having a complete mind to explore, in its current state as the result of all the states it ever was, and as the beginning of all the dreams and states it could encompass. Potential and past forms of consciousness merge, and the experience of the instant is all but untethered from the clock. I don't quite understand the concept anymore, but I have noticed with my current—strictly and consciously normalized—mind that the experience of time during reading versus watching TV is markedly different. I don't have an explanation for this, but the effect is similar, at least in the way a raindrop is similar to a dinosaur.

There is nothing more validating than this kind of enlightenment, because it removes all need for validation. For the most part, I haven't needed validation since, even though I'm back on the usual level of reality. When things get bad, or someone's judging me for whatever reason, I just shrug and think, "Well, I saw the other side of the universe, so fuck you."

Why was this a problem?

Jun once related to me what is now my favorite quote: "Drugs are a revelation we're not ready for."

I had the revelation.

I was not ready for it.

The problem with destroying symbolism is that if you want to go back to your day job, you have to put it back together, and if you're unpracticed in this sort of thing, you'll probably get it wrong.

The dawn finds me sitting on the roof in a thunderstorm, trying to coax a bird out of hiding. I'm not crazy yet.[3] I've always loved thunderstorms, rain, and birds, so it's not impossible I would do something like this today, except I'd complain more about being damp afterwards. I'm communing with the beauty of the world as it rages above my head, beginning to touch the infinite possible universes at right angles to our measly four dimensions.

I can't sleep. It's day four.

The previous night, before everyone except me fell asleep, the roommate doing God knows what in his bedroom made a brief appearance to the rest of us. He came in, wearing only rolled up cargo pants and a hemp necklace. He sat down, staring into the distance.

---

[3] Promise. Truth be told, I occasionally have trouble convincing people I'm not crazy now, but I know the difference, and I wasn't crazy yet.

"I think . . . I need to go into the woods."

"Okay," said Jun.

The kid stared at the ground for a while, then got up and slowly waddled back to his room. I have no idea what happened to him, but I suspect he was heading down a similar path to mine, he just had two teenage girls to go with him.[4] Later that night, while I was in the recliner, staring at the ceiling, I heard a noise, and discovered he had crawled into the living room and was rooting around in my bag. I sat up and he skittered away like a guilty Gollum. Glad as I was to have not been robbed, saving a few baubles and fifteen dollars worth of pot from an insane hippy wasn't worth the cost I was paying each sleepless hour.

I crawled in from the roof and tackled a new day. I'm still proud of myself for holding it together as long as I did. I was still sane, despite the stress, drugs, and sleeplessness. But the balance was tipping. I tried to take care of myself that day,[5] because, in the voice of Samuel L. Jackson, I needed to go. The fuck. To sleep. We hit the Berkfest tent city. The next two days were spent wandering between the hippy festival and the stoner apartment; the memories start to get a little cloudy here, so I'm just tacking together the best bits I can confidently say happened.

The tent city was all it promised to be, packed with surprisingly attractive girls and laughably spaced-out guys,[6] all equally welcoming. We wandered into ten-person tents with multiple arched entrances, where we'd sit and chat and smoke with whomever was inside. We played hacky sack, and I did it competently if not expertly. This was another skill I never had before and haven't had since.

I bought some glow sticks that night and did glow stick dances. Thanks to the Tai Chi videos my grandmother sent me when I was a kid, I had a natural talent for this, and it's one of the few skills I

---

[4] I constantly wonder what I did so wrong in my youth that everybody around me got so much more action than I did.

[5] As much as a reckless twenty-year-old can.

[6] Hippy communities are almost always like this.

kept for a few years, and I deeply resent the rave scene for imploding so catastrophically that glow sticks became the decade's sign of being a loser. The glow stick vendors would ask me to stay nearby so they could shout, "Buy our glow sticks so you can be like this guy!"

I fell in love with those glowing strands that you can bend into loops. I discovered I could hold the ends of one strand with a looped strand on it, and sort of hula hoop it up one arm, then down and up the other. I thought it was the coolest thing since air-conditioning, and I don't know what the general consensus was, but at some point a couple of girls went up to Jun.

"Is he okay?" one asked.

"I'm not sure," replied Jun.

I wish you could hear his voice. I didn't care. I was fine. Perfectly fine. Better than ever. I was fucking enlightened.

Here's Jun's take:

> So when you're with a friend when he's going through an experience like that, there is a certain amount of emotional ambivalence involved. Like any other reasonably well-educated young person who's been around drugs, and the tripping culture, you figure out pretty quickly when someone close to you is legitimately slipping their marbles. You want to think everything's okay, but you know it's really, really not.
>
> Affectively, he was just a little too sincerely fascinated with everything. Everything he was saying at the time just reeked of acceptance and gentle insight, and he said it with the kind of sincerity usually reserved for events like watching the sun rise. That's all well and good, but you get the sense of "he can't possibly fucking keep this up." Anyone who's done a drug like acid knows it's goddamn exhausting. It's the sensory equivalent to running a marathon; your filters for perceptual intake are on a paid vacation, and you're taking it aaaaaalll in.

Although we should have probably tackled and sedated him, forcing him to sleep, we didn't (so easy to say in hindsight). We let things run their course. I could say we did it out of a sense of respect for his autonomy, or his personal process, or something like that. In truth, we just didn't know what the "right" thing to do was. It would have been easier to call men in white coats if he hadn't been so damn nice and positive and zen about everything; I think part of me really did want to believe that this was just a friend going through a beautiful spiritual experience. You want sincerely to believe that the change you see in them has a positive and authentic core. Plus, he was doing some really cool shit. He isn't just writing that he suddenly got better at reflex-based tasks, or could suddenly and improbably dance at a festival, with rhythm and abandon, when we all well knew that he was way too reserved to have actually PRACTICED that, he was just doing it spontaneously. And doing it well. That's the important bit.

That was the nice part of this story. There's a not-so-nice part. Remember Leary? Set and setting? Part of me thinks he was just lucky for a while to be in a reasonably good space, in a good place, at a good time.

Things took a darker turn on the last day. I decided to supplement my travel budget with a little drug slinging, so we walked down what was nicknamed "Drug Alley," a wide and muddy swath of vendors selling bongs and bowls and fruit juice and pretty much anything else a turn-of-the-millennium hippy could want. Shady looking semi-hippies and ravers in hemp clothing weaved through the crowd, muttering, "Molly, molly, acid, e, KB, molly."[7] I find a particularly shady-looking kid and buy a vial of acid off him for a hundred bucks.[8] He runs off and we walk back up Drug Alley. On the way, we see a guy lean over to his girlfriend, who is staring blankly into the distance. He talks to her and she doesn't respond. He shouts at her and she doesn't blink. He starts slapping her, harder and harder. She doesn't respond. We walk by, like everybody else.

Once home, we relax with a final round of video games before we all drive back up to Maine in the morning. At some point, one of the girls accompanying Gollum came in and asked to buy a couple of hits of my newly acquired acid. The deal is she'll give me ten bucks, stick out her tongue, and I'll squeeze out two drops of liquid LSD on it. I take her money, and she holds her tongue out, slightly upturned to catch it. Just as the first drop is coming out, she turns her tongue down, which causes me to jump just enough to squeeze much, much harder than I intended to.

I'd say she got her money's worth,[9] in that about two or three drops worth hit her tongue. The other ten to fifteen drops landed on my arm. We apologized to each other, she seemed satisfied, and I lunged for the nearest thing that could clean the acid off my skin. As anyone who's watched *SLC Punk* knows, acid does not need to be ingested to take effect.

Jun and I have discussed this over the years, and we're not completely convinced the acid was real. It didn't matter; my state of mind was such that if you held a sign with big enough letters spell-

---

[7] Translation: "Really good ecstasy, really good ecstasy, LSD, okay ecstasy, really good pot, really good ecstasy."

[8] Acid comes in several varieties. Crystal, liquid, paper, and gel, last I knew, though I heard a rumor many years ago that gel tabs were on the outs, and I haven't researched since. A vial is a small glass container or an eye dropper holding somewhere between one and two hundred hits, and you can sell a hit for five bucks to the right person.

[9] Especially since I didn't charge her due to the snafu. Astoundingly, I managed to sell not one hit of the purchased acid, and remain history's worst drug peddler.

ing "YOU JUST TOOK FIFTEEN MORE HITS OF ACID" in front of me it probably would have had the same effect as the real thing. I hadn't slept in six days. The importance of this moment was that I accepted, to my detriment, that I was not going to be okay. Not immediately seeking medical help was the latest in a long series of bad decisions, but on the other hand, I still had to remain calm.

I think Jun was getting worried at this point, but he'd seen worse. When I told him about it, he said, "That's really not good."

I just shrugged and settled in for the ride.

Through the Looking Coke Mirror

You're never aware of the moment when you fall asleep. You just let your mind wander until it doesn't come back. Then you enter an alien world of rules, never guessing for a moment that there was a dramatic change in the way you approach the universe that congeals just behind your senses. We run around all the time looking for evidence to support or disprove the things we think, but what most people don't realize is that all of us, in order to continue thinking in the accepted human way, must assume that the way in which we interpret the world is correct. Otherwise, we can make no judgments, no decisions, and have nothing on which to base an action. Even if you think you are constantly wrong about everything and know it, you have to make the judgment that you are wrong with that tiny lump of noggin flesh. We are all permanently locked in our private set of mechanisms for seeing the world, and it's a prison with no doors. If those mechanisms change, there's no way to know, and there's no way to double check, nothing else to which you can compare your one, single, unique continuum of thought.

I know, in retrospect, I was crazy, and now I'm not, in exactly the same way that I know the upsetting dream I had last night was a dream, even though I didn't know it at the time.

One of the things I hate most these days is when people say, "Oh, everybody's a little crazy." This is not true. There is crazy, and there's not crazy, and regardless of how you feel about someone, they're either operating on generally the same assumptions you are (sane), or they're operating on a vastly different set of rules that they may or may not have managed to plug into the social milieu like the rest of us (crazy). People think everybody's a little crazy because they confuse eccentricity and various defense mechanisms or alternate viewpoints with true madness, and lump it all together on a sliding scale. This is wrong. There is an entire range of states of mind, but there is a hazy line, past which you are insane, and prior to it, there's some hope. Having been there, I can spot crazy in about two minutes of conversation. There are a lot more of them among us than most people think. I'm not trying to make anyone paranoid: crazy people aren't dangerous if they've integrated their madness into everyday life. But you have friends that you put up with who are absolutely nuts, and you think they're just shy or weird, and you probably know someone who you think is nuts who is just shy or weird. Maybe you can tell. Most people can't. Nor can they see crazy coming when it's creeping up.

I never noticed the moment I crossed into dreamland. I don't think it's a fine enough distinction to pinpoint a moment between what we call "awake" and "asleep" even though we know the difference between these iconic states of consciousness. In our own lives, we remember a few cues to tell us when we probably fell asleep, just before we stopped bothering to put the world together in our heads.

I'm not sure exactly where it all fell apart, but I think I remember the last time I checked the clock.

Once I started to accept that I was totally fucked and only a miracle or a truly epic act of will could save me, I just got on with it. I was, stupidly, banking on the act of will, because I don't believe in miracles. What I should have considered was getting to a hospital, but I was on the enlightenment kick and really thought I could bring it home, not realizing I was rapidly losing my purchase on reality.

I decided to maximize the profit of my acid purchase by buying sugar cubes and making sugar cube hits. If you are a drug dealer[1] dealing in acid,[2] the absolute worst thing you can do to your dreams of unbarred, unguarded living quarters is drop a bunch of LSD on sugar cubes, since when you're caught with acid, the amount you have is calculated by weight. Federally—and it would have been a federal offense, because I immediately crossed state lines—trafficking one to nine grams of acid is punishable by not less than five years in jail. Above that, not less than ten years, but it's okay, because it's not more than life in prison. I took two or three grams and turned them into about half a pound.

Those of you who have done or do acid and grew up or are growing up in some remote, relatively copless, low-crime area, or a cop-ridden, extremely high crime area, probably understand why I would make this decision, even if you're laughing about it. For those of you who have never been in circumstances like this, just consider that when you're young and invincible, and not really dealing as a lifestyle, and have never paid any notable legal price for your actions, moving what is to you a paltry amount of drugs doesn't seem like that big a deal. Consider, I was with a bevy of fellow part-time drugs users, most of whom were my former classmates at Simon's Rock, supposedly the go-to hotspot for the crème de la crème of today's youth. Nobody stopped me. Nobody even said it was a bad idea. There was some discussion over profit possibilities, and whether this was the best way to go about it. The point is, no one present was qualified to take care of me.

Off we went, packing me, Jun, Duke, Euro Trash, and Hippy Mainer into a four person car along with my multiple life sentences and a variety of other drugs and drug paraphernalia. I'd just met Hippy Mainer and she owned the camp we would be staying at once we arrived. I think Jun was dating her, or did later, or something like that; I lost track of a lot of story lines over the next couple of months. Hippy Mainer, Jun, and I packed into the backseat. It was an exercise in yoga and lack of homophobia, which isn't that

---

[1] Bad idea.

[2] Bad idea.

hard when you're all around twenty years old and have gone to the same bleeding liberal arts school and you're all stoned or tripping.

I don't remember the details of the conversations, except that the music was good, the vibe was chill, and the night air felt nice. The press of limbs in the back was a strange, non-sexual thrill as we all remained comfortable and un-awkward, even while marveling at our ability to not be awkward.

Then the cops pulled us over. I've called everyone I could get in touch with on short notice,[3] and nobody remembers exactly why. If Duke was driving, that's why, since Duke liked to drive 90 miles per hour on twisting back roads with a beer in one hand and a cigarette in the other while adjusting his CD player and making small talk about Jazz theory, but I expect Euro Trash was driving, because we all wanted to live.

Everyone was nervous except me. Why wasn't I nervous? First, because I was stupid, and didn't understand the gravity emitting from the bag of now crushed sugar cubes I'd shoved under the passenger seat when the lights came up behind us. Second, because I was still Remaining Calm. It was pretty much all I had left. Third, because I was starting to lose my grip. To compare it to drifting off to sleep, this is the point where I'm on the couch, catching scenes in the movie here and there, but not really following the plot anymore.

All of us have faced the cops in some inebriated state before, so everybody knows what to do, which is nothing. Do everything the cops say, show complete respect for their authority, and give them every impression that you are proud of them for protecting your loved ones and you understand you've just crossed the line and are willing, nay, eager, to take one for America as long as our boys in blue keep doing their job. It was clearly going to be a while, so we all hopped out of the car, with the permission of our nice, law-enforcing, gentle, my-aren't-you-handsome-and-so-dignified cops. Since I was somewhere between the real world and the Great Beyond, I was the most relaxed, since I knew everything would be

---

[3] Everyone being Jun.

fine. I stretched, did a little yoga, some contact juggling, and even persuaded Jun to do some martial arts practice with me.

I remember this practice vividly. It's called push hands: you and your opponent find your footing, place your forward feet against each other, then try to make the other person move either of their feet, and you have to do everything slowly. It takes a lot to be in a position where you're about to face-plant the ground and you still have to move slowly, but it's an excellent practice for understanding center of gravity, how your limbs bend, and how much a slow moving elbow can hurt. Jun and I had been doing a fair amount of this, and he was excellent, I was okay, probably best at it against him because he was my sole opponent most of the time.

Even taking into account trip time, this practice was slow. We barely moved, each minor muscle twitch sensed and countered by the opponent, before the arm had moved an inch. We measured our tactical advantage by each other's breathing. I did this because of my preternatural acid awareness; he did it because he was just really good at stuff like that. I think we were there for five, ten minutes, though it was probably less. Eventually I saw an opening and dove for it, way too fast, triggering Jun's kung-fu reflexes, and he hurled me to the ground. I stood, out of breath, at once chastised and honored.

I like to imagine the cops' conversation.

"Buncha kids."

"Yup. Probably from that hippy thing."

"Probably on drugs."

"Definitely stoned."

"That ain't so bad."

"Think they're carrying?"

"Dunno. Think they'd be more wigged out if they were."

"Probably."

"Yup."

"Lotta other kids on stuff tonight. These   .   .   . wait a minute . . ."

"Yeah, I see it too."

"That big Asian fella fighting that scrawny white kid?"

"They're doin' it awful slow."

"Yoga?"

"Doesn't look like yoga. My wife started doin' yoga, and it don't look nothin' like that."

"They're really not moving much."

"Maybe one of em's got a knife?"

"Nope, no knife."

"Their friends seem okay with it."

"Hmm."

"Oh, there goes the little white kid."

"Ayuh. Got twitchy."

"Shame."

"College kids. Screw it, send 'em home."

Or at least, that's the best explanation I have for why they let us go. I think someone else, possibly even a sober someone, was talking to the cops, and we had Hippy Mainer, who obviously wouldn't harm a hair on an endangered species' head, even if she was happy to drive schedule one drugs through three states.

Jun called me after reading the first draft of this and mentioned something I'd forgotten, and it's so ridiculous I wouldn't have believed it if I'd remembered it myself. Apparently, the cops did shine a light around our car, and asked me what my leather pouch full of acid laced sugar cubes was. At this point, the cubes had been ground into a pile of their component sugar grains, so I opened it up, looked the cop in the eye, and said, "Sugar."

The cop looked at the bag of white powder, looked at me like I was an idiot for trying to pull something like that, dipped his finger in the pouch, sniffed at it, then tasted it.

"It is sugar. Why do you have a bag of sugar?"

"I like sugar."

The cop shook his head and walked off. I have no idea if he got a surprise an hour later, but cop, if you're reading this, and you suddenly lost it for eight hours on a nightshift, I'm sorry.[4]

We packed it in and made it to the camp.

The camp was amazing. Gaslight and unfinished wood floors, and a trail down to the beach in Lamoine, Maine. Beaches in the

---

[4] And you owe me five bucks.

summer in Maine are some of the best places to be in any state of mind. Sitting on the beach under the stars melting beer bottles into lamps over a campfire? You can guess.

I wonder why I haven't done this since, as it's pretty fun to melt glass over a campfire. It's never hot enough to burst or liquefy, but you can, over the course of an hour, gently nudge a Corona bottle into the background of a Dali painting. We did this for three or four hours.

I remember the fire licking over the edges of the glass as it bent and flowed over itself. I remember the sparks jumping up in the middle of our circle of unlimited patience and quiet. The sparks flew into the stars, and when the shooting stars came down, sometimes you couldn't tell the difference. Fire, water, earth and sky bled together, and I could see the humming shroud of God between all things.

This was my seventh day without sleep.

The next morning I sat on the porch, lotus style, at dawn. No thunderstorm this time. This is the beginning of the part I'm not supposed to remember, according to the psychiatric profession, but I remember more of it than I care to.[5]

---

[5] I have an exceptionally odd memory. My girlfriend is right to be frustrated with the fact that I'll ask her the same question about our weekend plans three times in a week, and telling me your name is a pointless exercise until I've met you four or five times and am expecting to see you again. On the other hand, I have distinct impressions of being pushed around in a stroller, and my first clear memory is from when I was about a year old. I also remember asking my dentist, with the aid of a pad of paper, if I could drink beer after just waking up from having all four of my wisdom teeth extracted under total anesthesia, even though he told me I wouldn't remember anything that happened an hour after waking. In fact, I remember waking up briefly in the middle of that procedure, while the dentist had his foot on the chair, both hands on the instrument that was pulling out my upper right wisdom tooth, and was swearing loudly. Despite an immodest relationship with alcohol throughout my 20s, I've only blacked out two or three times, usually right before I went to bed anyway. So, for better and often worse, my episodic memory is abnormally resistant to interruption, possibly at the expense of my factual memory, which is a small junk drawer with a hole in the back.

This part was okay. I remember the color of every leaf on the trees around me. I remember the sky, the feel of the wood and the breeze. I was crossing the desert between sanity and madness, and the last few days had been so pleasant a journey, I simply walked on, seeking it, trying to find out what was on the other side, untying myself from the dock of reality. The universe was floating by in frames and staccato impressions, and I felt like I could navigate the splitting quantum universes bursting into existence a trillion times a second. I felt like I was a bodhisattva.[6] From a skeptical standpoint, I may as well have been.

The night before, I had slept with Hippy Mainer. Sadly, this was neither true in the literal sense nor the euphemistic sense. I didn't get any sleep, and there was no sex. The fact that I ended up in bed with a girl I hardly knew is a little mysterious even now. We drew straws. I don't think this is as deplorable as it sounds, though it may have been. At the time, I thought it was a complex illusion designed to give me a spiritual experience.[7] In retrospect, I believe drawing straws was about who would get to sleep in the queen size bed—and incidentally share it with the person who owned the camp—versus the twin bunk beds.[8] I snuggled up to her and there seemed to be no complaint, though I can't imagine my chaste but extra-friendly physicality was welcome. We had just spent a car ride entangled in a manner I rarely achieve with the people I sleep with, so it wasn't overtly sexual, but I was assuming an intimacy she couldn't possibly have felt.

I remember describing it the next day:

"It was like I could feel every part of her body."

---

[6] Loosely, "enlightenment-being." I encourage you to research this on your own, but briefly, from wikipedia: "a bodhisattva is anyone who, motivated by great compassion, has generated *bodhicitta*, which is a spontaneous wish to attain Buddhahood for the benefit of all sentient beings."

[7] Madness is extremely solipsistic.

[8] I didn't have a good sense of complicated relationships when sober at this juncture in my life. I had no idea what was going on.

This statement probably had something to do with why my bag of possibly acid-laced sugar vanished. But it didn't even begin to describe how I felt over the course of another sleepless night cuddling with this girl.[9] I felt her heartbeat, and the changes in her skin temperature. I listened to each breath, and felt every muscle twitch, and I loved each tiny variation in the experience, not in the sense that I was in love with this girl, but in the sense that I loved everything all the time by this point. I hadn't yet attached symbols and plots to my new waterfall of consciousness, so everything was moments and slow, timeless beauty.

The moment on the porch was probably the first moment I started looking for meaning and purpose, after the lengthy lack of both. Buddha nature, if such a beast there be, is not achieved overnight, or even over seven nights. The quantum flux of the universe . . . what the hell. Maybe I did pick a universe and find a way to it. My life's great now. All I know is that I was trying to rebuild a system of meaning based on what I'd experienced, and I got it horribly wrong. Maybe if I'd headed for the woods, like Gollum boy, I would have started a cult, slept with some underage girls, and been shot by the FBI like a good American shaman.

Instead I stayed with my friends. Or my friends stayed with me, thank something. I heard them talking quietly behind me, and my analysis of that situation drifted among thinking they were government agents keeping an eye on me, disciples following their savior (me), and thinking they weren't talking about me at all because I was distracted by something else. Whatever I thought, they were looking out for me. The day of my morning meditation, they even accompanied me on the journey to visit my parents.

My parents hadn't seen me since the day with Jake. As related by my mom:

---

[9] I would really have to ask her about this, but I have no idea how to find her. The facts are less memorable than the delusions, but I think we were mutually cuddling the way stoned hippies do, so it wasn't necessarily creepy and one-sided, just heavily tilted to one side.

I got a call from Jake's mother telling me that you had dropped some acid with Jake, he was in the hospital and maybe I should see what was going on with you. I took this as a sincere desire to warn me that you were in trouble. In retrospect, I'm guessing she also wanted to make sure I knew what a bad parent I was to have raised the person who led her sweet baby down the road to perdition. Fair enough. At any rate, you had disappeared by then and weren't answering your phone. We had no idea where you were during that week in Massachusetts. So we worried but couldn't do much.

So I hopped in a car with Jun and Duke to visit my parents and attempt to explain myself.

They greeted me laughing. I explained a bit, with Jun's help, and managed to get the conversation around to lighter things. How, I don't know. I ended up trying to play my dad's violin, we caught up in general, and everything was fine, and then we all packed up and went back to camp.

During this conversation, I had one of my first well-rounded delusions. I realized that age was simply the mind expanding into more and more adjacent realities, where all things are possible, and the reason people tend to get more distractible as they age is simply because they're spending more time in alternate realities, so they sometimes forget which one they're in.

Of course this is crazy. But think of this as a metaphor for aging giving you a greater backlog of information and a wider set of mental skills with which to hypothesize and imagine and remember. Then it makes perfect sense, right? Now forget that it's a metaphor. Now you're crazy. Or better, don't take away the metaphor yet, just build a whole new metaphor on top of the old one, then another one on top of that, then do it really, really fast, and you have no idea where you started. Now try to work your way back, and find the fundamental meaning of all the words you used and where they came from and where the real meaning started.

Oh, whoops. It never did, and now you're a neurotic black hole of contradictions. The level at which you nominally communicated was just social agreement. But you've been so obsessed with your meanings and symbols and metaphors you've forgotten what the agreement was, and you're so looped out of your gourd you can't remember who you are or what it was like to consistently believe the same thing for more than an hour. You've lost all the rational cutoff points that used to make you stop and focus on what's going on outside of you instead of the model of the world in your head.

Some hours later, Duke dropped me off at my place back in Bar Harbor. As far as the world was concerned, once Jake and I were accounted for and seemingly all right, everything was back to normal.

Me? Well, nobody was looking after me anymore. And I could do whatever I wanted. I had half a pack of cigarettes, a pair of shades, and I was on a mission from God.

I was insane.

Meanwhile, In My Brain

LSD is so powerful its doses are measured in millionths of a gram. Twenty-five of those are enough to produce an effect; 150 will send you on a solid psychedelic trip (150 mcgs is less than the acceptable amount of cyanide per liter in our drinking water). You lose more weight in skin cells every minute. If you live near a major highway, as I do, more smog probably settles on your skin every minute. Even after this minuscule amount of LSD gets into your blood stream, only a small portion of it makes it past the blood/brain barrier, because your brain really doesn't want extra chemicals floating around.[1]

Norm Dinerman, an attending physician in emergency medicine at Eastern Maine Medical, describes the brain as an "electrical and neurochemical bouillabaisse." The brain is a soup of inhibiting and disinhibiting forces; like an ingredient will suppress some aspect of taste in a soup while bringing out another, anything you add to your brain is going to activate and suppress various activities.

LSD is very similar to serotonin, and serotonin is a busy chemical in your brain: it's a neurotransmitter, or a chemical that transmits impulses between neurons, and helps regulate learning and mood, among other things. Initially, LSD was thought to inhibit serotonin, but many other things inhibit serotonin, and very few of them stop time and turn sound into light. In fact, inhibited

---

[1] Furthermore, it does not stay in your spine forever, does not form crystals in your body, and usually doesn't contain strychnine. LSD is detectable in urine for a few days after you take it, and no one is going to do a spinal tap on you.

serotonin tends to weaken emotional bonding instincts, so something more profound is clearly going on if the most common reaction to LSD is grokking universal love. Of course it's far more complicated than that: LSD may inhibit some of the initial serotonin cell-firing, but certain cells that are activated by serotonin prefer LSD, so even though it's technically preventing serotonin from docking in its usual receptor, it ends up over-activating the whole serotonergic system. Meanwhile, LSD is screwing with your dopamine receptors. Dopamine, very simplistically, makes you happy, and LSD over-activates your dopaminergic system, a system already a little confused since your overactive serotonergic system is supposed to be regulating it. What does all this mean? God knows, but your brain is hopped up and very confused, whether or not you are.

Glutamate is another neurotransmitter that's vital to our synaptic plasticity, or the ability of our neural connections to strengthen and weaken as we think. Hence, it's important in learning, memory, and the general activation of your brain. LSD classically breaks down your ability to filter incoming sense data, which is definitely true in a sense (so to speak), but LSD and other hallucinogens also create a massive release of glutamate in the thalamus, which is one of the key brain structures involved in getting signals to your cortex, which is where you do your thinking, so your brain is getting a sensory overload because the thing with which it judges senses is over-reporting before the senses even get to it. Glutamate levels are also already on the rise in your cortex, so it would seem like more is going on even without the jump in sense memos.

In *On Intelligence*, for the purposes of building a new conceptual framework for artificial intelligence research, Jeff Hawkins describes the neocortex as a six-layered pattern storage and recognition system. The cortex is an incomprehensibly complicated structure, which is good, because its processes and structural potential account for the whole of every mammalian thought, and bad, because we've spent a lot of time trying to comprehend it. Sense data processed by our basic intake hits the bottommost layer and fires patterns of neurons, denoting basic data like color, shape, pitch, or roughness of a surface on your right thumb. These patterns move up through the layers, firing wider patterns. At the topmost layer, you have broad concepts combining all the sensory input patterns into concepts, which can then be sent down through the other layers as a kind of map, though lots of input is already mapped effectively at lower levels and doesn't need to strain this Platonic region of the brain. Sensory data comes in, finds its pattern somewhere, and sends out motor control commands. Information runs up and down the hierarchy in the process of recognition and forms a memory pattern that can inform motor responses.

This isn't a literal picture of the cortex—the connections and systems are much more intricate—but it's helpful to think of it as high-level cortical processes that are firing all sorts of things in your brain and making you think about stuff, and low-level cortical processes that deal with things in the background.

> The sensation of sudden comprehension, the "aha!" moment, can be understood by this model. Imagine you are looking at an ambiguous picture. Filled with blobs of ink and scattered lines, it doesn't look like anything. It doesn't make sense. Confusion occurs when the cortex can't find any memory that matches with the input. New inputs race all the way up the cortical hierarchy. High-level cortex tries lots of different hypotheses but, as these predictions race down the hierarchy, each and every one conflicts with the input and the cortex is forced to try again. During this time of confusion your brain is totally occupied with understanding the picture. Finally, you make a high-level prediction that is the right one. When this happens, the prediction starts at the top of the cortical hierarchy and succeeds in propagating all the way to the bottom, chunk, chunk, chunk, chunk, chunk. In less than a second, each region is given a sequence that fits the data. No more errors rise to the top.

I agree with Hawkins later point that "consciousness is simply what it feels like to have a cortex." LSD starts a chain reaction that alters this experience of the cortex, which means LSD is doing something radical to the cortical process. An LSD trip is a constant stream of "aha!" moments and complete disorientation, as if every step you took put you in a different country with a Babel fish and a copy of *The Hitchhiker's Guide to the Galaxy*. The patterns firing up from the bottom are overactive and mixing with each other indiscriminately, the models being passed down are coping as fast as they can with revamped theories and a massive restructuring of expectations. Suddenly everything is getting to the uppermost cortex as both sensate and idea. Hawkins suggests there are invariant models capable of reacting to sense data at all levels of the cortex; if we have a strong enough pattern in the lower levels, we, in a sense, don't think about it. The motor coordination is automatic. This stops happening when you're tripping; there's nothing you're not experiencing thinking about. It's as if the scope of thinking and the experience of the process contains all layers of cortex, or that there's now no distinction between your experiences of each layer. Both the experience of incoming data and the process of forming memory models along these layers are disrupted, accelerated, and amplified. Assuming Hawkins's model, the cortical hierarchy seems to disappear: you can't automate or ignore any of the data or reactions because the data is firing all over the place. Meanwhile, the lower-level distinctions between the senses are virtually gone and you can no longer tell the difference between an abstract idea and a sense registration.

The basis of our intelligence lies in the plasticity of our brain, which allows us to modify our response mechanisms. For a brief period, acid turns this plastic into liquid.

After all this settled down a bit, and the acid, if not the psychological echo, was solidly out of my system, my lobes—or "brain meats" in the jargon—started malfunctioning.[2]

The parietal lobe is responsible for integrating your senses, understanding numbers, and processing visual and spacial relationships. It also seems to be responsible for a kind of sixth sense: the awareness of your body. Damage to parietal lobes, or lack of data to them, results in the loss of this sense: if your hand is behind your back, you don't know where it is, and you can't walk without looking at your feet.[3] You have no concept of your physical self.

The parietal lobe and their neighbors, the temporal lobes, do a lot of work to allow you to operate in the world, and interesting things happen to them after prolonged sleep deprivation. The parietal lobe becomes overactive, which appears to produce better short-term memory, but the theory is it becomes overactive because it's having a harder time doing its job. The temporal lobes, on the other hand, stop reacting, which inhibits the ability to put emotional reactions in context. Though you can still talk, learn, and do math, ability in all of these degrades, and prolonged sleep deprivation seems to reshuffle which parts of your brain you use for what: the normal regions for these tasks don't get activated, but you can still do them. Alertness and attention degrade steadily, along with creativity, apparently, although whether it was my brain or the lingering effects of the LSD, creativity did not become a problem for me.

The military, naturally, is at the forefront of sleep deprivation research, or fatigue management, since there's a fairly direct correla-

---

[2] Researching brain areas quickly becomes a morbid exercise, since almost all the evidence for certain regions doing certain things comes from patients who lost function in that area of the brain through seizure or trauma, but my favorite fact about the temporal lobes is that if you damage the left one, you have trouble recognizing words, and if you damage the right one, you can't shut up.

[3] For a detailed account of what happens when your parietal function goes wonky, read "The Disembodied Lady" from *The Man Who Mistook His Wife for a Hat*, by Oliver Sacks.

tion between sleep deprivation and unacceptable losses. A lot of the research revolves around studying situational awareness, or SA, since having SA appears to be the difference between being exceptionally effective on the battlefield and littering it with your corpse.[4]

Studies show conflicting results in SA function after short-term sleep deprivation, and immediate inductive and deductive reasoning seem to hold together as the brain drafts new neurons to compensate for the ones that are tuning out. There is some consensus that it becomes harder to incorporate new information and distinguish relevant data from other sense data, trains of thought, memories, and assumptions.

The functioning of the hippocampus, which is responsible for storing long-term memories, becomes impaired, which may in part[5] explain this phenomenon. Some research on mice suggests that to compensate for this loss, the brain shifts its learning strategy mechanism to rely more heavily on the dorsal striatum, which is associated with reward-based decision making. In other words, since the ability to expand the global model of the brain is hindered, it reverts to more immediate strategies for achieving its goals. This could explain the decaying connection between the real world and my mind, as though I could function, I wasn't storing things properly. Degeneration of the prefrontal cortex and alterations in the amygdala steadily degrade the ability to recognize and express emotions, further separating me from the world as we agree upon it. This also suggests a doubling, or maybe feedback, effect: as the prefrontal cortex is losing the ability to identify data relevant to the

---

[4] The research is filled with gems like this: "Additionally, a comparison of SA data collected under baseline versus sleep-deprived conditions provided insight into the complexity of understanding the SA construct as well as the potential task and situation-dependent nature of the construct." Loosely translated: "We made the problem harder. You're welcome."

[5] Don't think I'm unaware of the plethora of qualifications like "in part," "maybe," "possibly," and "suggests," in this chapter. This is your brain on research.

situation, the amygdala is losing the ability to understand whether or not a situation is relevant in the first place.

The body can rest and repair itself without sleep, but the brain, at least in most people, cannot. There are exceptions: I personally know someone who just doesn't sleep, and shows no ill-effects, apart from some chronic depression, which may be unrelated. There are reports of people who needed less sleep after certain events or drugs. For most of us, our neurons need shutdown periods, as they don't rest the way a muscle does. They're in a constant state of alertness until you go to sleep, though meditation can produce similar recuperative states.

Executive functioning (the part of your cognition you think you control) declines as a result of sleep deprivation, as evidenced by degraded ability to do tasks that require it. There's evidence that this is not caused by the immediate dissolution of higher-order functioning, but by the degradation of non-executive, or automatic functioning. This forces the executive, cross-regional processes of the brain to work overtime to compensate. In a perhaps strained metaphor, when the internet connection goes out in an IT office, everybody pulls out their phones and connects to the internet through them at slower speeds. Total output decreases, more resources are being consumed, and everybody's pissed, but the staff didn't suddenly get dumber or do worse work, it's just that their ability to do their work has been hampered. Back to the brain, the higher functioning of the brain has to work harder and harder to deal with steadily decaying support systems.

So acid scrambled my mechanism for consciousness, stress set it on fire, and mediation and relaxation just swept everything out the door, leaving me with a tabula rasa where my estimation of reality used to be. The herculean task of rebuilding a sense of the real fell upon my executive functions, which were already scrambling to compensate for the fact that my brain's automatic systems were shutting down.

So what are the early signs of psychosis?

> Specifically, deficits in the speed of processing, executive functioning, sustained attention/

vigilance, working memory, verbal learning and memory, reasoning and problem solving, verbal comprehension and social cognition have been replicated across several studies.[6]

Psychosis seems to be linked to damage and malfunctioning of the prefrontal and temporal regions of the brain. As the effect of not sleeping hinders functioning in these areas similar to the way actual damage would hinder them, psychotic symptoms become a matter of time. Jun also suggested that part of the process was the stress—and my reaction to it over the next few days—threw me into a manic episode, which eventually devolved into a total break with reality.

The brain is much like particle physics, in that the more you know, the less sense it seems to make. I hope this has helped you make less sense of the effects of LSD, sleep deprivation, mania, and psychosis, but one thing is almost definitely true: whether or not there is something wrong or limited about the brain that psychedelics can help fix, psychosis means it's broken.

---

[6] *Early Signs, Diagnosis and Therapeutics of the Prodromal Phase of Schizophrenia and Related Psychotic Disorders,* by Molly Larson, Elaine Walker, and Michael Compton. More bibliographic information on this, and the rest of the sources for this chapter, in the bibliography.

The Mission

It's amazing how long you can run around doing crazy things before people catch up to you. The only people I fear in this world are psychopaths, because society has no defense against them. The famous ones kill dozens, sometimes hundreds of people, and these are just the sub-par psychos who need to be up close for the kill and have childhood issues. The rest of them are running nations and armies and businesses. Psychopaths are better at all these things because they don't care what happens to anyone around them. I've relied on my friend Amy, who's worked in the psychiatric field for a while, for details:

> A psychopath is someone with pervasive antisocial personality traits, though these traits may not be obvious. Other people are 'things' to a psychopath, and concepts of guilt and remorse are completely foreign to them. They have no capacity for empathy or love or sadness, not toward themselves or others, though they do feel anger, hatred and disgust; they generally don't feel fear, as in believing they are superior to everything else, they have nothing to fear. Psychopaths are almost always 'loners,' but they are often very charming—think Ted Bundy. They are unable to maintain close or long-term relationships as a result of their inability to acknowledge the needs, let alone individuality, of others.

This is quite distant from someone suffering from psychosis or having a psychotic episode. I had a psychotic episode. As Amy points out, there's no such thing as a psychotic, there are people suffering from psychosis, and these people are not psychopaths. The popular put down "psycho" exacerbates the confusion. Now, someone who is going through psychosis may kill you just as horribly as a psychopath, but they did it for different reasons. The person with psychosis thinks you're a demon or something, the psychopath just thinks you're in the way, or too ugly.

Amy on psychotic breaks:

> A psychotic break is a sudden break with reality in which the symptoms of psychosis are present—people who have no underlying genetic predispositions, 'organic' or 'functional' factors, experience these, as do people with psychotic disorders. Whether you're someone who's lived with schizophrenia for fifteen years or a perfectly sane Dutch housewife, a psychotic break is caused by a sudden trauma (watching your child be obliterated by a high-speed train) or significantly increased stress (out of smokes AND money, this, for most people suffering from schizophrenia, is something very seriously bad). The symptoms experienced by people suffering from psychotic breaks are no different from those experienced by sufferers of a persistent psychotic disorder or drug-induced psychosis, and as with drug-induced psychosis, if you've suffered one psychotic break, you're more susceptible to suffering others in the future. A psychotic break IS NOT the same thing as a nervous breakdown; it's a break from reality, whereas a nervous breakdown is your realization that your personal reality is crumbling away from you. With a psychotic break you likely wouldn't care about your personal reality and might be thrilled to have it crumble.

The good news is I never was nor shall ever be a psychopath. The bad news is I'm much more likely to snap again than your average Joe. You may understand why I tried not to think about this for six years and waited another five to write about it.

What the psychopath and the person having an episode have in common is they're not following the rules as we know them, one because he doesn't care, the other because he no longer understands them. It takes a while to catch them because nobody believes—can't believe—that someone has thrown away every last rule of being a social animal.

The Mission is a bit of a misnomer. There were many missions, and none had a meaningful endgame, or at least none of them had a probable endgame. But something was really, desperately important and I had to do something about it, for the sake of the world, for the sake of all worlds! Whatever that something was was a little shaky, but I was confident I would sort it out.

The next few days are a bit of a blur.

The best of it was the 69 car. It was a bright summer morning, and I sat outside with my loaner bass guitar, taking in the autonomy. My disciples had led me to the quest and I only had to figure out what to do with it. The sun beat down in waves, and there was, randomly, a jalopy parked outside my apartment, painted in dusty blue with an orange 69 on each side. My vision was simple. My roommate was a consummate DJ, and he would start the party here, and it would join with the other DJs starting parties along the east coast, and each party would grow, and the dances would merge as the beats beat out the newer, funkier rhythm of life across the Eastern seaboard, and I would help make the connections and sew up the edges in this hippy heaven. The 69 car was just the evidence, the concrete object that proved this heaven was on its way. There's a touch to the visual experience of an acid trip that makes the world look as if you've been wearing dusty glasses your whole life and you've just taken them off and gotten LASIK. This was still there, even though whatever the acid might still have been doing to me was overwhelmed by the not sleeping for nine days. I was way beyond visuals and simple LSD revelation; every photon was the story of a star, and every breeze was a message from the universe. Everything meant something vital to the grand puzzle I was chosen to unravel. Each note I inexpertly plucked out of my shitty bass was key, and had to be the exact note to carry the message back to the breeze, the sun, and every living thing on Earth so we could build heaven. This also involved a girl I was friends with in college, who was kind of the queen of the druggies, so we'll call her LA Queen. For some reason, in this hippy heaven, she was the absolute most important being in the universe, and I had to find her as soon as possible so we could oversee this project together. Her being in California didn't help, but we do not do these things because they are easy.

I decided I had to become a man.[1] And to become a man, I had to put away childish things. I went to my apartment and threw out my security blanket, some photographs, the broken remains of a shell that my first crush painted for me, a few other irreplaceable tokens from my past, and the three or four porn magazines. Porn turned out to be not as engaging as you might think, though it did inspire me to think that the dominatrix in one of the magazines was waiting on the island across the sandbar and I had to go find her. Fortunately, the morning I realized this, it was high tide, and I couldn't walk across water yet.[2]

Later, I ran into a waitress from one of my jobs. This girl had a boyfriend and an obvious crush on me, and though I liked her well enough, I wasn't going to let that come to term. At least, sane I wouldn't have. Crazy, I made it extremely easy for her to drive me around and eventually end up back at my place, where I somehow managed to put on a condom and fuck her brains (or more precisely my brains) out on the floor of my apartment.

---

[1] Yes, at 20. This is funny, but I'm not sure if it's funny because I was so young or because I was so old. America fucks you like that.

[2] Though I tried.

I give two thumbs up to sex while insane. You're not just having sex with a girl, you're having sex with the essence of womanhood, all women, you are fulfilling the purpose of your being and all being, you are touching the goddess, the creator of all things, you are the giving seed, the father, the son, the HOLY SHIT THE UNIVERSE EXPLODED.

She wandered off and I didn't see her until a few months later when all this was over. It turned out that sleeping with me did put the last nail in her relationship, and discovering I had been crazy at the time did not improve her mood or our friendship.

I stole my roommate's bike and rode a few miles out of town. Here, I was like Corwin, from the Amber Chronicles, by Roger Zelazny. I recommend the first five books in this series, not so much the second five. This is relatively obscure sci-fi, so I'll sum it up: the universe is an infinite number of shadow universes stretching between The Courts of Chaos and Amber, which holds the pattern. All universes are some mix of the chasm in the Courts, representing entropy, and the pattern in Amber, representing order. The inhabitants of the Courts and Amber can move through the intervening universes, or shadows, by altering particular features of the landscape in their minds, so to get back to Amber, they'll just insert features of Amber into their journey, change the color of the sky, put a forest around the next hill, and so on, until they're home, or wherever they want to be.

This is what I thought I was doing. The fact that the landscape didn't change at all from the landscape I'd travelled down a thousand times didn't phase me, as I could pick out certain new things I'd never noticed before to support my improbable thesis.

I bought some scratch tickets and scratched them the way a monk would rake a rock garden, thinking that the undiscovered key to scratch tickets was pure focus, an act of will: with each scratch, you had to select the branching universe within which there would be winning symbols underneath. Even by crazy-logic standards, I should have been selecting this universe before I got to the store, but whaddyagonnado. When the scratch tickets inevitably disappointed, I thought this was a lesson in humility from some god, and I stashed the tickets to check them later for other messages.

I called a cab after that, since taxis were the secret navigators of the shadow universes, and could take me wherever I needed to be. While waiting, an acquaintance stopped off in his car to grab a few things and offered to give me a ride. I said no, since I had the cab, and since this person was obviously a temptation to set me on the wrong path. The more insistent he got, the more I was convinced he was a trickster demon and a thief,[3] so I waved him off. He shrugged and drove away, and I got my cab. The cabbie took me back through the shadow universes until I got home. My roommate was very confused about where his bike had been.

Once home, I gathered my objects of power. Among them was a piece of iridescent glass with a face on it. It was junk tourist fodder in the real world, but to me it was my soul, or the source of my power. I walked down to the shore and dropped it in a wishing fountain, thinking I had contributed my especially important soul's power as fuel for the wishes of others. I walked back feeling high and mighty, then saw a much cooler fountain in the middle of a kind of inner-block mall. This fountain had pretty rocks in it, so I thought that was a better place for my soul, and I ran back, plucked it out of the wishing fountain, and placed it on a rock in the nicer one. Because the nicer one was the fount of the world, where being began. To hell with other people's wishes.

Near this nice fountain was the restaurant I had quit working just before everything started,[4] and I wanted that job back, because I had decided that the true love of my life was my old manager at that job, Rose. We'd gotten along pretty well at work, until I'd ruined her day by quitting and whining about how much I hated it. Honestly, I hated Viper Lady, the other manager. Even though she turned out to be pretty good company when not at work, working

---

[3] He may very well have been a thief. There was a lot of that going around, but I don't think he intended to rob me on the spot.

[4] Just prior to all this, I was waiting tables at two restaurants and washing dishes at a third. My Fridays and Saturdays consisted of waking up, waiting tables from ten to three, going home, changing, doing dishes from four to nine, going home, showering and changing, then waiting tables from ten to three in the morning. It was not a good life.

with her, and having those giant, angry eyes bulging out of her over-tanned skin while she stabbed at you with ridiculously long nails and yelled at you with a smoke-hardened voice before she even understood the situation, was too much.[5]

Rose and I had no attraction to each other at all, that I can recall. She liked big men, and I'm barely above hipster and supermodel on the sapling scale. I liked other twigs, and she was full-figured (in an attractive way, not the euphemistic way). She was also twenty-nine, and considered me a boy, and I considered her out of my age range. We had good smoke breaks together, and that was about it. I have no idea how I got to soulmate from this foundation, but there you go.

I went out to get my job back and halfway there, I was accosted by an unbelievably drunk fifty-year-old woman. She may have been a hard forty. She wanted some action. She was barely walking straight so I figured I had to help her, while removing her hands from me as she tried to get frisky. I eventually sat her down outside the restaurant where I still had a job, at least until the exact moment I showed up with an unbelievably drunk fifty-year-old

---

[5] Or at least, that's who I thought Rose was when I first wrote this. It turns out Rose's identity was much more complicated. I went to the restaurant after writing the first edition and asked if Rose was working there, and they said she worked at the Florida location, so I said, "Ah, rats," and walked off. A block later I realized Rose was actually Viper Lady's name, and during my delusion, I had assumed that two managers for one restaurant equates to both of them being aspects of a single person. I assume I took Rose's name because Rose seemed more authoritative, but far less likable, so the actual person, or the favored aspect, was the manager I liked whose name I can't recall. A decade later, I've managed to conflate the delusional memory with the real one, even though I had seen the manager I'm talking about after the fact and even remembered her name, so it's a good example of how malleable memory actually is.

woman on my arm. My coworkers were duly unimpressed. My boss was stoned, because he was always stoned.[6]

"I don't know what to do with her!"

My boss gave me an evil red eye. "Throw her back?"

At that point, Drunk Woman fell off the bench I'd put her on and I called the cops. The cops showed up—thankfully not the cops I'd run into the previous week—and started looking after her.

"How do you know her?"

"I don't."

"How did you meet her?"

"She jumped me on the sidewalk five minutes ago."

"Uh huh. What's she on?"

"I have no idea. Looks drunk."

The cop shrugged and said he'd handle it. I think they were making her touch her nose when I left to continue my mission.

I met Rose out back while she was on a smoke break.

"Oh ho. What do you want?"

"My job back."

"Oh really?"

"Yeah."

"That takes balls."

Shrug.

"I have to ask Viper Lady."

Viper Lady said no, but Rose just told me I had balls! I went skipping out, knowing that I had finally found my soulmate. I was only mildly perturbed when I ran into Drunk Woman again.

"Come on. Don't cha wanna gets a drinksh?"

I sighed and sat down next to her.

"I can't."

"Why not?"

---

[6] This job consisted of working from ten at night to three in the morning, and since we were the only food source available at that time of night, we got the drunk runoff from all the bars. To allay the difficulties in serving the extremely drunk, we had a "safety meeting" in the walk-in freezer every night at midnight, where we smoked an ample "agenda" which allowed us to screw with the drunk people in good humor.

"I found my soulmate. I'm in love."

"Really?"

She held my hand.

"Really."

"Thas shweet."

I looked down at her arm and noticed a tattoo of a rose on her arm. Of course! Now everything made sense: this was Rose in a disguise, here to test my dedication.[7] I gave her a sly smile and said, "It is."

"Aright," she said, and smiled back. I got up and left her on the bench, waving to me.

I'm sure there's an explanation for what happened next, but it was one of the very strange things that I cannot work out. I don't ascribe supernatural qualities to these things, since I don't completely trust my memory and I absolutely don't trust the interpretative powers I was exercising at that time, but two seconds later I turned around to make sure she hadn't passed out again, and she was gone. I looked around. She was nowhere to be seen. How this woman, who was barely able to walk, managed to cover the one hundred feet it would take to get out of my field of view, or fall somewhere I wouldn't notice her in open ground, I'll never know. At the time, it confirmed my theory that she was Rose's spirit-form testing me.

I didn't show up for my next shift at my remaining restaurant job, and they didn't call. I never saw anybody from that job again, aside from the waitress I'd slept with a couple of nights before, which was too bad, because the waitress I actually wanted to sleep with—before I lost the ability to discern distinct identities in other people—was this cute Russian named Anastasia, who seemed to like me because I put up with her extremely broken English for more than twenty minutes at a time. We even had a date lined up to go whale watching. Once I forgot about my soulmate,[8] I realized

---

[7] This was particularly crazy logic. Drunk Woman would not have tested my dedication to monogamy if I was single and stumbling wasted.

[8] This took about an hour, tops.

I had to go with Anastasia to the ocean to see the whales. Actually, let me reiterate:

I.
Had to Go.
With the lady Anastasia.
To the Ocean.[9]
To See.
With the Power of my Eyes.
The Whales.

Traveling back in time would be involved. Why or how was unimportant, as Anastasia, being a magical princess, would figure it out somehow.

The next time the whale watch boat went off, I chased after it, but I was too late. I shouted "Anastasia!" in front of some confused tourists. I assumed I'd simply missed the boat, and she was on to her quest without me. At the time, I had a pewter ring with whales carved into it. I consistently wear a ring on my right ring finger; this was the first. It had been dipped in the waters of several oceans, been with me when I lost my virginity, and blessed by the pope.[10] I assumed this ring was part of her nature, so I threw it into the sea after her, so she'd have her talisman on whatever journey she was on. I didn't even know if she was on the boat. Well, no, I knew she was on the boat; there was just no actual evidence of the fact, as there was no evidence for most of the things I believed at that point. I think I thought she was actually a whale,[11] and had to go back to her people.

So that was the end of that, and I never saw her again. To think, had I just not done acid, this whole summer might have

---

[9] At Tanagra.

[10] This isn't that hard. You just go to the Vatican, stick something in an envelope, and the pope does a mass blessing over the envelopes every Tuesday or something, then they send it back to you.

[11] This is not flattering, and in fact she was the usual kind of stick figure I run after.

been the story of me hooking up with my hot Russian coworker.[12] Oh well. On to the next obsession.

I got back into my LA Queen trip. Since the actual LA Queen was probably in LA, I had to slap her identity onto whomever was at hand, and that was a girl whose name I can't remember, so we'll call her Jess, since I've known a lot of hot girls named Jess. My relationship with Jess, prior to this point, consisted of us working together at the job I quit, an occasional conversation, her pity and condescension, and me staring at her ass. I'm not even an ass man, but this was a great ass.

So I went to the restaurant and asked for her, since it wasn't creepy at all, no, she was LA Queen in disguise, and was just waiting for me to figure that out. Keep in mind I just quit my job at this restaurant, asked for it back, didn't get it, and had been running all over town acting weird for the last few days. There is no possible way word of my goings on hadn't spread all over town. They sat me down with a couple of dinner rolls and said she was busy, then twenty minutes later told me she had left. Looking back, they probably put me someplace they could keep an eye on me and told her she could leave early. I didn't grasp this at all, so I went to where I knew she lived, still thinking she was someone else.

When I finally caught up to her, she took one look at me and decided I was tripping out, and just a harmless shy kid with a crush. One hundred hours prior, she would have been right, and to her credit, she was close. She had no idea I thought she was someone else. She talked to me patiently, asked me if I was tripping, which I denied, and I tried to mumble my way through the infinitely complex explanation for my behavior in a way that would make sense but still follow the rules of The Game.

She wasn't having it. She patted me on the shoulder and said I had to go away.

Suddenly I realized that she wasn't LA Queen, she was my twin sister! How could I not have realized? It was so obvious. Before she ran upstairs, I tried to confirm my theory.

"Are you my twin sister?"

_____

[12] And to this very day, despite all efforts, I've never slept with a Russian.

She laughed. "Uh, no. Jesus."

And she vanished. I would love to get her version of this story, but sans fame on my part and saintly patience on hers, I have no way to find or convince her, if she even remembers.

I went home. Bereft of women to obsess over, I started drumming up more fiction from childhood to imprint on my consciousness. What better than *The Hitchhiker's Guide to the Galaxy*?

I don't know what exactly my mission was when I walked out of town. I went to the local college. I was drifting, swapping delusions with abandon, but I knew this wasn't my world, and when I ended up in the College of the Atlantic parking lot and saw a Ford, I knew that Ford Prefect was a metaphor for a car, a car to the galaxy.[13] I tried to break into one,[14] but to no avail. I heard a car coming into the parking lot, so I hid under metaphor Ford until it passed.

I saw the stars. They were calling to me. I could see the depth between the far and the near, the blackness and the hidden galaxies behind the blackness.

I called a friend. I can't remember his name either, and haven't kept in touch. He was a thirty-something musician Jake and I had hung out with for a while until he said he needed to hang out with friends his own age. I respect that, looking back, but he was kind of an awkward dick about it. I wish I could look him up. All I recall was calling him on my cell phone and saying something along the lines of:

"I need your help. I'm on a mission. Can I come over?"

"Uh . . . phew . . . um, Pete, are you okay?"

"I'm fine."

"Okay, look, I don't think that's a good idea. I think you need to go home and get some rest. Okay?"

---

[13] For what it's worth, Ford Prefect did actually get his name from the Ford model Prefect.

[14] I do actually know how to break into cars, but I've only ever done it for friends and myself when one of us locked the keys in by accident. I didn't even have to break into the car that eventually earned my probation during this little episode. Foreshadowing.

"Okay."

And I hung up.

I wandered back toward home. The conflicting universes I was living in were breaking all over my head, and I had no idea what to do. I decided there were two paths, one leading to the hippy heaven and all earthly pleasure with LA Queen, one leading into the night, the stars, and some secret on the far end of the darkness. And I had to choose. I was walking through the woods near College of the Atlantic, along a path running to a bridge over a stream, and as I knew I had to make this decision, I looked up for a sign.

I saw a shooting star. And I saw it split into two shooting stars above me.

For all my delusions, I never saw anything that wasn't there. Aside from the strange taste to my visual landscape and the intensity of everything I saw and the meanings I attributed to it, there were no hallucinations. No green aliens, no dinosaurs or trees attacking me. No ghosts or lizards or people turning into bats. No people who weren't really there. The documentation and witness reports generally agree that every physical thing I saw was also seen by reliable witnesses, and even if I thought a pen was a wand with which to rewrite the future and past, I did actually see a pen and understand it was a writing instrument.

There was no one with me to verify the splitting star. But I have every reason to believe it happened. Nowadays I write it off as an astonishing meteorological coincidence. At the time, it was the universe telling me that I didn't have to make the choice. I got two wishes. I could follow both paths, and all paths, forever. I could have everything. I could do anything.

The Naked Guy

An LSD trip is not a model psychosis. I have no doubt they are physiologically related, but the subjective experience of delusional thinking is as different from acid as acid is from being drunk. It's the inability to communicate subjective experience, and the occasional ability of acid to induce psychosis, that causes people to think they're the same experience.

One of the common themes in psychedelic reports is the feeling, during and after, that under it all there is an authentic self beneath it all. LSD amplifies You. Psychosis nullifies You by removing all coherent sense of self, which is not the same as temporarily nuking your ego. That central core of being, the illusion of the operator, becomes malleable and out of control, changing without regard to reason or evidence.

When I related the short version of this part of the story to some friends in Bar Harbor, three years after the fact, two of them dropped their cigarettes and said, "Oh my god, YOU'RE the naked guy!" I don't go to Bar Harbor much anymore, so I don't know how long the story lasted, but it survived at least five or six years past my time.

When I first related this part of the story to my dad, he just said, "Lucky you didn't think you were a bird."

Another sleepless night. I had to figure out what to do with the message from the stars. I chose to drink my roommate's soul.

As mentioned before, my roommate was black, and I happened to have a bottle of Blackstone merlot sitting around. Clearly, it was the holder of my roommate's soul, and in order to become him, and achieve whatever it was I was bent on achieving, I had to drink his soul. Because everything with the word "black" in it is clearly connected to anything possessing the property of being black, right?[1] I consumed most of the bottle, then at the last minute realized this was a trick implanted in my mind by The Evil, and I needed JD to complete my mission, so I stopped about two gulps from the bottom and left it on the table.

The next couple of hours are hazy. I recall wandering around my room in nothing but a pair of shorts, desperately trying to figure out the next step. I was reading the patterns in my rug, looking over my remaining possessions with a dark light, and scattering change on the floor in some kind of capitalist I Ch'ing. The coins told me nothing, but then staring out the window told me I had to sleep with the Earth Mother.

Unfortunately for everyone, I decided my roommate's on and off girlfriend was the Earth Mother. Of all the hippies I've met under forty in my day, Earth Mother was the closest to the real thing. Impeccably chill, lazily wise, constantly stoned, efficiently crunchy, and into quiet moments on the beach. We were decent friends at that point.

That evening, my roommate was hanging out with a couple of friends in the living room, and Earth Mother was already trying to pass out. 'Twas not to be. I ran out of my room in my shorts, went into my roommate's room, and hopped into bed with her.

JD later described the conversation he had with one of his friends after I did this.

Friend of JD: "What the fuck?"

JD (lighting bowl): "She can take care of herself."

Once I was in bed, Earth Mother looked over.

---

[1] Some interesting implicit racism here. It's not like everything that was white ran together for me. Maybe it's defensible in that the white over black population in Bar Harbor is about a million to one during the summer, but I can only offer up psychotic episode plus middle-class guilt.

"Hey, Pete."

I said nothing.

"You need something?"

I started crying, and gripping her arm.

"Okay, Pete, you're scaring me."

I backed off, confused. What was I supposed to be doing here? I'd forgotten, but it was really important.

"Okay. Let's go outside."

I jumped up, she sighed and wrapped the sheet around herself, then led me outside into the night.

Once we were outside, she looked up at the stars, then looked at me. "Nice night. Why don't you take a walk, get some air."

And she went inside. That was the last I ever saw of her, and out of everybody, I'm saddest about that, because we had a good rapport, and I never got the chance to explain how nuts I was.

I didn't go for a walk right away. I went to my neighbors' apartments, but there had been a sort of exodus recently, what with the summer ending and the work drying up. This is probably for the best. With no one to get orders from, I started walking down the road.

I felt dehydrated. This is probably from consuming nothing but a bottle of red wine all day, but at the time, I thought it was because my body was aging rapidly. I started walking like an old man, hunched over, crouched, the moisture being sucked out of my body like I'd just opened the arc of the covenant. I felt I was aging and dying in a second, then I was regressing back through my genes, and I was suddenly a monkey.

This is where I stripped off my clothes and started making monkey noises. At two in the morning on the main drag of Bar Harbor. I ran about six blocks, and my first witnesses turned a corner in front of me.

"What the fuck . . . ?" was the first response.

"Fucking right dude!" was the second, then they started cheering and clapping.

Being a monkey, I was afraid.

There's a small square in Bar Harbor, that's gated off during the night. There's a walkway above it, separated by a two-foot gap of wood. In order to escape the witnesses, I lunged over to the gate, climbed up it, jumped up and grabbed the railing along the walkway, hoisted myself over, ran around the walkway on all fours to the other side, hopped over the rail, and shimmied down one of the pillars on the other side.

I've often gone back to look at that gate and consider how incredibly stupid it would be to do something like that even if I was in shape, and I wasn't. Had I missed grabbing the lip above the gate, I would have fallen backwards about ten feet and broken my fall with the back of my skull on the sidewalk.

I made it, which is the important thing.[2] I ran across the parking lot behind the square, and dashed down to the end of a pier. I sat, crouched, at the very edge, above a fifteen-foot drop to the water below, and then I thought I was a fish.

I knew I had to truly, truly believe I was a fish, and once I did, I could jump, swim to the center of the Earth, and restart creation as it should have been, once I took on the primal form, the first life, the first hint of awareness. This was what needed to be done.

When I was a kid, I saw a Jem cartoon where one of the characters had been dosed with a hallucinogen. Of course, they didn't say it was a hallucinogen, since they weren't in business of spreading accurate information; they were in the business of telling children all drugs will wreck your life. At some point she's dancing around like a drunken teenager on a balcony, shouting, "Wheeee, I can fly, I can fly!"

This is not how it works.

I sat for a long time, breathing the universe in with each breath, breathing out the air of creation and acceptance. I felt my hands merge in front of me. I felt my fins grow out. I felt my legs turning scaly, a tail growing.

I tipped myself, ever so slowly, off the end of the pier.

---

[2] Kind of. I'm not sure what the important thing was that night.

The sensation of falling and the oncoming water was as close to the feeling of the end of everything that is me that I can imagine experiencing. I don't expect to top it until I actually die.[3]

When I hit the icy ocean water,[4] I had the last moment of clarity I would have for the next two and a half months. My thought was:

FUCK THIS IS COLD.

The cold water did something intense, albeit brief, to my brain, and at the very least delivered some accurate data to my survival instincts.

I have no idea how, but I climbed back up the pier without so much as a splinter. I got to the top, and started breathing, heavily, leaning over the edge. I breathed, and the madness took over again, I was dead, dying, crossing over, reborn, seeing the universe, insane, what the hell.

A truck pulled into the parking lot and shined its high beams on me. Someone shouted from it, "Hey, are you the naked guy?"

"Yeah!" I gasped. "That's me."

"You okay, man? You need any help?"

"No, I'm fine. Thank you."

"Aright dude."

And they drove away.

I made my way back, hiding in bushes, since I'd fooled the first patrol, but clearly there were men in pickup trucks with shotguns trying to kill me and stop the mission. The now very unclear mission. I picked up my clothes and made it back to my apartment, where I tried to put it all together.

---

[3] And hopefully not even then, as I'd much prefer to tap out in my sleep or during an orgasm involving the Dallas cheerleaders.

[4] Water in Maine is frigid all the way through summer.

People Finally Start Catching On

I've spent much of my life trying to describe how psychosis works to people who've never done good acid. Trippers get it for the most part; I just say, "Like the weird thoughts you have while tripping but you never stop believing." Belief is a big part of it: all capacity for skepticism and doubt is gone. It's confirmation bias on crack. It's like being three years old with no parents to explain things or tell you when you're wrong. But it's not just that. When I say I thought I was a fish, a part of me knew that my body had not changed in any specific way, I just believed, absolutely, that it would if I summoned the image strongly enough, and when nothing happened, I found a new story to follow. If a delusion got so out of control that it required superphysical proof that wasn't coming, I'd adapt the delusion or move on to another one.

Most of the attributes and identities I imbued in the people and things around me required no proof. It wasn't that a person was growing horns or summoning spirits, it was that I reevaluated what "person" and "spirits" and "summoning" meant, enough to attach them to any individual or object, but not enough to separate them from their roots. Etymology, homonyms, alliteration, fiction, and history all became paths for attaching meaning and substance to the signs on my autobahn of thought. It didn't help that I was particularly well read, and had been studying ontology and semantics over the previous year. My mind was packed with superficial knowledge and tricks for arbitrarily removing and reattaching meaning.

That's one of the most important lessons I took from this. It's also the saddest. Few people have ever believed in anything as totally as I believed in a litany of demonstrably false beliefs. I'm left with the doubt about this life, occasionally wondering if I did die at the end of that pier, or even during my first trip, and this is Leary's afterlife, or if I'm strapped to a bed somewhere on an IV drip. But I will never believe in anything again, because I've seen how easily the mechanism for belief can be tripped.[1]

There are two works that I've read that accurately capture the experience of being crazy. The first is *The Invisibles*, which I recommend to anybody. *The Invisibles* is the description of the world where every dream is a gateway and every drug is right, and especially in the beginning, the hazy line between magic and "maybe I just wasn't looking" is almost perfectly scratched into the mirror. The other is Jesus's inner struggle in *The Last Temptation of Christ*.

I managed to dry off. People were after me. Men with shotguns. Because I was an agent of the re-creation of the world. Or because I was traveling in an alien galaxy. Whatever. I had to plan my next move.

Around dawn, my next move was to equip myself. Running around naked wouldn't do. I'd failed in the Regression of the Fish, so I had to seek out the next path. I donned black slacks, my dress shoes, a blue button-down shirt, a belt, yellow-tinted shades, and an antique army coat, black, knee length, with red crosses sewn into the cuffs and collar. I also took some totems: a piece of tigereye, a few coins, some other junk that didn't do me much good. I had one of those Nokia brick cell phones that everybody had back then, which had become the most fascinating object in the universe.

---

[1] This is also why I patiently try to explain to conspiracy theorists that their beliefs are psychotic.

We'll never know, but if I'd had an iPhone I probably never would have left my apartment.[2]

I set off in the foggy morning. A few blocks down the road, I realized I was a vampire, and since I was essentially wearing the uniform for a local restaurant, I assumed the restaurant was the vampire lair. I cruised in as the waiters were getting ready for the morning shift, headed to the upstairs bar, and drank the cold drink that was sitting there. I think it was an Irish coffee. Then I sat, waiting for my vampire minions to collect.

Eventually, the owner of the restaurant found me. I got a lot of sympathy during this, because I was pale and gaunt due to barely eating during the last two weeks, and I had a thousand-mile stare usually reserved for war veterans. I also rarely said anything that was obviously insane, because I understood that all language was complex code for what was really going on that only the initiated understood, so I had to talk and respond "normally."

"Hello?" said the manager.

"Hi . . ." I said.

My natural empathy[3] saw the concern in his eyes, and I felt sad. He must have picked up on this.

"Are you okay?"

"I don't think so."

I was as far from okay as you can really get, but I said it for different reasons. My vampire minions hadn't come to me, so maybe I wasn't a vampire, so I had to figure out what I was.

"Do you want to go to the hospital?"

"Okay," I said, and followed him.

---

[2] This may not be true. I'm sure I could have imbued all my iPhone apps with infinitely complex purpose, but I've found that when tripping, media-rich experiences are the most boring. *The Matrix*, for instance, has so much going on, your brain focuses on sorting out the sensory input, and has less time to screw around with it. The most interesting thing when tripping is low lighting and wood grain.

[3] Which is stronger than most people's and stayed strong throughout the whole episode.

Someday I need to find this human being and thank him for one of the most amazing acts of kindness performed by a total stranger. I was a possibly dangerous crazy person who had just cruised into his restaurant, and he took me to the hospital, instead of calling the police or just beating the hell out of me.[4] He dropped me off outside the emergency room, and I turned myself in for the first time.

At this point, his concern had convinced me I'd done something really bad. I decided it was because I had killed Jake, which was the only reason I could feel this bad.

This is not totally out of the blue; Jake has a condition which allows him to suck in his chest to the point where there's a hole in the middle of it in which a medium-sized person could fit his fist. I decided that hole hadn't been there because it was genetic and had always been there; it was there because I punched through his rib cage and crushed his heart. Why had I done this? Because I was on a crack bender.

Since Jake is still alive, it's pretty obvious that I did not do this, but this is what I told the doctor when I turned myself in. He was nonplussed. He stuck his finger up my ass to check for something drug-related, I don't know what, but I distinctly remember the sensation, and it was a little bit like being stabbed in the gut by God. Having had another proctologist root around for more normal medical reasons, I can say proctology is best experienced while sober.[5] He told me not to use my cell phone while in the hospital, so of course that was the first thing I did. Here's my mom:

---

[4] Which wouldn't have been wise. Never fight crazy people. It's one step short of fighting the Terminator; they won't interpret the pain they receive or the damage they do correctly, so unless you make it physically impossible for them to go on, they won't stop, and they may not know when they're killing you.

[5] Though still not on my top-ten list of things to do.

> I was in my office in the garage when Sam[6] came
> out and said you had called the house. He said you
> sounded "kinda strange" and told him you were
> planning to drive your truck (a phantom truck?)
> to California. I immediately took off for Bar Har-
> bor to find you.

I'm dim on the precise delusion, but I think I was back on the one that involved LA Queen. This would not be the last time I needed to get to California. Aside from LA Queen, I was born in San Francisco, so there was probably some return-to-the-scene-of-the-crime symbolism involved.

The doctor came back in and yelled at me for using my cell phone, but failed to confiscate it. He told me to sit tight and he'd be right back. He was calling the police, but they would be frustrated yet again, since as soon as he left, I wandered out the other door and escaped via the service entrance.

I distinctly remember the next delusion: I was Doctor Who. Since it was a foggy morning, I took that as a sign that I was wandering back through time, to undo the wrongs wronged and make sure the rights kept on righting. I rearranged my visual experience to place me in the Victorian age, and eventually got as far as the Middle Ages before the morning traffic made that thought untenable. I managed to get back to my apartment.

Back to my mom, since I don't remember the details of getting home:

> I spent an hour or so looking for you and asking
> around—picking up rumors of a kid fitting your
> description and acting weird. Eventually I parked
> in front of your apartment and waited until you
> wandered back there. I bundled you into the car
> and took you home. You wanted to get some stuff
> from the apartment so we went in for a few min-
> utes. Your cool DJ roommate was there and told

---

[6] My brother.

me he thought you were really depressed. It would have been more helpful if he'd told me you were stark raving mad but he either didn't realize that or was trying to spare my feelings.

Anyway, I took you home to Hancock. You were pretty quiet and seemed kind of dazed and not too coherent. At one point you said something like, "I don't know who I am." I took this to be existential angst rather than the literal truth it turned out to be. I've often wondered how I could have failed to realize that my own son was psychotic. In my defense, my experience with drugs was limited to weed and alcohol and I had no inkling of the potential for the kind of experience you're describing. Maybe if Tom[7] had been there he'd have recognized what was happening, but he was at work in Augusta. So I put you to bed and went to bed myself. At this point, I demonstrated my total misjudgment of the situation by taking a sleeping pill (dealing with my own insomniac tendencies in those days). Ambien is a pretty benevolent drug that leaves no hangover, but it makes you completely unable to function—or even stand up—until it wears off about six hours after you take it. So when Sam knocked on my door and said you were in your room sobbing I didn't get up to check on you.

Here are some of the details I do remember. I got home, and spent a good amount of time crying, as I had failed in my mission, and this was clearly some kind of posthumous penance, and I had to get through it to deal with the next stage of my existence. My mom went off to do something in her office, near our house, and I wandered around this strange new place, which was also the place I grew up in for eight years.

---

[7] My dad.

I saw my mom's hormone pills on the kitchen counter, which happened to be spherical. Since there were only two of them in the container, I realized I'd failed in my missions because I'd lost my balls,[8] and here they were, so I just had to take them and everything would be all right. I have no idea what the effect of taking female hormones is supposed to be when you're male and insane, but what it did to me was make me hear voices behind the narration on the book tape my brother put on when I went to bed. Here's my brother:

> I am so innocent of drugs that I was three years out of college before I could pick up the smell of pot on my own. The sixteen-year-old me had no idea how to take care of someone on a bad acid trip. I basically went from kind of paying attention to *Tales of the City* to having a Miss Madrigal party in my room.
>
> I can explain the book tape. It seemed like an awesome idea at the time. Some of our earliest childhood memories are of listening to *The Hitchhiker's Guide to the Galaxy* on these warbly old tapes. I thought the soothing voice of Douglas Adams reading words we'd fallen asleep to a thousand times would bring him back to the real world, or something. I think I began to suspect my plan had gone awry when I looked up at the loft where he was and had the creepy feeling that someone I had never met was looking at me with my brother's eyes. I must have fallen asleep shortly after that, because when I woke in the morning, Barb[9] was knocking on my door telling me to get up, and Peter was gone.
>
> At least I didn't play the Ray Bradbury tapes.

---

[8] Had I taken a logical leap to "marbles," much of the following might have been averted.

[9] My mom.

My brother had the right idea, but I was way, way past the point where nostalgia could have settled my mind. The voice behind the Douglas Adams' voice told me the universe had ended around this house. Everything was slowly collapsing, the stars were winking out, and the end of everything was unfolding beyond the skylight.

One of the continuing themes during this period was thinking I hadn't survived my first acid trip, and the past few years had just been Leary's afterlife, and I was just reaching the end game of a five-second hallucination, a la *Jacob's Ladder*. Though this delusion ebbed and flowed among my other delusions, it never failed to create a sense of dread and urgency, both to avoid the million-dimensional knot and to do whatever it is you're supposed to do on the dividing line between life and death. So regardless of what I was thinking, it absolutely had to be done, immediately, because there was the reoccurring possibility that I was living the last microseconds of my mortal existence. The whispered ending of the universe did nothing to alleviate this feeling.

I got up. I went to the TV and put on the Matrix, and realized this world was a fake, not precisely in the Matrix way, but the Matrix was a code telling me I had to save the universe, and all this paltry physical bullshit wasn't real. I think I put my head against the screen to better understand the message. I was Neo, lacking only my Trinity.

Fortunately, I had been infatuated with a goth-esque girl who was my neighbor the previous year, so that was my Trinity, and every time my cell phone did anything even slightly out of the ordinary, it was her contacting me. Since she's going to show up a lot in the future, we'll just keep calling her Trinity.

I needed to get a move on. Step one was to restart the universe.[10] In order to do that, I had to get my physical essence integrated into the physical world, since I was the nub of Real Reality to which the ashes of the old universe were clinging. I took the keys to my mom's car, and drove to the shore, where I spit into the

---

[10] Again.

ocean. I still think this shows a fair amount of intelligence given the delusional rules I was abiding by. If you have an ice-nine situation relying on your body fluids to save creation, step one is definitely spitting in the ocean.

From there, I drove to Southwest Harbor, and en route decided I was Shannon.

Shannon was a friend of mine who occasionally had okay parties, and, more importantly, rich parents with an amazing house, a sauna, a pool table, and a 36-inch TV with surround sound.[11] I had done my job, achieved my mission, and it was time to reap my reward as a former Florida DJ retiring to the woods. He really was a DJ in Florida for a while, and remember I already had a hard-on for world-saving DJs.

I drive to a parking lot in Southwest Harbor, and low and behold, there is my phantom truck. I park my parents' car, get into the truck, and start rooting around. Since I skipped getting dressed on my way out of my parents' house, I'm only wearing underwear and a pair of shorts. After I put on the shades sitting on the dashboard, I find a lockbox and start trying to open it.

"Hey!" says the woman I assume owned the truck.

"Hello," I say, without a care in the world.

"Get the hell out of my truck!"

"Oh, okay," I say, realizing this was not my phantom truck, honest mistake.

She looks at me disbelieving.

"Um. Those are mine."

"Oh, sorry." I hand her the shades.

"That's mine too."

"What?"

She points at the lockbox.

"Oh, sorry." I hand her the lockbox.

"Maybe you should turn yourself in to the police."

"That sound like a good idea," I say, and now I'm sad again, as I'm picking up on her anger and confusion. "Where are they?"

"Right over there."

---

[11] Remember this is 2000. That shit was badass. Especially in Maine.

I smile at her, say, "Thank you!" and turn myself in for the second time in twenty-four hours.

I give the police much the same story I'd given the doctor, except this time, my name is Shannon, I'd killed Jake during a heroin bender that I couldn't remember, and I'd done every drug known to man in the last month. You can't buy that kind of on-the-spot creativity. The only surviving report I could find just says this:

> Reported person claiming to have killed someone.
> 406 advised that subject was still under the influence of LSD from night of 8/22. Spoke w/family of "victim" who stated he was alive and well.

Of course my chemical situation was far worse than that. I assume that given my behavior, everybody was just going on what they already knew, which was Jake had flipped out on acid and maybe I'd done it again and was doing what Jake had done. Here's my mom, upon discovering her car was missing:

> All I could do at that point was call the police. I dialed 911 and was routed to the Sheriff's Department. I told them you'd taken my car and I was afraid you were suicidal (still not understanding what was going on with you). The dispatcher sent out an APB (or whatever they call it these days) and kept me on the phone for a few minutes. While we were talking he got a response from a cop in Southwest Harbor. The cop was standing outside the police station leaning against a car to take down the information about my car when he suddenly realized that it was my car he was leaning on. He'd just returned from the hospital in Bar Harbor, where he'd taken a kid he'd found wandering around the parking lot in his underwear acting crazy. My baby. I got a ride to Southwest Harbor, picked up the car and headed for the hospital.

The people at the hospital were happy to find out who you were, since you had been unable to tell them. This was the moment I finally realized how crazy you were. You didn't know who you were, who I was, where you were, what year it was—possibly what century it was.

They took me back to the same hospital I'd turned myself in to the first time, where the very same doctor saw me, and he was not happy.

"I told you to stay put!"

"Yeah . . ."

They brought in somebody from some emergency mental outreach program in Bar Harbor, who recognized my state of mind immediately. She was very nice and helpful, and had a tattoo of a rose on her arm, so obviously Rose had come to my aid in a new body.

I spent about an hour sobbing, because at this point I'd gotten enough negative reinforcement to convince me I had in fact died on the pier and was now in Hell. I felt nothing but fear, disappointment, and helplessness. I was doomed to spend the rest of eternity in this room, alone, with the occasional person stopping in to tell me there was nothing they could do.

Fortunately, there was something people could do. Back to my mom:

> They were trying to find a bed in a mental health hospital for you and so far were having no luck. I called Norm and asked for help. Occasionally it turns out to be helpful when one's Old Boyfriend Network includes a local emergency room director. He spoke to the ER liaison with Acadia Hospital in Bangor, which had claimed not to have any beds available. Turned out they could scare up a bed as a favor to Norm. I went to the Army/ Navy store and bought you some clothes and they

put you in an ambulance and sent you off to Bangor.

Odd little vignette here: What with all the phone calls to Tom, Sam and Norm passing on information and trying to sort things out, my cell phone had died. So I switched to using yours. You had changed the settings in your phone so everything was in French—an odd choice since you didn't speak a word of French. You had also turned off the ringer. My limited command of the language and general stress level meant I couldn't figure out how to turn the ringer back on. So I had to stand outside the hospital staring at the phone while I waited for people to call me back. Theatre of the Absurd.

I still don't speak a word of French. I know there was a very good reason for changing the language on my phone, but I don't remember what it was. The ringer was off because the cell phone was my means of moving through all these strange universes, and I had to do it silently.

All that mattered now was that I was going to the institution.

They strapped me down in the ambulance. It was very red. After my stint in Hell, this was my rebirth. The ambulance was the afterlife metaphor for taking me to another womb. The EMTs were angels or devils or spirits, coaxing me back to pre-consciousness, lulling me to the form of a fetus, taking me to my next life, where I could try it all again, because I'd failed so miserably in this one. I was about to be reincarnated.

In a mental institution.

Interlude: Admission Report[1]

PATIENT'S NAME: WELCH, PETER H.
SEX: M.
ADMIT DATE: 8/24/2000.
HANDEDNESS: He is ambidextrous.[2]
ALLERGIES: Allergies to dust, pollen, cats, and dogs.

PAST MEDICAL HISTORY: He denies any recent exposure
to infectious process, but states that he was exposed
to HIV when he was 18 years old. He states that a
friend of his was cutting himself, that he wanted his
friend to stop cutting himself, and that he licked
his friend's blood.[3] When asked if this person had
HIV, he said he thought so.[4] He has a history of a
head injury. He states he was dropped when he was
little.[5] He tripped and fell onto a concrete floor at

_____

[1] This is a best-of compilation of the records I received from Acadia Hospital. I've included all the original documentation in appendix D.

[2] Dexterous as I am, this is not technically true, though I may have said so.

[3] It was a liberal arts school.

[4] He only mentioned the possibility after I licked the blood. Turns out he didn't, and it turns out HIV can't survive in open air, so even if he did, odds of transmission were dismal.

[5] According to my parents.

the age of 4 and lost consciousness.[6] He is unable to
give me any other medical history.

PAST PSYCHIATRIC HISTORY: According to the patient's
mother, when he was 6 years old, he had a psychiatric
evaluation due to depression and anxiety. He participated in family therapy and improved. As a teenager,
mother remembers him as having been on and off depressed but never to the point of requiring treatment.

SURGERIES: Tonsillectomy at age 7, appendectomy at
age 8.[7]

FAMILY HISTORY: He is unable to tell me his mother's
or father's ages. When asked how old they were, he
told me 150. According to him they are both alive and
well, but he has a brother age 25, a brother age 21,
and a sister age 21 with no health problems.[8]

SOCIAL HISTORY: He has been living at _____ Street
in Bar Harbor. He attended MDI High School, but left
after his sophomore year. He has worked as a waiter,
dishwasher, tennis instructor, and a bartender.[9] He
states he also has taught math and English.[10]

CONDITION AT ADMISSION: Upon admission, Peter presented as a disheveled, withdrawn, guarded, and un-

---

[6] I still remember this, but it may be a fake memory.

[7] I must have told them this. The tonsils came out around 9, and I still
have an appendix.

[8] I don't know where these siblings came from. I have one brother, who
was 16 at the time.

[9] True, true, true, false.

[10] Sort of.

derweight young Caucasian male.[11] He had very poor eye
contact, minimal cooperation with the interview.
There was significant psychomotor retardation to the
point of near catatonia.[12] For prolonged periods of
time during the interview, he would remain almost motionless with closed eyes. When moving, he would do
it extremely slowly. His speech was spontaneous,[13]
fluent, hypophonic,[14] and monotone, without much inflection and minimal emotional content. His mood was
detached, and affect flat. Though processes were with
significant circumstantiality, tangentiality, and
loosening of associations. At times, he was positive
for thought blocking.[15] His thought content was with
vague delusions of persecution. He had positive visual and auditory hallucinations.[16] He denied in an
inconsistent manner suicidal and homicidal thoughts
or plans. His cognition was difficult to assess because of poor compliance. He appeared alert and ori-
entated to person and place, but not to time. When
asked the date, he initially replied February 28,

---

[11] They would have said this if I'd shown up sane and sober with a Ph.D. dissertation in my hands.

[12] I thought I was dead, and dead people don't move much.

[13] Deferring to my friend Amy for professional insight. Amy's notes: Which, to me, contradicts observations that you were responding to internal stimuli before answering.

[14] Amy's notes: soft or weak voice.

[15] Wikipedia says, "Thought blocking, a phenomenon that occurs in people with psychiatric illnesses (usually schizophrenia), occurs when a person's speech is suddenly interrupted by silences that may last a few seconds to a minute or longer." Amy clarifies: It means you weren't saying whatever popped into your head and seemed to be actively trying to push it away.

[16] Not true, though I can understand why they thought so.

1980,[17] and then later on, January 1, 2000.[18] Capacity to focus, sustain and shift attention, as well as the ability to present the events of recent days in a sequential manner, were severely impaired. His insight and judgment were quite poor.[19]

IDENTIFYING INFORMATION: Peter Hunt Welch is a 20-year-old single Caucasian male who was residing in Bar Harbor, Maine this summer. He is a University of Maine at Orono student with no prior psychiatric history, who was admitted to the Acadia Hospital on an involuntary basis[20][21] due to an acute level of confusion and disorganization, both behaviorally and cognitively. He was evaluated at MDI and was transferred from that facility due to psychosis, impulse thoughts, delusions, and disorientation. He was felt to be a risk to himself and others due to his high level of disorganization and disorientation and

---

[17] This has to do with a complicated delusion involving being reborn; that's my actual date of birth.

[18] Another delusion involving the restart of the universe on one of my generation's original doomsday dates.

[19] They nailed that one.

[20] This, according to the insurance companies, wasn't precisely true, since I signed myself in when I was initially admitted. My dad later pointed out to the insurance company, "When my son signed himself in, the only person he put on his visitors list was his dead ex-girlfriend. If you want to take this to court, let me know." The insurance company didn't call back.

[21] Amy's notes: And if you hadn't signed yourself in, you probably wouldn't have been hospitalized at all because it's incredibly difficult to get someone involuntarily committed unless they've been seen multiple times in the same emergency department within a relatively short period of time and they have been very, very disruptive. Seriously—I've had clients who were threatening my life, destroying property, and significantly injuring themselves get discharged from the ER back to me before the end of my shift.

impulsivity.[22] He did not know where he was. He believed that he had murdered his friend by sucking out
his soul.[23] The patient was also reporting, upon admission, that he could see, smell, hear and touch
God. She has an acid smoky smell.[24] Patient is an unreliable historian.[25] He initially denied any alcohol
or drug use, but later on admitted to having had LSD
on several occasions. He also acknowledged the use of
heroin, crack, cocaine, mushrooms, ecstasy, speed,
etc.[26][27][28] Just prior to his admission to Acadia Hospital, he had been displaying markedly abnormal behavior with confusion, illogical statements, and appearing disoriented, and as if walking in a daze.
When asked about sexual activity, he does not discuss
whether he prefers males or females, but states that
he has used condoms,[29] and he has been sexually active. He reported unusual experiences like having
seen the earth and the bottom of the sea. He stated
that almost continuously he is able to see around him

---

[22] Sometimes people still say this about me.

[23] My means of killing Jake had evolved somewhat.

[24] Prove me wrong.

[25] Hah!

[26] False, false, false, true, false, true, etc.? Etcetera in a substance abuse report? Was I boring them?

[27] Amy's notes: No, they reached a point where they felt you were listing off every drug you could think of and listed only what they thought there was a good chance you'd used.

[28] Response to Amy's notes: Not entirely; they listed a bunch for me to confirm and then told my parents and my doctors that I'd been on them.

[29] Probably in the trash can somewhere.

many of his friends.[30] He acknowledged the presence of
thought broadcasting but denied thought insertion or
withdrawal.[31] He also denied any ideas of reference.[32]

PHYSICAL EXAMINATION: General: This is a very emaci-
ated, 20-year-old who is awakened for the physical.
He is somewhat sedated. He is very spacey. He appears
to be responding to internal stimuli and stares. No
eye contact. He is cooperative. He has been making
inappropriate hypersexual comments, so much of this
physical examination is also limited, due to that
fact.[33] Height is 5 feet 8 inches.[34] Weight is 123-1/4
pounds.[35] Temperature is 37,[36] pulse 60, respiration
16, blood pressure 108/80. Head: Normocephalic.[37] No
lesions or tenderness. Skin: There is some slight facial acne. Patient appears to have a tinea infection
of his arms, back, and chest.[38] Eyes: Pupils are

---

[30] This is probably where they got the visual hallucinations from. It wasn't
that I saw extra people, I just thought that the strangers around me were
my friends in different bodies.

[31] Because my thought-fu is the strongest.

[32] I have no clue what this means, so Wikipedia again: "Ideas of reference
and delusions of reference involve people having a belief or perception
that irrelevant, unrelated or innocuous phenomena in the world refer to
them directly or have special personal significance: 'the notion that everything one perceives in the world relates to one's own destiny'." Yep.

[33] Oh to be a fly on that wall. I don't remember what I said, but I'll explain the probable reason for saying it in the next chapter.

[34] I don't know how they got this so wrong. I'm 6 feet tall. Must have been
slouching.

[35] Hadn't eaten much in the last two weeks.

[36] I assume Celsius.

[37] Just check Wikipedia yourself.

[38] Tinea is ringworm.

equal, round, and reactive to light and accommodation.[39]

NEUROLOGICAL EXAMINATION: The patient is not oriented to time, place, person, or situation. He appears to be responding to internal stimuli.[40] He hesitates for several moments before being able to answer questions.[41] He has trouble retrieving information.[42] Cranial nerves I-XII are intact. Cranial Nerve I: The patient is able to detect peppermint.[43]

DIAGNOSES:
AXIS I:
1. Psychosis, NOS (not otherwise specified).
2. Rule out substance-induced delirium, probably due to LSD (lysergic acid diethylamide).
3. Rule out substance-induced psychosis.
4. Rule out schizophrenia.
5. Rule out schizoaffective disorder.

---

[39] This goes on, but it's boring.

[40] Amy's notes: Means you're talking to the voices in your head. If you watch me closely, most days you can see me doing this too.

[41] Amy's notes: Which is why they think you're responding to internal stimuli—they think you're getting your responses approved before giving them, or something like that.

[42] Amy's notes: They test this by showing you pictures and giving you lists of words and after 10+ minutes, asking you to recall the pictures or words. Heinously, they also test this by having you count backward from 100 by sevens.

[43] I included the first nerve because it's so awesome and weird that they verify its function by my ability to detect peppermint. I'm skipping the rest of the nerves here; see the appendix.

6. LSD, heroin, cocaine, mushrooms, ecstasy, and amphetamine abuse.[44]
AXIS II: Deferred.[45]
AXIS III: Status post tonsillectomy; history of multiple sinus infections.
AXIS IV: Psychological stressors: Severe - Suicide of
friend, recent relationship breakup, and family arguments.
AXIS V: Global Assessment of Functioning: Current:
15.[46][47]

PLAN: Admit patient to 3-south. Monitor for psychosis
and cognitive difficulties. Physical exam and labs.
Start Risperdal 1.5 mg twice a day[48] and Thorazine 100
mg q.i.d. p.r.n.[49] to help with agitation, irritability, and explosive behavior. Initiate a Valium
protocol.[50] Start multivitamins one q.d. and thiamine
100 mg q.d. Involve in the milieu. Obtain more information from family.

THIS REPORT IS STRICTLY CONFIDENTIAL.
Redisclosure is prohibited by law.

---

[44] Amy's notes: #1 is always the "actual diagnosis"—it's what they would have sent to the insurance company—all the "rule out" options are what you might be suffering from if the first one proves incorrect.

[45] Amy's notes: Means they suspect you have a personality disorder, but they can't or won't speculate on which one; it's very difficult to identify personality disorders in actively psychotic people.

[46] This is low.

[47] Amy's notes: No, it's *very* low. Most people I deal with in crisis still have a GAF score around 30. GAF is measured on a 0 to 100 scale and any-thing under a score of 50 is criteria for inpatient hospitalization in Maine.

[48] Amy's notes: This is a lot, starting doses are usually 0.25mg – 0.5mg.

[49] Amy's notes: QID = four times a day; PRN = as needed.

[50] Amy's notes: Can I have a Valium protocol now?

NOTE: This information has been disclosed to you from records whose confidentiality is protected by federal law. Federal regulations (42CFR part 2) prohibit you from making any further disclosure of it without the specific written consent of the person to whom it pertains, or as otherwise permitted by such regulations. A general authorization for the release of medical or other information is NOT sufficient for this purpose.

PERMISSION REQUEST: I would like to ask myself if it's okay to include my medical records in a book to entertain total strangers. I need explicit permission.

PERMISSION APPROVAL: Because of our tautological relationship, I hereby explicitly grant myself the right to publish this information in whatever form I please.

Welcome to the Nuthouse

In much the same way I have mixed feelings about LSD, I have mixed feelings about the psychiatric profession. Most people do. The facts were these: I needed to be off the streets and under watch. I probably needed to be medicated. Other crazy people are possibly not the best company for a crazy person. Nobody really understands what psychoactive medication is actually doing to people; it's scattershot aimed at symptoms.[1] Most medications cause side effects, and those side effects are medicated with other medications with side effects, and voilà: you're taking five pills. I know people who can't function without medication, and have been frustrated with friends who habitually stop taking them and become bipolar wrecks within a week. I know friends who never needed drugs, but were on them for three years before they managed to wean themselves and recover their personalities. All drugs can create habitual forms of dependency, whether they're chemically addictive or not. Marijuana is famously non-addictive, and just as infamous for the obvious lifestyle dependencies people build around it. Most prescription drugs are significantly worse for you and more addictive. People have been trying to medicate me for anxiety and depression my whole life, and I've never let them do it, since I wouldn't be able to maintain the dissatisfaction with life I need to continue to write. I also learned how to deal with those problems on my own, for the most part, and the occasional panic attack is a small price to pay for the neurotic urges that force me to keep busy. When I was institutionalized, I needed to be medicated, because I was dangerous. But

---

[1] This may have improved in the last ten years, but I doubt it.

there's something important about the anti-psychotics and all the other mood stabilizing drugs they put me on: not one of them made me less crazy. All they did was prevent me from acting on anything, or speaking up. In fact, I developed more elaborate delusions during my time in the nuthouse, because my inactivity meant I got less feedback about what I was thinking, so less opportunity to have some external input. The whole time I was there, only my dad piped up with, "You know that's crazy, right?" providing me brief moments of me thinking, "Oh shit, there's something wrong."

My mom's take:

> Acadia Hospital is the mental hospital for people with health insurance and connections to local doctors. I still believe it was lucky you didn't end up in one of the crummy state hospitals, but I remain unimpressed by the treatment you received. The focus seemed to be on getting you to stop acting crazy, not on getting you to stop being crazy. They put you on anti-psychotic drugs, the chief effect of which is to make you do anything anyone tells you to do. No wonder mental hospital staff love those drugs—they make their lives so much easier. But they seemed to not be paying attention to your actual experience. I arrived one day to see you and they met me with grave expressions and told me you'd been stealing things from the other patients. When I went to your room you said, "The strangest thing happened today. I walked into my room and there was a really nice pair of shoes there. I put them on and they fit great so I walked around wearing them for a while. Then I went back to my room to take a nap and when I woke up they were gone." So this is what actually happened: All the rooms looked exactly alike. They had moved you to a new room by moving your stuff while you were in a group session. You had gone back to your original room

and found the shoes that belonged to another patient, but you didn't understand that this wasn't your room any more. The staff's conclusion: Peter is a thief. Peter's conclusion: shoes appear and disappear with no explanation.

The doctors' reports of me being responsive or clear-eyed or making progress only came about because they told me what they wanted, medicated my thought-to-action connections into oblivion, and provided a dearth of stimuli in which I could form a comprehensive delusion better suited to my environment. The times I left my environment, it tended to fall apart, which I think was ultimately better, because painful as it was and crazy as I acted, I needed the incongruity of the real world and my delusions brought to a head. Being in an institution with doctors who talk around you and nurses who think they're in on your jokes and a bunch of other crazy people who actually are in on your jokes[2] is not a place to rebuild reality. What they achieved was to teach me to give less evidence of insanity. I suppose that's all they can do, because they had no way to look into my head. They could only decrease the probability that I would kill myself or someone else in the future, and get me to act according to their terms, even if their terms weren't an especially useful set of terms in the outside world. I don't begrudge them their efforts, nor am I unappreciative. But I recovered because I was lucky, not because I was treated, though had I not been treated, I'd probably be dead.

So I can explain the inappropriate hypersexual remarks, even if I don't remember what they were. When they unstrapped me in Heaven, Hell, or Purgatory, or the reincarnation zone or the *Defending Your Life*[3] afterlife, or wherever, they put me in a room for a

---

[2] Or at least laughing at something at the same time as you.

[3] I highly recommend this movie. Keep an eye out for Shirley McLain.

physical, and in walks this cute redheaded nurse in her late twenties. I of course thought she was my girlfriend from college who committed suicide the year before, which made perfect sense since I was dead. Naturally, I put her on the visitors list and left it at that. My other friends and family were still alive, so they couldn't visit me, and though Jake was dead, I'd killed him, so I assumed he wouldn't want to see me just yet.

After I was processed, they put me in the common area. The first day is very blurry for me, but I remember I was underwater, and had to breath through a straw. I wandered around in my shorts, sucking on the straw, and at one point wrapped a towel around my hand and tried to punch through the plexiglass door that locked us all in. It didn't go so well, and a scared looking nurse came up to me and said, "You shouldn't do that, because it makes people nervous." I nodded, but couldn't respond because I was still breathing through the straw. Eventually my mom showed up with clothes.

Here's my mom:

> When I arrived at Acadia Hospital shortly after the ambulance, they wouldn't even confirm that you'd been admitted. The privacy laws meant I wasn't entitled to any information about you unless you authorized it. I stood there clearly prepared to make a scene and finally someone realized it was a stupid pretense and I might have useful information for the doctors so they escorted me to the ward where a doctor was conducting an intake interview. You obligingly told them you had taken every kind of drug you'd ever heard of during the past week, which they carefully wrote down. (You assured me later that this was not true but the staff at the hospital remained convinced you were a heroin addict.) You also told them you'd had sex with your mother. Thanks very much for sharing

> that little Oedipal fantasy—they started giving me
> the hairy eyeball.[4]

The problem with the drug thing at this point was that I was trying to be accommodating, and thought my past was different than it was, so every time they asked me if I'd done something, I just said "yes" and worked it into my backstory. Anyway, the staff put me in a room with my clothes and told me to get dressed. This was a moment that makes it clear why I needed supervision: unbeknownst to anyone until the moment this writing goes public, when they left me alone to change, I was on a destroyer-god kick, and it was my duty to lay waste to the world, but I needed energy, so I grabbed my wand of power[5] and was about to urinate into a light socket to recharge. Fortunately, the tie on my new pants was too difficult to undo, so I just pissed myself and decided that was good enough.[6]

I was under 24-hour watch the first couple of days. My first night I wandered around with one of my guards, and hung out under a spot in the hallway with eight lights arranged in a circle in the ceiling. This spot was alternately the Tardis, a transporter, and the eight suns of a different planet during my stay. I tried to steal a nurse's watch off his wrist. Not so successful.

Eventually, and finally, I went to bed, and I slept. For the first time in two weeks. This didn't cure me. I had no dreams that I recall, and when I woke, I assumed my brief unconsciousness was me going back in time to fix an old college relationship, and the world would be savagely different. It was and it wasn't. I got breakfast. I was still in the afterlife.

---

[4] Told you this was unabridged. I have no idea where this idea came from, but I assume it was because I'd been reading Freud in the last couple of months.

[5] You guessed it.

[6] Counting the number of times I should have died in these three months is a futile exercise.

I watched TV for the rest of the day, believing I was causing all the tragedies in the news.

I can't break down the next few weeks chronologically, so the next few chapters will be describing relationships and a few key events.

Here are some introductions to the people who stuck out:

Truckette

Truckette was a tits-to-the-wall ex-trucker and construction worker. I have no idea why she was in there unless it was about drugs, or unless her entire past was a lie and she was making it up as she went. She told stories about bailing out of oversized gravel trucks as they barreled over cliffs. She was a drunk, a fighter, and a wall of a woman. Writing this now, I think she may have been pulling a *One Flew Over the Cuckoo's Nest*.

The Wrestler

This guy was the stereotypical gentle giant. He was an amateur wrestler who was in for trying to kill himself. He had the personality of Woody Allen on heavy sedatives. He was about two hundred pounds, mostly muscle, and all nerves.

Other Thin Guy

This nickname makes sense if you're from Maine. Other Thin Guy didn't talk much, and I never found out what he was in for, but I felt we had a bond because we were both underweight.

Bad Marriage

This is probably unfair, as I have no idea what her marriage was like. She came in with her husband and gave a teary report of never having stood up for herself. Naturally, they put her in a room with Truckette, and within a week she was swearing like a sailor and not putting up with "any of this goddamn bullshit." When I visited the institution a year later, she was the only person I recognized.

Shitty Friend

This is also unfair, but as my mom mentioned, when they moved my room, I went into what was then someone else's, and it belonged to Shitty Friend—a shy, bespectacled girl, probably in her mid twenties. In addition to the shoes, I found a tape recorder. On the tape recorder was what sounded like an answering machine message, with an angry female voice screaming, "I can't believe you did this shit, what the fuck were you thinking, you fucking bitch?" I don't know what this was about, and since Shitty Friend was so demure most of the time, I expect the actual shitty friend owned the voice on the recording.

Pocahontas

Probably wasn't Powhatan; most likely she was Penobscot, maybe Passamaquoddy. She was a crack addict with a husband who had taken her kid away. She was about forty, and looked good for a non-crack-addicted forty, and I was smitten on sight. Because she was a Native American goddess, of course.

So.

There we were, all deemed unacceptable to society, and mostly left alone with each other, although under constant watch. We had puzzles and group therapy and awful snacks at our disposal. It was a cauldron of madness with no context outside the calibrated probing of the psychiatrists overseeing our cases. Our meals, smoke breaks, and activities were regimented and led by variously competent nurses, many of whom were former or future patients.

One other weird thing started here. It was likely a combination of cloudy weather, extensive outdoor lighting at night, and me just not noticing, but from the point I entered the institution until I made a full recovery, many weeks later, I didn't see a single star.

The Milieu

People often talk about getting on the same wavelength when tripping. As if their minds had merged or they were telepathic. I do grant that LSD can create a hyperawareness of signals usually reserved for the subconscious, but this does not lead to telepathy or the merging of souls. The actual communication of thought is still constrained to the standard mediums, even if it seems otherwise. Emotionally, you bond in a unique way with your fellow trippers, because you're modulating your reactions much more subtly and accurately than usual, but behind the scenes, each of your brains are working away on their own narratives, and creating symbolism compatible with the environment.

When you're nuts, and deprived of your ability to doubt and reason against evidence, the same thing can happen. The processes running your emotions are now running your logic centers, and you're more receptive to signals you can no longer interpret.

The most important things about the institution were the smoking areas. The medical community has long recognized that you cannot deny crazy people their cigarettes.[1] It's not especially safe to deny a non-crazy smoker their cigarettes, but addiction

---

[1] Turns out they took away cigarettes the year after I left. This probably has something to do with Bad Marriage, for reasons that will become apparent.

aside, something about nicotine allows people suffering from schizophrenia and psychosis to keep it together a little better.

There were two smoking rooms that were available at designated times. There was a smallish one with benches around the side of the walls that I associated with time traveling and being at the center of the Earth. There was a larger one with picnic tables I associated with being at the center of the sun and making decisions about how the world would work. There was probably some time traveling there too.[2] I remember having conversations about essentially nothing, but I knew from the laughter and banter that we were subtly making decisions about the fate of the world and the future of meaning. Since all our smoke breaks were two to three hours apart, we generally chain-smoked two or more cigarettes. In the beginning, I smoked two at once. Cigarettes were emblems of power, and the brand of cigarette was very important; when I was a robot, for instance, I had to smoke menthols, because the cold shot to the throat was more machine friendly.[3] Camels were traveling cigarettes, and I stared at the little logo on the paper many times, wondering where the camel would take me.

At one point, they brought in a girl who was barely coherent, with her 24-hour guardian. She was wearing one of those "Can't sleep, clowns will eat me" T-shirts, which should be illegal in mental institutions. She wandered in, smoked half her cigarette, and kept asking what day it was. This worked nicely into my delusions of indeterminate timelines, so I figured she was just like me in the Quest to Achieve the Mission, but at an earlier point, and having a harder time.

I was having a hard time too. I had to get to the next stage of my mission. I packed all my things: the pens that rewrite the future and past, the three marble spheres that gave me power over the sun, the night, and the stars, and the journal in which the newer testament would be written. I dressed, smoothed my pants, tightened my belt, put on my coat, and went to the nurse's station to check out.

----

[2] I was very big on time traveling.

[3] This was the first and last time I smoked menthols on a regular basis.

"Hello?" said the nurse.

"I'm ready to go."

Long pause.

"You can't leave just yet."

"Oh?"

"Yeah."

"Okay."

And I went back to my room. Clearly I wasn't prepared enough. I gathered my chi, made sure my soul was in the right place, unpacked and repacked all my things, because order was important, and went back out.

I'll spare you the next conversation, because it was exactly the same as the first one.

As was the next.

And the next.

And the next.

Sometimes I was just repacking and readjusting my outfit. Sometimes I went back and created an entirely new delusion, usually something to do with California or Doctor Who, or both. Regardless of how I redid my outfit, my packing, or my mind, the nurse's answer was always the same. I only hope I gave her a story to tell when she got home.

Eventually I gave up and got another night's sleep. Didn't do much for my state of mind, but at least my body was resting.

The first group meeting was odd. Truckette said she was feeling fine, but not ready to go anywhere. A kid with glasses who got transferred that day said he was hearing voices. The doctor asked him if he had racing thoughts. He said yes. I still wonder how anyone can self-diagnose racing thoughts, since the speed of thought is how we track experiential time. In retrospect, my thoughts were doing mach 10, but I didn't notice. I just wondered why everybody was talking so slowly. Pocahontas said she felt out of sorts. I said I was just fine. Shitty Friend said she was depressed.

INPATIENT PROGRESS NOTE. DOS: 08/25/2000

```
The patient came to doctor's group. He
was distant, detached, at times intru-
sive. Appearing disoriented to time and
situation. Not reacting when I explained
that he took another patient's belong-
ings. Unchanged loosening of associa-
tions and thought blocking. Vague perse-
cutory ideas. Possible perceptual dis-
turbances. Compliant with medications.
Labs refused by patient.⁴
```

My dad came to visit me during this first week. My dad was as god, in various forms, as a dad generally is to a son's Freudian mentality, except in this case my dad was specifically Odin, since needing glasses is as good as trading an eye. You know. For wisdom.[5]

I was eating lunch in the TV room when my dad first came, and he had to watch me pour a serving of salt down my throat. I thought I just had a new understanding of the basic nutrients that would make me immortal. I remember my dad making an expression he'd never made, looking away with a slight gasp, wincing in disgust. At the time I thought he just wasn't ready to see me ascend to a higher plane of being. Now I look back and see his reaction as a rare moment of despair. He saw his son as I was at that moment: in all the ways we judge one another day to day, I was hardly human. That expression, not of disappointment, not of anger, not of chagrin, but of so much shock that my father couldn't look at me, haunts me to this day.[6]

---

[4] What would you do if you thought there was a shadow society trying to interfere with your efforts to save the world and a stranger came to you with a needle and asked for blood?

[5] Imagine Tim Robbins in *The Hudsucker Proxy* saying those last two sentences.

[6] I like to think this has made me a better person, but since I'm The Asshole at my local bar, I think it just made me a better Welch.

```
INPATIENT PROGRESS NOTE. DOS: 08/28/2000

The patient came to doctor's group. He
was more friendly and cooperative. Ap-
pearing oriented to place and time as
well as to person.7 Thought processes
remaining tangential and loose.8 He ex-
pressed his concerns about taking away
joy from people.9 Vague persecutory and
referential thoughts. Maintaining good
behavioral control. Compliant with medi-
cations. Normal CBC, CMP, and TSH re-
flex.
```

I don't know how I got Trinity to come visit me. I may have texted her, she may have found out through other means. Trinity was a pale wisp of a girl, with short, black hair and an asocial disposition. As far as acid went, she swallowed ten-strips as soon as she bought them and locked herself in her room. She drank dextromethorphan cough syrups daily; she had bags full of empty bottles in her closet. She had tried to kill herself a few times, didn't like to be touched, and made a point of distinguishing herself as asocial, not antisocial. It's not that she avoided other people; she just didn't need them and didn't especially care if they lived or died. I've met cutters before, but her arms were pure scar tissue from the backs of her hands to her shoulders. Because of the severity of her diabetes, she was waiting, miserably, asocially and asexually, to go blind and die. She was one of the people who worked at Acadia occasionally, when she wasn't a patient herself.

---

7 I was quite well oriented. Place: the summit of the worlds. Time: 2,400,021,987 A.D. Person: I was a computer, and my doctor was Loki.

8 He just didn't get my jokes.

9 This reminds me of a girl I dated a couple of times who called me a chisucker. She turned out to be brain-damaged.

Naturally, I was infatuated even before I lost my mind. After getting it back, I would battle Crow Abilities for her indifferent heart, and I would lose. But that was yet to come.

She came in and we talked about nothing. I may have professed eternal love. I was into doing that. I think I assumed this would be a conjugal visit, but 'twas not to be. Before she ran out, she kissed me once on the lips, just for an instant.

It was another one of those universe-collapsing moments. Happily, I didn't shit myself this time. I would say the kiss re-charged my madness. It was a brief moment when a delusion almost kind of worked out, or at least seemed to be going in the right direction.

The rest of the time I waited, ate packets of salt when no one was looking, stared at the walls, and paced, gathering imaginary power. Maybe I was getting better.

INPATIENT PROGRESS NOTE. DOS: 08/29/2000

He came to Doctor's Group.[10] Significant improvement in his psychotic condition. Less evidence for persecutory and referential ideas.[11] Speech is spontaneous, fluent, and focused. Affect is euthymic. The patient is compliant with medications and becoming quite active in the milieu.

That night we played cards for cigarettes. It's possible I was dropping some of my delusions in favor of company and good times, and for the love of Pocahontas. I distinctly remember doing

---

[10] I don't know why these openings vary among "He came to Doctor's Group" and "The patient was seen in doctor's group" and "The patient came to doctor's group." May have been different people making the reports.

[11] I felt less persecuted because I think I was the Metatron at this point. Archangels don't get persecuted. They do the persecuting.

the math at the end of a round of Spades, and being completely wrong, but convincing everybody else I was right.

I was well-liked by patients and staff. Although I didn't tell them, everybody was an angel or a deity or some other perfect representation of a concept, and I hung on every word, utterly fascinated by whatever wisdom or secrets they were imparting. I stared deeply into everyone's eyes, nodded and smiled at everything they said, did whatever anyone told me to do, respected all authority, and generally made each person I interacted with feel like they were the wisest, most wonderful and beautiful person in the world.

INPATIENT PROGRESS NOTE. DOS: 08/30/2000

The patient was seen in doctor's group. He was pleasant and easily engaged. Good eye contact. Appropriate interaction. He was stating that he feels much better. Sleep and appetite normalizing. Thought process is much better organized and focused,[12] given though at times long lags and circumstantiality is present.[13] Thought processes do not show evidence of overt delusions. He denied perceptual disturbances.

Later that afternoon, I spent a good half hour spitting in the toilet, due to acid reflux. I watched my saliva unravel in the water, and because of its dim resemblance to the theorized bubble structure of the universe, I knew I was creating little universes to go on if I couldn't save the one I was in.

INPATIENT PROGRESS NOTE. DOS: 08/31/2000

He was seen in Doctor's Group. He is continuing to improve in his cognition

---

[12] I was an android.

[13] A poorly programmed android.

```
and psychosis. Minimal referential
thinking. Thought process is quite logi-
cal and goal directed. Appearing to
minimize the whole experience, and espe-
cially the use of street drugs.14 Won-
dering about discharge and his return to
school. Appropriate and active in the
milieu. Compliant with his medications
and denying side effects.

PLAN: Continue with the current psycho-
tropics. May go tonight on a pass with
his parents. Also encourage a weekend
pass and target discharge for the begin-
ning of next week.
```

I had an English class once, where the teacher was charming and meant well, but when we were covering Othello, she brought a lot of material about the objectification of women into class. Othello is as complex a work of the Bard as any other, and it was distressing to have our entire class's focus narrowed to the fact that he killed his wife because "his wife was an object to him." Little mention of class, race, jealousy, the illogical nature of the male mind in the face of sex or power, or any of the other dramatic and psychological themes wrapped up in Othello.

Once I noticed what she was doing, I stopped reading the play. I just waited for her to tell us to turn to page X, whereupon I flipped to that page, bookmarked it, and went back to doing my math homework. When the time came to write the paper, I flipped to all the pages I bookmarked, pulled a quote at random, then typed up some filler between the quotes pertaining to the objectification of women.

She read my paper aloud in front of the class, citing it as the finest work she'd read on Othello in her years teaching the class.

---

14 Although still quite insane, I was trying to tell them I had never done the drugs I didn't do but told them I did. This is apparently minimizing the experience.

I tell this story because I was doing essentially the same thing with my doctors in the institution.

```
INPATIENT PROGRESS NOTE. DOS: 08/31/2000

He was seen in Doctor's Group and on a
one-to-one basis. Quite friendly and
engaging. Making attempts to integrate
his unusual perceptual disturbances. No
evidence for overt delusional thinking.
Denying suicidal or homicidal thoughts
or plans. Cognitively intact.[15]

PLAN: Continue with the current psycho-
tropic medications. Weekend pass dis-
cussed with team and approved. Engage in
milieu and group therapy.
```

I'm sure the overnight pass was interesting, but I only remember one, small moment.

My parents' house is on a pseudo-island called Hancock Point. It's a small subsistence fishing town with a pox of summer rich people, and my family falls right between these demographics. I mapped the bulk of my episodic memory to summers spent in this town, before we officially moved there and I had to map my memory according to schools and drug incidents. One particular summer stands out as involving my first True Love.

Six years after that summer, my family and I were walking around the shore road on my day pass, and I was intent on getting to the house where I'd first fallen in love, knowing that my childhood infatuation would be there, even though it was off season and she hadn't summered in that house in years.

When we came upon the house, my dad leaned over and said, "I mean, you couldn't possibly expect Name Changed to be here, right?"

---

[15] True, true, true, false, true, false.

How my dad knew the exact insane delusion I was having at the time, I don't know. My dad is far from crazy, but for some reason he seemed to pick up on the alternate realities I was creating every few minutes and called me out on them. I said, "No, of course not," but he was absolutely right.

What with all the new stimuli and my family being unsympathetic to my delusions, the carefully nurtured alternate reality I'd built in the nuthouse began to give way, and I had to consider the implications of my dad pointing out I was crazy every couple of hours. These were helpful jolts to my dreamworld; they were like blurry half-awakenings when I could see that nothing I was thinking made any sense. It wasn't enough to snap me out of it, but it was enough to make me consider whatever I was imagining at the moment might not be real.

Although I was sleeping regularly by this point, I wasn't dreaming, as far as I know. I mean, why bother? Whatever dreams supposedly achieve in sleep was getting taken care of during my waking hours.

However, sleep was clearly doing something, because after they kept me awake the next night in preparation for an EEG, I managed to commit my first felony.

Grand Theft Auto: Orono Dreams

Say you had a kid in a mental institution who lost his mind because he didn't sleep for two weeks. Say he seems to be keeping things together, and is scheduled for release. Would you schedule him for a sleep-deprived EEG and keep him up all night?

To be fair, they didn't know it was the sleep deprivation that drove me over the edge. They were trying to figure out if something more terrible than a run-of-the-mill psychotic break was going on. Also, though they were aware of my apparently deteriorating condition after the weekend pass, they didn't think it would be as much of a problem as it became.

I don't really feel responsible for any particular decision I made after I spilled acid on myself. I feel wholly responsible for getting myself to that point, so I'm culpable in all the events, but in the actual moment I just had alternative theories of ownership, and I was trying to save the world, for Christ's sake. All great heroes ignore petty laws when the world needs saving. Also, I didn't know I was breaking the law.

Other Thin Guy was also scheduled for an EEG so they put us in the main room to keep each other awake for the night. I think we mostly watched TV and played Scrabble, which I had a surprisingly good handle on, all things considered.

I got back on the *Hitchhiker's Guide* kick, but at least this time I had maps. The three colored balls I'd been using for contact juggling. I couldn't believe it took me so long to figure out what they really were. They were black with night sky-ish patterns in various colors: blue, for the Moon Map, yellow for the Sun Map, white for the Star Map. Of course the Moon and Sun maps weren't maps of the moon and sun, they were maps of the galaxy in their Moon and Sun aspects.[1] I was examining them at around 3:00 A.M., and since it was dark out, I knew the Sun aspect map would be useless, so I threw it in the trash. Other Thin Guy found this hilarious.

By dawn, I was thoroughly armed with the knowledge conveyed to me in the Scrabble games, and was ready for my ascension. We each had a nurse guard, and went out in some kind of bus. I don't think it was an ambulance.

We got to the hospital, and I went in for my EEG. They lay me down in a dark room, and started sticking things to my head. The gel on the sensors was cold, and because of the deliberate way they applied pressure to attach them, I was convinced they were sticking rounded metal rods about a quarter inch in diameter into my brain, about half an inch deep.[2] The absence of my skull cracking in a dozen places would have convinced sane me this probably wasn't the case, but I didn't bother to confirm the theory. It was quiet, and they told me to close my eyes for a few minutes, then open them for a few more minutes.

This blew my mind. With the spikes in my head and the lilting voice of the technician, I was being changed, altered on an existential level. My brain was being remapped to adapt to some godlike form, with which to smite and bless, and various other things gods are good at.

I was in a trance as the nurse walked me out to have a smoke while we waited for the bus to come back. I sat on a terrace at the hospital and had a Camel light,[3] which gave me the final piece of

---

[1] If this makes no sense at all—and it doesn't—the closest literal description of what I think I thought the concept of "aspect" was is in *Lord of Light*, by Roger Zelazny.

[2] I distinctly remember the sensation and these measurements.

[3] The traveller's cigarette.

the puzzle. I was an avenging dragon,[4] and had to go find LA Queen, again, except now she was also an alien, and I had to persuade her people to join in the ascension of conscious beings instead of ruling over humans.[5]

We walked out of the smoking balcony while I was in this condition. When we went down the stairs and into the pickup area, the nurse—in one of the not-so-savvy decisions of her career—walked in front on me. She said:

"There's our ride."

She was talking about the crazy bus that had just pulled up. What I saw, at the moment she said this, was the hot little black number that had just parked. In real life, it was a taxi. In my delusion, it was My Ride. The taxi driver walked by me without looking at me, but I knew he was giving me license to take his wheels. I got in the car. I spent a good amount of time checking out the interior, while my nurse was probably freaking out wondering how I'd vanished. I examined the cell phone, as it was my conduit to the masters of the universe, whoever they were. Amazingly, the keys were in the ignition, so when I finally focused, it was easy to start the car and get moving.

BAM! Grand theft auto.

I immediately drove the wrong way out the emergency access ramp for ambulances. An attendant ran toward me screaming "Hey, hey, HEY!" but I ignored him, since he was obviously on the side of the government forces trying to stop me. If an ambulance had been coming the other way at the time, this story would have a very dif-

---

[4] Lack of scales, wings, and fiery breath notwithstanding.

[5] My obsession with LA Queen would make you think I'd been in love with this girl my whole life. I wasn't; she was one of the girls in college I had a brief crush on, and their numbers are legion. I got over it when I got a real girlfriend and had a descent friendship with her until we drifted apart. I don't know why my brain fixated on her so often while I was crazy, though she did have great hair, but it may be due to the fact that she was present during my first trip, when my brain exploded. Apparently she's imprinted on my consciousness in some way that's susceptible to delusional obsession.

ferent ending, if it were written at all. The access ramp led to route 2 going the wrong direction, so I drove the wrong way down the road for a couple of minutes before I decided I should blend in, at which point I made a U-turn in traffic and headed for the University of Maine, since I'd been meaning to get back to school all week.

Once I got near the school, I pulled into a field and took stock of my vehicle. Aside from the infinitely fascinating cell phone,[6] there were some maps and a crowbar in the trunk. Good. That was everything I needed to get to California. I stuck a map in my pocket and drove on.

I decided this car wasn't going to make it, so I pulled into the parking lot of the school chapel looking to make a deal. I wandered in, and asked whose car was in the parking lot. Turned out to be the receptionist's, so I asked if she wanted to trade. She blinked at me, then smiled and said no.

There were some other people wandering around and one of them asked me if I wanted some water. I said yes, drank it, then thanked them and left. They called the cops.

I walked down the road toward the main campus. I knew I was being followed, but as long as I walked along the shadows of the power lines, nobody could see me. I walked up to a sorority and knocked. A sorority girl answered and I asked for a glass of water.

"This is a sorority, try the frat next door."[7]

I hit the frat, and, predictably, a frat kid answered, and was much friendlier. He gave me a glass of water and I sat on the couch for a while, doubtlessly weirding people out as I offered to trade my map for various things. Eventually I moved on, and hit some of the sophomore housing, where I ran into some people I almost knew. I say "almost" because they were Boyz in the Woodz types who listened to nothing but Eminem and tried to have homies, even though they just sat around doing what everybody does in Maine at that age, which is stay inside all winter drinking cheap beer with underage girls and lying about their sexual history.

---

[6] They'd taken my cell phone away in the institution, so it had been a while since I could get messages from outside the matrix.

[7] Bitch.

I was generally quiet, since I was figuring out my quest, but at some point, a girl asked me:

"So what's up?"

"Just broke out of a mental institution."

Awkward chuckles.

"No, really," she said.

"Really. I just grabbed a car and broke out of a mental institution."

Silence.

"Can I bum a smoke?"

She gave me a menthol and went back to her room. I smoked it and left, probably without a word.

So the students weren't going to be especially interesting. I wandered around the class areas, and finally decided to go into the little concert theatre building, where I walked into a theatre class.

"Do you belong here?" asked the teacher.

This was a tough question.

"Where's here?"

"Playwriting 200."

"Yes."

"Ah, good, good. We're filling up."

I sat and was bedazzled by the complex information on acting and narrative and story, and all the secret weapons the teacher was giving me to become a spy and a history re-maker. At some point, he said, "One of the most important things is to know when to stop and make a good exit," so I took that as my cue and left.

I was getting close to the philosophy department building, and that's where I knew my next bit of information was, because therein lay God.

God God. The big Christian one, who I now knew was my ethics teacher from the previous year. His name was Oscar Remick, and he was the best teacher I ever had. A quintessential scholar. Unfailingly respectful of the dignity of his students and all human beings. He could lecture for an hour and a half and it was gripping to a roomful of hung-over students. He taught a full round of classes the day he died of cancer, at his desk. If I didn't already have such a good actual father, he would have been the strong father figure they're always harping about in after-school specials.

He wasn't there. I went to the bathroom, and somehow locked myself in. This was especially troubling, since there is no lock on the door. Maybe I was just too crazy to work a doorknob, but I'd just driven a car GTA style down a busy road, so this fact still bugs me out. I had to go out the window.

If you've never read *The Hitchhiker's Guide*, there's a scene I have to describe. Zaphod Beeblebrox is trying to find Zarniwoop, and he eventually gets to Zarniwoop's office, where he's been told to go out the window. In the book, this is because going out the window means he's going into a custom universe designed especially for him. So this is what I assumed was happening to me: Oscar Remick had locked the door with his God powers, and I was supposed to go out the window into my own designer universe. In moments of ontological doubt, I wonder if this actually happened.

I walked to the student union with uncertain purpose. I didn't make it. At roughly noon, two hours after my escape, when two thousand students were getting out of class and heading to lunch at exactly the building I was in front of, the cops drove a cruiser onto the grass and arrested me.

My first thought was, "Ah, my ride's here." I can't say that thought changed in any particular way over the next twenty minutes. A cop I recognized from previous semesters got out of the car and said, "Sir, please come over here."

"Sure," I said.

I wanted to make him comfortable, since he seemed nervous. I thought he was nervous because he was arresting a dragon, as was his duty, but there was no guarantee I wouldn't fry him. He was nervous because there was a countywide APB out for me, describing me as mentally unstable. He directed me to get face down on the hood of the car, at which point he cuffed and frisked me. Satisfied that I had no weapons,[8] he stuffed me in the back of the cruiser.

---

[8] He didn't know about the tigereye stone in my pocket.

For several years, I wondered why I'd never met anybody who'd seen that happen. I met many people in my remaining college days, and I always asked if they'd seen me cuffed and stuffed in front of the student union. Not one person recalled it. Four years later, it finally hit me: the people who saw it don't talk to me.[9]

On the ride, I asked the cop how he was doing and what all the funky gadgets in the car were for. He responded to most of my inquiries by asking me to sit back and not get my face so close to the grate. He drove me straight back to the mental institution, where a bunch of people I'd become aquatinted with were considerably less happy to see me.

I had graduated from voluntary to involuntary patient.

---

[9] And they knew my name, since I made the first police beat of that year's campus newspaper, so they could avoid me at a distance.

Assassin-Demon-Hunter-God-Angel-Thingy, Interrupted

When I first wrote about this on my website, somebody asked this:

> I just don't understand what is going on in the
> brain when all this is happening. I mean I've done
> LSD and I can relate to the crazy thought patterns
> and temporary insane feeling, but its like it just
> didn't wear off for you. How is it that when you
> are in a nut-house, you don't all of a sudden come
> to, and realize, "Oh shit, this is a nut-house . . . I
> must be insane!"

The answer is to me, it wasn't a nuthouse. To my mind, there was no such thing as crazy, or it didn't mean to me what it meant before or since. I'm going to try to beat some sense out of this metaphor: Imagine the whole possibility of thought and sensory experience is a floor, with a pendulum hanging above it. The pendulum is your awareness, stream of consciousness, short-term memory, whatever. There's a roughly demarcated circle in the center of the floor that represents the usual, acceptable arcs of the pendulum. It swings around conversations, practical matters, the occasional flight of fancy, creativity, skepticism, belief, and so on. It has a reasonable sway and curve that matches most of the other pendulums, and the fact that all these paths are generally similar to one another, and not too out of control, allows them to communicate and function.[1] An acid trip is like giving the pendulum a gentle shove, so it roams around a larger orbit, but one that's still related to the circle of everyday understanding.

Now, to the end of one of the pendulums, we're going to staple a small, screaming child with a rocket engine handcuffed to its wrist. The path of this pendulum is now careening wildly all over the floor, rapidly tracing paths nowhere near the circle, utterly unpredictable and out of control, constrained only by its mechanical nature. Sure, the rocket-powered child might occasionally send the pendulum into the circle, but only for brief moments.

In that circle lay the pattern of interpretation that told me I was a mortal human boy in a mental institution. It might occur to me, but only as a fleeting thought before my internal narrative shot off in another direction. I no longer had the ability to hold on to my mind and turn thoughts over in a measured way, because there was a screaming child with a rocket stapled to my brain.

My next report:

INPATIENT PROGRESS NOTE. DOS: 09/05/2000

He would perseverate on certain themes,
especially related to the positive experience of having been on LSD. Even
though he was alert and oriented to person and place, he seemed to have difficulty with the exact time frame.[2] Later
in the morning, he was sent to Eastern

---

[1] To what end, who cares, and how pendulums communicate, I don't know, but bear with me.

[2] This bugs me. When a person seems to be "oriented to person and place" yet thinks it's 1783, maybe they have an insane story running in their head and they're just humoring you on a few details?

> Maine Medical Center for an EEG. After-
> wards, he eloped, taking one of the cars
> from valet parking. He was brought back
> in the afternoon by the police. He ad-
> mitted to having used some marijuana[3]
> and having gone to some classes and to
> see his ethics teacher. At the time he
> was quite withdrawn, anxious, irritable,
> avoiding eye contact, and appearing even
> more disorganized in his thinking and
> behaviors.

We had some therapy groups. These were the kind of classes a vegan New Yorker would take to get back to whatever it is they want to get back to after two years in the financial district. There was some perfunctory yoga, some anger management, and a woman who taught us how to press our joints together to strengthen them.[4] This is the only one I remember clearly, which should tell you something.

At one point they brought in a woman who I never saw out of her bed. She was in her late eighties, at least. They wheeled her in, and wherever she went a hush followed. She never said anything I could hear. She spent the night in the room across from me, and died a few hours into it. They wheeled her body out in the night, but we were all awake for it.

The next time my parents visited, that I remember, I was al-lowed outside again. My dad had been getting reports of what they thought my delusions were, and apparently got the one about me thinking I was God, so he mentioned, "Well, divinity runs in the

---

[3] They asked me, "Did you use marijuana?" And I said no. Then they asked, "Are you sure?" and I decided they were right, and that the menthol I had smoked was marijuana, so I admitted to yet another drug experience I hadn't had. I'm not trying to decry the efforts of the psychiatric profes-sion, but I want to point out that most of the time, it has no idea what's going on.

[4] She would be disappointed if not horrified that in the decade after meet-ing her, I've cracked my wrists a thousand times each.

Welch family." Probably not the best thing to say, but I admire the effort to maintain a sense of humor.

At one point during a doctor's group, I thought the entire world had been melted into liquid metal by the expanding sun, and all reality was just electromagnetic static in this ball of iron. This led to a very complicated delusion involving me being a kind of incidental assassin, and my job was to end people's normal lives through extremely indirect means—so indirect, as a matter of fact, that I was already responsible for many deaths, despite not having left the ward for two weeks. This way, they could understand that consciousness was just an electric dream, and we could create a new universe while the old one was ending. The notes from that meeting describe me as "friendly and cognitively intact." Also, my next targets were my family members, because my name was Peter Hunt Welch, and if you read Hunt as a command, it all makes perfect sense. Oh, also, my true name wasn't Peter, it was "Peer" because Trinity's real last name could be creatively rearranged to spell something phonetically similar to "fog our tea," and I thought that meant that by joining Trinity, the T in my name would be removed, and I would become Peer, the singular peer of all humans in the world, the second coming of a truly egalitarian Jesus. I thought I was destined to die at forty-two as this Christ figure, but I also worked in the idea that death just involved moving to the woods and slowly drifting into the universal consciousness.

INPATIENT PROGRESS NOTE. DOS: 09/11/2000

Interpretation of the EEG became available. It showed the presence of left temporal intermittent theta waves.[5] The case was discussed with Dr. _____, who stated the importance of reviewing

---

[5] I don't know what this means. All they told me was there was an irregularity in my temporal lobe. I spoke with a neurology student who read this excerpt and some other records, and he said this is probably something inherently weird about my brain and not caused by either the drugs or the sleep deprivation.

```
the clinical situation and the need for
repeat EEG after at least two or three
months of sobriety.⁶
```

There was a level system written on a whiteboard at the front of the ward. All the patients' names had a number from 1 to 4 next to them. Level 4's could go outside, go on passes, and were slated for release in the near future. Level 1's were on 24-hour watch and couldn't even eat meals in the cafeteria. I'm sure it was meant to help the staff figure out what was what when they came on duty, but it functioned as a crazy scorecard for the rest of us. I repeatedly thought it was describing our positions on an angel hierarchy, from cherub to archangel, and level 4 meant you were close to ascension, which made perfect sense since level 4's tended to leave shortly after making the grade. I was one of the very few people who made it to level 4 and got dropped back to a level 1 in the space of three hours. I spent most of my time there as a level 3.

In order to garner my powers and prove my worth as a level 4, I adopted a kind of uniform. I had some yellow shades that I wore because they gave me ESP. I took two key rings, looped them together, and wore them around my right middle and ring fingers, to focus my electromagnetic powers. I also always kept the green Pen of Creation and the red Pen of Destruction on me, so I could re-write the universe around me as I saw fit. This served to maintain some consistent delusional stories. Objects seemed to be the only things that shifted meaning in a predictable manner, so they kept me grounded to some degree, and in a sense, they did garner my powers and help me get to a level 4. Go figure.

They certainly helped me defeat The Wrestler in push hands. This is the same thing I was doing with Jun outside the car on the ride back from Berkfest, and I do have some mediocre skill in it,⁷

---

⁶ This never happened. Makes me think I should get an EEG soon.

⁷ Though it doesn't look like it when I do it with Jun. Jun at one point took down the push hands champion of the world. True, only in one out of nine, and in the next round, the champion sprained Jun's wrist with two fingers, but still.

enough to surprise The Wrestler by taking him down in about thirty consecutive rounds. He was twice my size, so at first he was just trying not to hurt me, then he was just confused, then angry, then impressed, so I taught him a few things. The staff was chewing their fingernails off wondering when somebody would break a bone or flip out, but our mutual friendliness and quiet personalities somehow convinced them that we could mock-fight in the middle of a mental institution and it would be okay. It seemed to be. I thought we both came away better people.

The ESP shades also helped me freak out the staff. I would ask them to start talking and then repeat their sentences back as they were saying them, about one or two syllables behind. They one and all told me to stop after ten words. I assumed I was reading their minds, probably on a 24k modem, which would account for the lag. I expect most people could do this with enough concentration, but there's no reason to practice unless you're crazy. Even when our adrenaline pumps up and seems to distort our sense of time, it's a function of memory, not actual activity: we can't perceive or do things any faster than normal, we just think we did. So my patchy, out-of-order sense of time that seemed like it was running through a flanger and a wah pedal wasn't giving me any extra powers, it was just the chemical imbalances encoding my experience into my neurons a little haphazardly.

It didn't help that I'd stolen my mother's watch, which didn't have hands or numbers, just a little LCD display that had pie sections light up, and it was broken. Aside from randomly lighting up various sections in no particular order, the five-minute section before noon or midnight was never on. Since I was born about five minutes before February 29, 1980, I decided there was some deep flaw in the space-time continuum having to do with my being born five minutes too early, and I had to heal the time gap. At least until my mom noticed I had the watch on and took it back, after which I just forgot about it.

My extreme disassociation from reality kept me at a distance from the stressors everybody else was dealing with. Bad Marriage, after learning how to swear, decided to take up smoking again. This led to her taking up collapsing on the way back from every smoke break.

The first time, everybody freaked out. Truckette kept it together and helped her up, the nurse started screaming into her walkie-talkie, The Wrestler started crying and ran off down the hallway, Shitty Friend backed up against the wall and stared without speaking. Pocahontas and I went to help Truckette.

The second time, pretty much the same thing happened. The third time, same thing, except Pocahontas, Truckette, and I were less impressed. The nurse was getting sick of it. Try as we might, we couldn't make her see the connection between cigarettes and passing out. We would patiently explain to her that she never collapsed otherwise. She only collapsed three minutes after finishing a cigarette, and she did it every single time. She railed at us, screamed at the nurses and called the whole hospital staff bastards for not letting her have a cigarette because there was no connection at all between her smoking and collapsing. I pitied the staff in this particular battle; a normal person would probably be more worried if they spontaneously collapsed without cause, instead of denying the obvious cause in order to keep smoking. As far as I know, it never got better, and she's collapsing to this day. I haven't quit yet.

Near the end of my stay, Truckette managed to collapse too. I have no idea why. At the time, I was seeing three of everybody. Not literally, there were just three aspects to everybody's nature, possibly based on an ego, superego, and id distinction, but it got more complicated than that. I would watch people's edges vibrate as the three aspects wavered and fought for dominance. So when I helped Truckette into a wheelchair and wheeled her back to the ward and she looked at me and said, "Jesus, there's three of you." I just nodded and said, "You'll be here soon."

Crazy Love

As already described, there's no sex like crazy sex. There's no joy like crazy joy. There's no fear like crazy fear. And there's absolutely no love like crazy love.

I've been in love exactly five times while sane. I don't believe in fate, meaning, or even free will; I think love is a poetic illusion built around pheromone-triggered chemical addictions. But it's my favorite illusion, and I dive in at every opportunity. I've been so in love, pre- and post-crazy, I've sacrificed everything I could think to sacrifice for just another day of it.

A piece of my mind, written under the influence of psychosis, extra theta waves, and whatever drugs they had me on, is still in love with Pocahontas. She drifts through my dreams to this day. I've never spoken of it in any detail to anyone, and this chapter is more for me than anyone else. I'll keep it short.

I don't know why I fell for Pocahontas so much harder than any of the various other women I decided I was in love with over the course of my insanity. She was the only person I remember who was always herself; though she represented different things or beings at different times, she had the only stable identity throughout the time I knew her. I never thought she was a dead friend or a relative from the future. Maybe it was because I was around her the longest.

The first time it became obvious to everyone that I was in love with Pocahontas was during the first week when I rolled onto her yoga mat while she was exercising. She left it for a moment to do a stretch, and I hit it like it was a sandbox filled with heroin. Everybody laughed at me, and she politely asked me to move, so I rolled off it, with a grin of perfect and insane contentment on my face.

In my more disorganized periods I would just smile at her and hope she talked to me, virtually wagging my tail every time she entered the room, since I had the emotional control of a heavily sedated puppy. In my less disorganized moments, I would engage her in conversation, and she started opening up to me a bit at a time. She mostly talked about how she missed her kid, and was trying to write a book about her experience, though the details were never clear, even after I found the first couple of pages of what she'd written.

I played the piano a lot, since I could almost play like a real piano player back then, and she listened. Everybody listened a bit in the beginning, but I was either playing one of the handful of things I'd learned, or hitting the notes very slowly and carefully according to some crazy math in my head, to avoid upsetting the celestial balance with bad vibrations. So it was less entertaining after a while, and even I got bored of it, but she listened the longest, and we started talking about music. She offered to teach me to play guitar once we got out, and that sounded good to me.

Once, she said she was going to church with Shitty Friend. She may have been kidding; I wasn't allowed out of the ward at the time, so I couldn't verify. She told me to play for their souls while they were gone. I immediately complied, and they came back five minutes later.

"That was quick . . ." I said.

"Yep. We were saved." And she winked at me.

I have no idea what they actually did, but I assumed I had saved their souls with my playing.[1]

---

[1] I'm not a good piano player. If I practiced for the rest of my life, I still wouldn't be able to do this even metaphorically.

As a pretty forty-year-old who had spent a solid chunk of her life addicted to drugs, she was probably about as mature as a twenty-five-year-old, so she still had five years on me. Once she decided she liked me, she flirted expertly, with dry wit that I completely misinterpreted, and sly smiles and winks. I have no idea what it meant to her. While I was crazy, nobody was crazy, and looking back, I was so crazy that everybody else was sane in comparison, but there were definitely some people who'd flown the coop. Later, I would get evidence that she was one of those people, but I don't know for sure.

All I know is I still remember her long, black hair, her delicate fingers and tired eyes. I remember seeing through layers and layers of personalities and angels and demons and aspects, every one of them more beautiful than the last, and light pouring out of her dark eyes every time she looked at me, as if there was a galaxy of dying stars behind them. More than once, the world was nothing but a void around me, and the universe was inside her and she had brought me out to look upon it—her, all creation, the goddess and the form of the cosmos.

Near the end, we were sitting across the table in the TV room, talking. She seemed more nervous than usual, and was playing with her ring. She took it off and handed it to me. I tried it on, and it fit my pinky perfectly. I smiled, took it off, and handed it back. She looked sad for a moment.

"If you were Indian, you would have kept it."

"Oh. I'm not."

She smiled and then we had to go to a meeting.

Released Back Into the Wild

Every place I went was relatively safe. My parents' house, a tourist town winding down for the season, a hippy festival with friends, a mental institution, and finally the University of Maine. If I'd been in Brooklyn when this all happened, I'd be one of those guys you see the police tasing in the subway. I doubt I would have survived, much less recovered. The thinking that led me to jump naked from a pier in the wee hours of the morning and try to urinate in an electrical outlet could just as easily have led me to believe I could stop a subway train with my head. Then again, aside from the rare exceptions, I did seem to have some tiny sense of self-preservation that kept me off window ledges, so maybe I would have just wandered down a subway tunnel and starved to death a month later.

Much as I love Brooklyn, I do a mental self-checkup at least once a day. If anything seems slightly amiss, I pour a stiff whiskey[1] and call someone to watch me. So far, they've all been false alarms or brief, anxiety-induced flashbacks. If it ever lasts longer than an hour, I'm catching the first flight to Bangor and checking myself back into Acadia.

This is from a report from an outpatient follow-up interview I had long after I had recovered:

---

[1] I quit whiskey in 2005. These are the only times I drink it.

> He states that he also believed that he
> was the living dead, and his job was to
> get people to quit smoking. He subse-
> quently was admitted to the Acadia Hos-
> pital. While obtaining an EEG he evi-
> dently eloped and stole a car from the
> parking lot. He states that he was expe-
> riencing a delusion to become a taxi
> driver and to go and do good deeds. He
> was stabilized on Risperdal, however, he
> reports that he was just as crazy when
> he left as when he went in.

I'm not sure how they decided I was okay. Enough good eye contact and apparent cognitive intactness, I guess. Also, my dad had been steadily coaching me in how to appear normal, and was doing a better job of it than the combined medical resources of Acadia Hospital. He would give me tips on when to shave, what to wear, what not to say to doctors or anyone else, and he told me to get a post-it, write "don't be stupid" on it and put it on my door. It occurs to me that this would be a fantastically insulting thing to say to somebody if they weren't obviously crazy, but it saved my ass at least a dozen times once I got back to college.

I remember my exit interview with the head doctor. I had decided long ago that he was The Devil, and we were to do long battle in the future, but he had lost his control over my growing power, and had to let me out of the afterlife holding center. He said I was doing fine and ready to go, and he shook my hand. He had a strong grip, and I was still wearing the key rings on my fingers, so it hurt a bit, and what I thought at the time was that the hellfire emitting from his hand seared the electromagnetic conducers into my aura, even as they protected me from his evil.

Those were my thoughts during the handshake that got me out of the mental institution.

Mental institutions are social institutions. They try to make people safe for society. Much as I harp on how little they did for my actual psychosis, they never pretended they could cure me, and told my family I would probably be crazy forever. Their job was to rehabilitate me to the point where I could be somebody else's problem, or at least function without constant supervision. All institutional psychology is ultimately economic behavioral psychology: How much money will it take to make this person less of an overt problem? If we can get $30,000 out of an HMO now, will it save taxpayers the $80,000 a year it would take to put them in jail? I don't deride anyone who tried to make me okay, even though they had no understanding of what was going on in my head and sent me back to college while I was still completely delusional. They medicated and trained me to not jump off piers and buildings or get in trouble with the police, and I thank every person who helped in that effort. I would like a psychological science that could untangle all the shitty wiring that was going on in my head connection by connection, but that's an unrealistic dream. They did what they could.

My case is rare only in the fact that I did finally snap out of this protracted psychosis, and can examine it from the perspective of sanity. Despite the industry knowing the following fact, there's a prevalent popular belief to the contrary: antipsychotic medication doesn't make anyone less psychotic. They just made me less active. Also, all the eye contact and friendly demeanor notes had nothing to do with my grasp on reality, they had to do with my mood and a dim grasp on what was expected of me.

I don't know how or why I came back, but I submit that it was not the gentle guidance of people trying to shoehorn me into useful-member-of-society mode, though they did a decent job of that. More likely, it was the constant challenges to my imagined reality, and the need to function in the real and complicated world that everybody else functions in. Dangerous as I potentially could have been, college probably cured me. Had I stayed in the mental institution, I never would have recovered.

I packed my things once more, since lo and behold I was actually leaving this time. I said my goodbyes, and traded phone numbers with Pocahontas. There were guitar lessons involved, after all, and I was as in love with her as it was—or is—possible for my brain to be.

They made me leave in a wheelchair. This was policy, and I still think it's weird. I've needed to be in a wheelchair a couple times in my life; they hadn't happened yet, and I was at no point physically disabled during my time at the hospital.[2]

I remember chatting with the nurse as she wheeled me out and called a cab; she was also someone from my past, I don't remember who. I had a smoke outside, and she mentioned something about choosing where you want to be and the kind of world you're going to live in. I was heading to college to conquer or save or bless or whatever it was. There was a very strong secret agent undercurrent, and the need to remain under the radar. Mostly, there was excitement to be free, and back in the much wider and more interesting world.[3] I had successfully navigated the afterlife halfway house or the NOC training program or the electrostatic assassins' guild hazing, and now I was out to complete some new mission or purpose and it was one of those turning moments, all portent and possibility. My brain was loose, not really holding on to anything, and I felt close to the meditative moment on the deck in Lamoine, like I was at the nexus of an infinite number of corridors made of slices of time in potential universes. When the nurse asked me what world I wanted to be in,[4] I had some tiny inkling that the world was not right, that there was something just a bit off.

I stamped out my cigarette and said, "This one," not really knowing what this world was, but know I wanted something solid and real, and "this world" was something good that I should be trying to find.

---

[2] Aside from being thirty pounds under weight when I got in. By the time I left, I was a normalish 150 lbs, since I got no exercise and ate little but carbs. A few months later, I would look in the mirror and feel fat, which is as disturbing as anything else.

[3] Orono. I was excited to be free in Orono. On a college campus. This is what great drugs can do to you.

[4] Or something like that. Whatever she said, it was a weird thing to say, especially to a delusional person.

As the taxi covered the ten-minute drive back to campus, I settled into full 007 mode. There was much to do.

Once I arrived at my room, it became clear that none of it would get done. My room was a tripper's paradise, even in its half-unpacked state. An oriental rug on the floor, beads and flashy little toys everywhere, a collection of tiny stone and metal animals that served as totems, little boxes filled with marbles and bits of turn-of-the-millennium technology, notes, drawings, a few stuffed animals that had survived my Need to Become a Man back in chapter Bar Harbor, a plastic key chain ring with a woman's torso and a baby in a ball that popped out of the stomach,[5] tapestries hung around the walls and ceilings, and more. My room was a perfect storm of LSD, middle-class taste and money, and rat-packing tendencies. I spent five hours arranging things, then another two rediscovering my recently returned cell phone.

I managed to stick the "don't be stupid" post-it to my door. I think I was running out to go achieve something about thirty or forty times in the first couple of days, only to be turned back by the notice that I might be about to demonstrate stupidity. It also occasionally turned me back when I was going to class, but that was still good advice, because my classes weren't classes to me. I had a hell of a line up for a crazy person: computer science 201, communications 102, the theater class I'd signed up for during my grand theft auto, a formal logic class, and some other less interesting bullshit.

I kept up with the theater class, and wrote a number of pieces it must have been painful for my classmates to read. I remember the worst of it, which was me titling each paragraph of my play synopsis with "Part 1, Para Uno, Primero" as if it was some kind of clever pun. It might have been, if everybody had been exactly as crazy as me, thinking the same things, and I'd been cleverer at the time. Nobody read their own work, so when I think back on the poor kid who had to read my nonsense during that class, I wince, and feel sorry for the both of us.

---

[5] One of the weirdest things I ever bought. I joked that it was an instant abortion keychain. This joke never made me any friends, but I thought it hilarious.

I never made it to a computer science class, and this may have been the most rational thing I did, since I was still a Luddite at the time, and would have been outed immediately.[6] The other classes were worlds of fun. Formal logic was the code of all codes, and I doubt anyone who truly loves the discipline feels differently. Even if I didn't understand a single thing in that class in a semantic manner, it did seem like I was being taught the language of the universe. I don't think formal logic is the language of the universe, but I do think there was something to discipline that spoke to my brain in a practical way.

Not so with the communications class. There, I wrote mad symbols, knowing beyond a shadow of a doubt that this class's sole purpose was to give us insight into the language of our alien visitors. I spent the first few classes of that course trying to crack the code of the otherworldly forces descending upon us.

I still hadn't seen stars.

Leaving my first communications class on a cloudy day, I felt the presence of aliens in the sky, waiting to descend. This was okay, somehow. It seemed like the clouds were constricting around the Earth, and I wondered who among the studentry were already aliens in disguise. One, I was sure of, and that was my friend Big Drug, whose charisma and weirdness made him a perfect alien invader. I called him fifteen times one day while he was out with his parents, taking every thing I saw as some kind of signal from him in a complex game of cat and cat. When I finally did run into him, the alien delusions had dissolved back into the standard 007 Jesus-bot sent from the future, so I didn't try to grill him on his species' plans.

After sending Big Drug the original version of this section, I asked him if he wanted a nickname besides Big Drug, and he replied, "No, that pretty much nails me back then." Then he reminded me of something else that happened.

Way back in my Simon's Rock years, I needed a pack of cigarettes. Lacking money, I implored a friend to help me. Since we were all around eighteen, he thought it was reasonable to demand

---

6 And now I'm a "Senior Software Engineer."

my soul in exchange for a pack of smokes. Seemed simple enough to me, so I wrote "I hereby give my soul to Dave in exchange for one pack of Camel Lights" on a scrap of paper and gave it to him.[7] A year later, my girlfriend at the time decided my soul would be part of my birthday present, and traded a crystal goblet to Dave to get it back, and for this I hold the best memories of her in my heart forever. I burned the paper, naturally.

This is only important because I did exactly the same thing two years later, trading a piece of paper dedicating my soul to Big Drug for a pack of smokes, although I think it was only 5% of my soul, since I'd become a savvier sinner in the interval between then and the first sale. While crazy, getting this piece of paper back was the most important thing in the world, since I was missing all sorts of time, meaning, and soul, so I went after him until he gave it back. As he describes it:

> You came up to me and said, "Do you still have my soul?" and I said, "Of course, it's in my wallet." Then you got wide-eyed and said, "Dude, I need it back," so I gave it to you, and you ATE IT. Still one of the funniest things I ever saw, even if you were crazy.

I eventually found my way to the computer lab, where I spent about an hour selecting my helpers from the Microsoft Office animations. That fucking paperclip was the most fascinating thing I'd ever seen, and I tried, futilely, to communicate with it properly, but it just bounced around saying the same thing. I flipped through the others, I forget what they were, but none had the dynamic personality you apparently get from being a bent piece of metal for holding paper together. When I got bored of talking to unresponsive and over-caffeinated help menus, I walked out and passed a pool table. I was about to play, but couldn't defend playing with balls that were actually planets and suns, because I might end the universe if I didn't know what I was doing.

---

[7] This is a lesson in the arbitrary nature of currency.

Here, I believed I was in Hell, but Hell was a fantasy playground, where everything was possible and death was a moot point, so it was time to have fun. This merged with my image of Heaven, and Heaven and Hell just became opposite views of the afterlife in general, encoded according to your ability to enjoy it.

There were many, many complicated delusions, though none more complex and socially perverse than the one that I'll be describing in the next chapter.

The last one I'll mention here is the closing eye. I was looking for my friend Crazy Biologist,[8] and never found him during my insanity, but I found the whiteboard on his door, and I drew a closed eye of Ra, which is one of the five things I can draw like an untalented eight-year-old. He asked me later why I drew it.

"Well, you remember the climax in Fight Club where he looks at Tyler Durden and says, 'My eyes are open' and shoots himself in the mouth, because he realizes Tyler is just a complicated escape from things he won't admit to himself? I was running around on all these cracked out delusions and according to The Rules I couldn't communicate with anyone properly or tell them what was going on in my head, and I probably couldn't have explained it if I was allowed, so it was like trying to send signals to the real world from a dream. When I went to your door, I was still insane, but I knew, for a few moments that something wasn't right, but I didn't know what, or even have the words or understanding to start figuring out what it was. I just knew I wasn't seeing things properly. So I remembered the Fight Club scene and drew that as a message to tell you, 'My eyes are closed.'"

---

[8] Not crazy like I was, but the kind of eccentric person people think is crazy, but is actually perfectly rational and just doesn't care what you think.

The Light and The Void

Emotion trumps reason. Always. You can stop yourself from screaming and curb the urge toward violence, but your thoughts are shaped by how you feel. You can throw some feedback into your hormones, but the impetus for even that effort is rooted in your mood. If you take someone and cut the link between the cerebral cortex and the emotional centers of the brain, that person can no longer make choices. Nothing has any more or less value than anything else, so judgments are pointless.

Regardless of the symbolic system I was entertaining with my brain meats, the feelings of the moment directed my actions. Sometimes I like to think I was regressing through human ancestry to the point in time when we thought the thunder was angry gods, and we didn't have the spoken word map of reason and science we have now. As much as I say our brains haven't changed in millennia, I wonder if they have, and psychosis is a form of regression. I'm also sure that the kind of experience I had, unchecked, leads to religious and cult leaders. The sureness of purpose and the complexity of the experience, once it's translated into language, bespeaks infinite existential mystery. Deciding what caffeine vehicle to buy at Starbucks bespeaks the same existential mystery, but you can describe the basic transaction in a sentence. When the basic transaction is some amorphous movement of semantic energy, it sounds a lot more exciting. And when this mystery exchange is described by someone who has lost the ability to distinguish between their dreams and needs, it can be as charismatic as Jim Morrison. But all this rewired meaning is still the slave of emotion. There are a million descriptions of love and hate because there have been a million people trying to rationalize and contain the temperature of their blood. It's still the same thing in the beginning.

My return to college came in the nick of time, just when I was running out of women with whom to develop deranged obsessions. Trinity lived downstairs from me, and, just as good, a girl I'll call Sirius was nearby. Sirius was another Native American, though you wouldn't know it to look at her, since she was a tiny blond girl with freckles. I'd recently read the Sandman end to end, in which Lucifer, the Devil, is commonly referred to as "The Morning Star, The Light Bringer," and Sirius's real name pertains to stars, so this set the stage for a very consistent delusion that Sirius was the Devil,[1] and a burning star in the heavens, creation and fiery destruction rolled into one over-caffeinated little girl. Sirius was, predictably, The Light.

We'd been friends the previous year, and she, like everyone else at the school who knew me personally, had no idea I was nuts. We hung out once or twice during this spell, and at one point she drove me and a couple of other kids out to her place to hang out and maybe play video games. We went for a walk for whatever reason, possibly none, and Sirius was coasting along on a long board, darting down alleys ahead of us, vanishing and reappearing, like devils do.

Because she was a flirt and had always been vaguely evil, she played her part perfectly. For instance, it was fine to hang out in her room while she was in a towel, as long as I could put up being teased about women in general. I remember few of the actual conversations, but it felt like it always feels to be teased by cute girls: like you're being bounced around on a fishhook. This was a fairly platonic interaction the previous year, and I'd gotten used to it. Now it was Lucifer herself testing my qualities as a plaything.

---

[1] A vast aesthetic improvement over the Devil's last form, my doctor in the institution.

Of course, I was also God, so when I was more confident, I had other plans for her.

Trinity should have known how far gone I was, but she later claimed not to. I can think of two possibilities: she was so unused to normal social interaction that she didn't know what was involved, and couldn't tell crazy behavior from all the other annoying human behavior she avoided, or she didn't care. It was probably a mix of both.

Trinity's uniquely extreme emotional barriers were just mountains to climb in normal circumstances. Now they were evidence that in the darkest depths of her soul, there was nothing. Being crazy, I could look deep inside reified metaphorical constructs, so I tried to look deeper and deeper into her eyes until I found the bottom.

This took about two weeks, during which I saw her more than I'd seen her the previous year.[2] Our interaction involved me staring at her face while she stared at the floor or the wall or her computer. I thought she was communicating to me with all the tiny muscle movements in her face. Occasionally we'd have a vaguely normal conversation. She decided to dye my hair, and since this was physical contact, I let her dye it red, white and blue, which stands as the single patriotic act of my life.[3] I did get a patriotic trip out of that until my next shower, since it was easy to wash out. It was boring. Sort of like being a Fox News show for a couple of hours.

She fluctuated in her ability to put up with me. I'm surprised she put up with me at all; a normal girl would have called the police. When she wasn't having it, I called her at all hours, slipped notes under her door, and went so far as to stick a note in a roll of duct tape and dangle it outside her window, though even crazy I realized this was a little beyond the pale.

I never found the bottom of her soul, but I got close. She was putting up with me by taking a nap, and told me I could stay. I couldn't touch her, so I sat on a chair next to her bed and closed my eyes. It was gray outside and there was no music. I sensed the world

---

[2] And I'd had a class with her the previous year.

[3] And it wasn't my idea, and I was crazy.

was slowing down, and this was the end of all things, not with a final moment, but with each human particle ceasing motion, choosing a final position. There they would lie, or sit, neither happy nor sad, as time leveled out into a gray desert, and we would all be alone with our thoughts for the stilled eternity, perhaps close to someone we would never again touch or speak to, or even see, only knowing their presence by the dim sound of even breathing. Just before the gas of the universe hit empty, I looked as far into Trinity's soul as I could, and found only more depth, the whole of her metaphysical being sucking down into a singularity, infinitely far away. Her soul was a black hole. She was The Void.

Amy describes it thus:

> I didn't consciously realize it at the time, but I sensed a tenuous fragility in Pete early in our friendship and felt fiercely protective of him, though I tried not to act like it because I thought that'd be weird. This was my only sense that gave me any indication that maybe things were not as stable as they seemed for Pete (notice I say 'for' and not 'with.' I think Pete was a constant for himself, and I tried to be as well, but the rest of the world, I think, seemed questionable to him). To my conscious perception, there didn't seem to be anything amiss, but subconsciously a silent alarm was blinking on and off. At no point was I more alerted to these feelings then at *any* point having to do with Trinity. His infatuation wandered back and forth over the border of obsession. It was complete and it was completely obvious to anyone who cared to see it for what it was. I didn't care to see it for what it was, but I couldn't help it, so I stayed witness and tried to make sure my friend didn't do something he'd later regret, or worse, something he wouldn't regret but would destroy him. I did my best to at least be civil with Trinity, out of respect for Pete and our friend-

ship—I somehow even agreed to watch out for her when he went to Amherst the following year (one of many things I've utterly failed at in my life). But I didn't like her, and wouldn't have even if Pete wasn't teetering on some unseen knife-edge for her, and I'm fairly sure she knew this but couldn't be bothered to particularly dislike me. We didn't spend much time together, though I seem to remember Pete trying to get the three of us together far more often than it actually worked out. Pete wanted to save Trinity and Trinity genuinely did not want to be saved, at least not at that time or by Pete, but I didn't intervene (much) because I also sensed that she didn't really have intentions to unleash her powers of manipulation on him. Her intentions toward him seemed to be more a natural byproduct of how she interacted with society as a whole, neither particularly good or bad, and Pete happened into the middle of it and was intoxicated.

I ricocheted between hanging out with The Light and stalking The Void. They were people, but they both existed in my head or in the aspects of people and things around me at all times. They were the poles of the universe, tying together many of my delusions. This says some odd things about me.

A) The poles of my universe were both girls I found attractive. I have no problem with this; I still approach the universe with the understanding that the only things that drive me to do anything are girls I find attractive.

B) Both of them represented destructive forces. The Light was a Shiva figure, destroyer and creator, good and evil, the snake that eats its tail, the wheel of karma, loss and living and loss again. Meanwhile, The Void was just that: the cessation of all energy in the universe, the nothing, the atheist death, the absence of a universe that ever was. Interestingly, I never chose a delusion based on a codified, abstract-yet-male lord of the universe with a benevolent set of rules, even though those figures were present at various times. I stuck with two emotionally difficult women and decided they each represented a different kind of meaninglessness in the universe, and meaning was a construct built somewhere between the light and the void. Since the metaphysical and the physical were indistinguishable to me, I saw the cosmos as that which came out of their dance.

C) I have a troubling fixation on short women. Neither of them was over 5'2". Pocahontas was at least 5'6", but she comprised the institution's entire attractive female population. Given sufficient capita, I start dipping below five feet tall.

In case you have any ideas that I was building an egalitarian, enlightened, and feminist-friendly mythology, trust me, I wasn't. People who know me have already figured out where this is going.

I only mentioned Trinity to my therapist as a girl I had a crush on who wouldn't marry me. My therapist was alternately my handler passing me mission agendas via coordinated eye movements, and an agent of the shadow government trying to keep me under control. Had I been honest with him, I'd have been sent straight back to the nuthouse, but I'm sorry I didn't relate my more interesting delusions. I'm sure he would have been entertained. Most of the time, I trusted him, because he had *Calvin and Hobbes* books in his office. When I recovered and was still seeing him, I decided he was gay and didn't know it. Now I think he was just a decent guy I never stopped making assumptions about. He was helpful in conversations like this:

"So . . . you've never had sex with this girl?"

"No."

"She kissed you once when you were at Acadia?"

"Yeah."

"And she doesn't like to be touched?"

"Right."

"Well . . . maybe marriage is a little bit further away than you think."

"Hmm."

While I was lying to my therapist, I was developing my role in this mythology, and that was to be a new kind of god that would perfect the dance between The Light and The Void, and that would be achieved by having lots of sex with both of them at the same time.

As frustrating as it was in the moment, I'm as relieved as I am about anything that I never even managed to get them in the same room together, because I might well have let slip my intentions and—since nobody knew how insane I was—immediately lost all my friends.

Fortunately, I only managed to get one in my room at a time. I got Sirius in there, who was friendly and hung out, though quickly bored because I never had many people around. Trinity came in occasionally, but preferred to stay in her own room as much as possible. I kept waiting for them to realize that I was here and they should both be there at the same time, but, unsurprisingly, they never did, since they had never met and never would. Clearly I could imagine them liking each other in my most outlandish fantasies, but in the real world, I doubt they would have put up with each other longer than two minutes.

Then again, I haven't heard from either of them in eight years, so maybe I should have gone for it.

The End

All things must come to an end. I hate this fact more than anything else. I even enjoy bad things. I'm fully on the technology band-wagon; I only hope we get around to making ourselves immortal before the god-fearing fanatics blow us up in a bid to get what we can have without all that mess. But I know that even if my body is perfected and technology becomes background magic, you can't account for everything. A star goes off without warning, a black hole that nobody saw swings through town, the heat death of the universe, the false vacuum wakes up,[1] the skin of the universe smacks up against the skin of a neighboring universe and reduces every particle to radiation. Something will happen. I will end, and my lifespan will never match the length of forever. Everything good or bad or somewhere in the middle ends, and we hope that some-thing else will begin, but maybe it won't. Something is happening now, dream or not, something may happen after it, might be better, might be worse. But it will happen then, and you and I won't be there.

The mental skills it takes to forget this and get on with it are what we call faith, addiction, and distraction.[2] For a while, I had a

---

[1] This is the most frightening. Turns out our vacuum might be a false vac-uum, and that little fact allows us to have things like particles and Pink Floyd. If the nature of things finds out about it, our universe ceases to be, in barely an instant.

[2] There also seems to be a weird set of people who are okay with nonexist-ence, but I don't understand them at all. I think it's a lack of creativity, but in truth, I envy them.

better option. I had the option only crazies and prophets and fanatics get: an answer for everything, and the knowledge I would be loved forever.

Then, one day, it was over.

The closer I get to the end, the cloudier my memory gets. I'm not sure what this suggests; I was either going crazier or the cocktail of drugs they had me on was kicking in harder, or it didn't mix well with whatever else I was doing at college once I was unsupervised.

I mapped each floor of the four-level dorm building to the four levels on the crazy scoreboard from the institution, and I once again spent most of my time on the third level, attempting to ascend. The fourth level was populated by hippy stoners who provided pot to the rest of the dorm. We called it trickle-down economics. Crazy, I assumed they were the movers and shakers of the world, and I spent a lot of time trying to figure out how to get up there, since just taking the elevator wasn't an option; I needed an invitation.

I met Crow Abilities here, decked out in ever-present prescription shades, fedora and trench coat, a paragon of gothhood, and I would introduce him to Trinity, and he fell in love with her as fast as I did. Since I was nuts, and kept flip-flopping on whether Trinity and I were destined to be together or in a three-way or whatever, I alternately told him stay away, she's mine, and go for it man, I was never really into her. Eventually he got fed up and said whatever dude, it's on, may the best man win. If you pick your way along the trail of blame, this exchange led to the complex relationship the three of us had for the rest of the year, which put her in the hospital and drove Crow and I apart.

This is when I first met Amy, and we became fast friends. She also didn't know I was crazy, though she probably perceived more of my disturbed thoughts than others. She became my instant off-the-books therapist, putting up with the things I'd say that were as close to what was actually going on in my head as I could get, and she reminded me time and again that the people around me were not the perfect godlike beings I gave them credit for, but mostly just a bunch of selfish assholes. As she remembers meeting me at the time:

> The thing that will always stand out most for me about when I first met Pete is that I approached him. This is very out of character for me, not because I'm particularly shy, but because, in my experience, I either don't want to know you or you don't want to know me, so it's easier to never meet. But to this day, I vividly (relative to other memories from that time in my life) remember our first meeting—it was on the stoop of York Hall sometime during the fall semester; I was 18, he was 20. I was out there smoking a cigarette when Pete came out and, being naturally suspicious, I gave him a once over. He looked right at me while I did so and it was his expression that made me approach him—it said, "Come talk to me, or don't, whatever you decide will be the right choice." This was not a look I generally received in those days so I was intrigued to learn about this man wearing the expression of non-committal acceptance and I initiated a conversation bland enough that I don't remember anything specific about it now, but interesting enough that we're still friends more than 10 years later. (Of course, there's also a strong likelihood that I was high at the time and the conversation was actually interesting and I'll just never remember it because I smoked that part of my brain off—it's like walling it off, but more difficult to break through.) I suppose, if I'm being completely honest, his being a skinny man with blond hair didn't hurt either, but any physical attraction became unimportant pretty quickly.
>
> What's more important is that nothing over the course of the ensuing months made me think

Pete was insane, at least not anymore than I was/
am, though, admittedly, I've always had an affinity
for what I refer to as the cleverly unbalanced. Later
learning this was the case led to my personal belief
that anyone who likes me upon first meeting me is
insane and it's a belief I hold to this day.

Looking back on all of this, I find it hysterical
that I had enrolled as a psychology major.

Amy in turn introduced me to X, a drummer and guitar player.
She said we had to meet because I pretended to play piano and he
could play guitar, so I was all for it, since music, literally, made the
world go round, instead of flat. X was a hardy drinker back then,
which I learned just after I heard about some kid from the previous
year who drank himself to death in a closet one weekend. It was
obvious to me that this kid was X, and the physical X I eventually
met was a ghost, and it was my job to lead him back to the land of
the living. I succeeded, and we started a band a year later, which we
should have called *X's Ghost* but I wasn't letting myself think about
all this stuff yet.

It amazes me that I managed to cobble together a functional,
supportive social life while having no handle at all on reality. I at-
tribute the new people I met to my continuing fascination with
every word anybody said, combined with my assumptions that everybody was some sort of powerful, perfect entity.[3]

Still, my introductions had no follow through. One stunningly
beautiful girl came to my door wondering if I'd ordered a pizza that
was delivered mistakenly to her room. After that first meeting, she
must have come back five or six times to introduce herself, say she
liked my room, look at my books, and ask if I wanted pizza. She
would say hi around campus, and generally acted like she was waiting for any sliver of an excuse to jump me. I politely but completely
blew her off, because I thought she was a spy of some sort, or we
were on opposite sides. More likely, my regular emotional habits of

---

[3] Except Big Drug, who was still an evil alien.

the day were holding steady throughout my insanity: pursue the unattainable and dangerous, run from the available and interested.

While experimenting with all these new beings in my life, I was adding and dropping classes with abandon, because classes weren't just lessons anymore, but alternate realities, and since I was either dead or immortal, there were no rational consequences to anything. All my narratives were semantic and ontological concepts slapped onto whatever or whomever I was looking at in the moment, so the practical consequences of a thought-out future were well beyond my reach.

Logic class was a mind blower, as mentioned before, and as little of the content as I understood, I credit this class with a piece of my recovery. The comment that two mutually exclusive things cannot both be true gave me pause. It was all well and good to ignore the specific examples people gave, like I could not simultaneously be in Paris and London, since of course I could, and was at the moment, because the nature of place was actually an imagined physicality of perceived locality, when in fact all places were one, and each place was simply a harmonic on the same string, so you could be anywhere. But the simplest form of the statement, that two mutually exclusive things cannot both be true because their relationship is mutually exclusive, could not be broken apart by my crazy super-logic into meaning something else. I turned that over a lot in my head.

Speaking of harmonics, I managed to befriend some musician druggies in a grad student's room that I wandered into because the door was open. This guy reminded me of my therapist, only because I thought he was gay and didn't know it yet, the difference being that this time I was right. It doesn't matter; what mattered was he let me play his electric guitar.

The first note I pulled out of this thing was the most earth-shattering noise I'd ever heard, because I could see the intention of my mind traveling through my spine to my fingers to move the muscles to pick this perfect note[4] on a string that sent its vibration as magnetism to electricity to a speaker to the air to my ear drums

---

[4] G.

to my brain to my intention, in the most beautiful feedback loop ever created. I managed to pick eight more notes of ecstasy before I couldn't take it, and I went back to my room and spent the next few hours meditating on music and vibration.

I used to credit this experience with my music ability, which isn't the best in the world, but it's far more than it should be for someone who didn't take it seriously until he was twenty. I don't anymore; I'm decent at music because I practiced a lot. But whatever massive rewiring happened during this experience definitely hit some harmony centers, because after I recovered, I still felt I understood music on a level that I never had before.

Before this, I always wanted a reason and a logic, and traceable, meaningful routes from any event to any other event, and things were steps in my head. Once I made a full recovery, there were no more steps, my thinking and understanding were, and are still, a constant flow. Everything is related, everything is arbitrary, everything is basically the same, nothing has any objective meaning, and everything is awesome in its flowing ability to exist and change. For better or for worse, I went from digital to analog, and haven't switched back. This is probably what let me pick up music, and for that matter, programming, afterwards. It probably lets me do most of what I do these days.

But even as I accept my thoughts as the stream they are now, there was no way to make sense of the raging torrent over the edge of the world they were back then.

A concept that nags at me still was the idea that people branch into different universes depending on their habits. I live in a predominantly rational universe of rules simply because I moved toward it and spent time around other people who moved toward it: it's not that the magical universes don't exist, it's just that I'll never see them because I branched off into a set of universes where magic doesn't happen. It's a metaphysical extrapolation of social tendencies: I tend to gravitate toward smokers and drinkers because I smoke and drink. Effectively, yoga classes may as well not exist for me except in myth. If I'd believed in ghosts and fairies and sought them out, I'd have moved into a world where I could have found them. Had I wanted God, I would have moved toward universes with God. This is a pleasant but perverse and unprovable hypothesis that accounts for everything. It was the last ditch effort to make sense of the unlimited universes I was experiencing all at once.

Possibly the final cohesive delusion that I recall was The Movie. I was looking for Trinity, as usual, since Trinity spent half her time avoiding me, and I went to the stadium during a football game. My primary story sources were *The Matrix* and *The Game*,[5] and I was realizing that my entire life, and everybody's life, was a joke until you hit twenty, the year in which you discovered that everyone and everything had been playing a trick on you, getting you to believe you were mortal and average and not the eternal being you could be. My game involved Trinity coming forth as my perfect compliment, and we would be married and live happily ever after in the real, immortal, perfect world that was always there, but that you only discovered once you broke through the meaningless pretend world. This previous life was being filmed by cameras at every corner, and *The Game* and *The Matrix* were movies based on other people's realities and ascensions, and all movies were simply lives of various people finding their way to The Truth. I arrived at the stadium to cheers and applause for the halftime show, asking for Trinity at every corner, knowing I had to find her and finally become a man and take my place in the council of something.

I didn't find her. I went back to my dorm room.

Things were starting to unravel, outside and in. It was getting harder to support the delusions under the pressure of the real world, and the rapid switching back and forth among fantasies was starting to make me doubt things.

I had cut my hair about a week before all this began. I went from having hair down to the small of my back[6] to having the close-cropped, two-inch hair I have now. I kept the ponytail out of sentimental value. I realized that by keeping this hair, I was tying myself to the old reality, and to escape and truly be free, I had to throw it out, so I did.

---

[5] A so-so Michael Douglas vehicle from 1997.

[6] Luxurious, baby-soft golden locks of hair. My hair was the envy of every girl I met between 16 and 20.

I started obsessively rearranging all the little trinkets in my room, the same way I packed and repacked all my belongings trying to leave the institution, but this time there was nowhere to go. None of my delusions were ending, nothing was being satisfied, there was no release or absolute truth that didn't have to be discarded and reevaluated. Every path wound around to nothing, and I had to find a new one, like being lost on a mountain, unable to find the summit.

I called Jake. I got his younger brother, but I thought it was Jake.

"Pete?"

"Hi, Jake . . ."

"Are you okay?"

"Are you alive?"

"Uh . . . yeah . . . are you—"

"I have to go."

I hung up.

I paced. I looked for help. I walked the campus at night, but it became dangerous. I couldn't trust anyone. I hid behind buildings, in dark corners of the libraries, in the back of the cafeteria, only speaking to people I knew, only if I thought they were real. Something was wrong! I knew something was wrong, and there were hints but no answers. It was the end of the world, this time in a bad way, in a way that would hurt me and everyone I loved.

My time continuity went completely out the window. I have no idea what happened in what order, and most of it's blocked in a fog of reoccurring images and thoughts I refuse to try to think my way through, even a decade later. I couldn't keep 24 hours straight.

As I moved around, I stopped feeling like I was the engine for my motion. The universe was simply opening up space in front of me and I was sucked into it. I had no choices or control.

I decided if I didn't go to the bathroom, my body would just recycle my waste,[7] and as long as I drank salted ginger ale—which to my mind was just the recipe for serotonin—I would be immor-

---

[7] Fortunately, nature called.

tal. Every action became at once effortless, because the universe was yanking me along, and infinitely complicated.

I started pointing my mind at itself, which is generally a bad idea, but I had to seek inward, because I started having the notion that whatever it was that was wrong might be in me, and not coming from the stars and the gods. I had no idea what, but since nothing was culminating, I got the shadow of a notion that I wasn't quite right in the head. I pulled even further from the world, trying to untangle the maze my mind had made for me over the last few months. I wasn't looking for a reason or a principle or a meaning, I was just looking for some common thread, something that was consistent, something that I'd missed but must have been holding me together, or at least driving me apart. I had the sensation of trying to find just the right Cheerio in a supermarket, not even knowing what made that Cheerio distinctive.

Then, about five or six weeks in, I was walking back to the dorm with Amy one evening, and she described a dream she'd had the night before. I realized that even though I'd been sleeping for two months, I hadn't had a dream. I said, "I want to dream again."

That's the last thing I remember for three days.

According to my mom, this happened during that period:

> One day you called me at my office and told me
> you thought you were dead. I told you to stay in
> your room and raced up to Orono, picked you up
> and brought you home. This time I knew enough
> to keep an eye on you.

All I know is that I woke up at home, and I was sane. I remembered having a dream as its plot faded.

I like to think at some point after I realized that the world no longer made sense and started rooting around in my own brain, I found the reboot switch. My REM program came back on and did overtime for three days, then let conscious-me back into the control room.

Not one of the psychiatrists and psychologists who saw me during those months thought I would recover. At the very best, I would be a heavily medicated, semi-crazy zombie for the rest of my life. It may have been the medication, it may have been the facts of the real world reasserting themselves, it may have been dumb, stupid luck. I like to think I thought my way out of the mire, but I wasn't there for the recovery. I do know I wanted something solid to hold onto. The endless complexity of madness never led to the promise of my brief enlightenment, and I had to find my way out if I ever wanted to progress toward anything substantial.

On the far side of the revelation turned hell, I awoke to find an Earth solid and unaltered. The world goes all the way through, the trees don't know your name, and the cosmos is busy with other things. The palpable truths and beauties that seduced my mind a neuron at a time fell silent and intangible. In the space of a half-remembered dream, the universe went from my kingdom, my lover, and myself, to the vast, empty, and uncaring noise it is today.

I mumbled my way through that first day of sanity, not making eye contact with my family, trying to get used to a mind that seemed barely functional, and a life that seemed impossibly empty. As I pieced together the memories as much as I could bear, and realized how close to death all of the things I'd done had brought me, I had the dim impression that I'd fought my way back to the real world. My rewards were a distraught and despairing family, a college that had significantly flipped in its appraisal of my academic potential, an entire county of police that knew my name, unemployment, unemployability in Bar Harbor, dozens of friends lost forever, and a felony soon to be on my record.

That night, I mixed myself a drink after my mom and brother had gone to bed, lit a cigarette, and went out to the deck. I looked up, and for the first time since I entered the institution, I saw the stars.

They looked cold, and far away.

Aftermath

I like being alive. You ever been asked that question, "Would you die to save ten strangers?" and you say no, so they keep bumping the number up until you have to pause and realize, "Wow, ten million people is like a small country," and you have to think about it? My unhesitating answer is always, "Not a chance." I might die to save my brother, but that's about it. I am the opposite of heroic. Maybe I'd show some bravery in the face of uncertain death, but show me certain death, and I will strangle as many puppies as it takes to avoid it.[1] This never comes up: immediate death is never certain[2] and almost nobody gets choices like these. This unflattering aspect of my personality is a cocktail of ego-preservation, nihilism, amorality, and an uncontrollable phobia of death. It's also because I love life, I find everything interesting, and I almost never get bored.

That said, this life sucks. You work through most of it, watch your body and relationships fall apart, and the reward for all your patience is slowly losing everything you love, possibly including your mind. In the end, if you're lucky, you have a few friends or relatives around and the possibility of a quick, painless death. God bless you if you have a god; I don't, and see no reason or evidence for one, aside from the social phenomenon hamstringing medical

---

[1] If it was certain death either way, I might take a second to make a speech or kill some bad guys. But the nuke would have to be thirty seconds from t-zero with no engineers in site.

[2] Except that once.

research and personal liberties. The universe is cold and empty, lightly sprinkled with friends, booze, and sex.

People make do. I've had a better run than most, and I have fun. But going from the most important person in the universe back to a shy twenty-year-old fuck-up isn't easy. Post-psychotic depression is common for just this reason, and I was no exception.

The next few months of my life consisted entirely of this routine: Wake up at seven to drive my brother to school. Drop him off, chain smoke on the way home. Go back to bed. Wake up at noon. Make coffee. Sit on the couch and watch a movie until I fall asleep. Drive back out around three to pick up my brother and bring him home. Go back to the couch. Wake up at seven to watch *Seinfeld* and *Frasier*, the highlight of my day. Fall asleep. Wake up at midnight to get a snack after everyone was asleep. Drag myself to bed. Sometimes jerk off halfheartedly, fall asleep in the middle as often as not. Other times, stare at the wall until two in the morning, trying not to think too hard.

My parents treated me with a light touch for a while. They thought I was pathetic, but then, I was. At least I wasn't crazy, though it was a while before they realized that. Hell, it was a while before I was confident it wasn't a brief moment of clarity.[3]

I did nothing. I didn't even read. I drank alone at night to get my brain to shut up as much as possible. Fortunately, I didn't go to jail. Here's my dad:

> After you managed to steal the car and get caught,[4] there was obviously the issue of "how to avoid having a crazy person's mistake give them a felony record." For reasons related entirely to my generally excellent karma, it turns out that the county DA where you stole the car played left field to my center field on my high school baseball team in Philadelphia, so I called him up with one of those "how have you been and let's make a deal"

---

[3] Four years, to be exact.

[4] It takes a lawyer to realize the getting caught part was the real problem.

opening lines. We agreed that it would be good not to have a felony on your record, but also that you should be punished enough so you wouldn't forget this little episode. He suggested a year's probation and a fine (essentially the deal another first-time offender would get, but with perhaps less negotiating time). When this was presented to the judge, with the assistant DA recommending the plea deal and you with no lawyer, the judge was a bit puzzled (he couldn't figure out this had all come out so "neatly"), but decided to trust the people involved and blessed it.

Another little sideshow was the bill from Acadia: the insurance company hadn't been notified "in time" (for the simple reason that you didn't know who you were), and the hospital wanted to stick Barb and me with the bill. We pointed out that since they let you in, and denied your parents access, it was their problem. I think eventually they worked it out with the insurance company after everyone decided to wake up and return to planet Earth.

I mentioned before that if I'd been in Brooklyn during this episode, I would have been dead within a week. One of my coworkers on my software development team is black, and he mentioned that I wouldn't have survived had I been black, either. There's more luck than location and skin color involved: I got the best available medical care through my mom's connections, and a quick deal from the DA through my father's. I returned to sanity as a lucky outlier, whether or not I had anything to do with it, and I survived because I was a white, connected, upper middle-class kid in a small town. I certainly didn't do anything to deserve coming out of this relatively unscathed.

I haven't done drugs in eight years. If you do the math, you'll note I did dabble around after all this. I never did a hallucinogen again, and I'm embarrassingly paranoid about leaving my drink unattended. I've gotten better, but if I'm not sure I or someone I trust has had an eye on my beer, I'll dump it and get another one. I'm not worried about being roofied, and I'm not too worried that someone's going to revenge dose me, but I am worried some idiot will try to give a friend a "present" and get the wrong drink. The odds of this are probably worse than winning the lottery, but the consequences are I have a 50/50 shot at losing my mind permanently, so I'm not without cause in my wariness. I won't even go into a house or apartment with LSD on the premises.

I quit kiddy crack and all other speed for unrelated reasons.[5] I smoked some weed after my probation was up, until one night two years later. I got high, watched some TV, and went to bed. And I couldn't sleep. No matter what I tried. Then sentences stopped forming properly in my head. Then the paranoia kicked in. I lived near Amy at the time, so I called her and she rushed over and took me back to her place, where I lay on her couch, moaning and scratching at myself, unable to think straight for three hours, until I slept. That was the last time I ingested a psychoactive drug, or any illegal drug. My drug use for the last eight years has been an annual dose of ibuprofen, self-medicating with alcohol to stop myself from thinking, and smoking because I'm addicted to nicotine. Slightly drunk is as altered as I get, aside from the occasional flashback, which so far has just led right back to slightly drunk.

My brain did a couple of strange things during my months of depression. Once, I woke up in the middle of the night, and instantly started falling back asleep like I was going off a cliff. It was like blacking out, but faster, and terrifying, feeling my mind lose consciousness in a second, and I resisted, and snapped awake, but just started falling again. This happened seven or eight times, and eventually I lost, and woke up in the morning, sweating. Less disturbingly, I was semi-sleeping during one of my longer nights, and I felt my awareness collapse into a point in the back of my head. I was aware of my body, but felt like it was a distant surface. I could move this little point around in my body and see how it felt to be

---

[5] Namely that doing speed is fucking stupid.

various distances from other parts of my body. Neither of these were dreams, and neither of them happened again.

The previous year, I'd been deep in some strange but academically viable philosophy research, combining all my -ology classes. The roots of whatever I was working on had something to do with the more positive acid trips I'd had, and there was a small mountain of dog-eared books next to my desk for most of the semester. I smoothed out all the folded corners and put them in my parents' attic. I didn't read a philosophy book for six years. I didn't read psychology, or expose myself to anything that remotely questioned reality. Every TV show that runs long enough has that one episode where the main character isn't sure what's real, and it's filmed in such a way to make you doubt right along with them. I couldn't watch these. I carefully protected my mind from all the patterns of thought related to creative interpretations of existence, any research about how the brain works, and anything else that could awaken the party waiting to start back up in my head. I waited until I was sure most of those synaptic connections were dead, because I didn't just snap on drugs. My path to madness was 90% organic, and anyone can get there without chemicals, by accident, at any moment. I've spent years training myself to keep my brain in the middle road, whatever it takes. I would like to quit smoking someday, but if I think for a second that the stress of quitting would unbalance me, I'm taking it right back up and I'll just have to deal with the cancer as it comes. Nothing in my life is more important than keeping my brain quiet, balanced, and reasonable. Writing this story was a slight risk, and it was hard, and it's as close as I ever intend to come to this experience.

As I've said before, I'm not 100% sure I'm not locked in a room somewhere. This isn't bad; everybody has the "maybe I'm a brain in a jar" moment. In fact, I'm doing better than most people, because I'm 99.999% sure, since the quality of consciousness now is as distinct from madness as waking is from dreaming, but there is enough of a disconnect between how my brain works now and how my brain worked before that I can't be sure. Because of all this, I can never completely trust my mind again, which means I can never completely trust anything again. There's no event that could make me wholly believe in something, because I believed virtually everything, and most of it was wrong. Seeing is not believing: believing is believing, and I can no longer do it. The flip side of this is I'm more confident in the mainstream reality than most people, because I know what it's like to not be in it.

Apart from some average teenage depression and the dash of ADD most people have, I had no mental illnesses before this. Apart from a mild case of PTSD and some unmedicated anxiety,[6] I haven't had any since. I was not genetically predisposed to psychosis. So far, it's been a one-time event.

Eventually, I recovered enough from my depression to go back to school. It took several months of forcing myself out of my room to meet people and pretend to have fun until it stuck and I started actually having fun. After a year or so, I had a life again.

My brother had his own fallout:

> Every step you took towards LSD, I became more The Dutiful Son who never does anything dangerous. I was doing what any little brother looking for an identity would have done, but my "rebellion" was a pretty boring one. The most interesting insight I got out of all this was how I could see and understand what caused my own personality to develop as it did. I had reacted just exactly the way any social behavior model would have predicted; I was not special and so was everyone else. On this account, all my friends in college thought I was super wise until I blew it and did something wonderfully stupid and predictable.
>
> One day in high school, probably 2001, I was at ease in the student lounge when someone made some offhand reference to LSD, and I lost my shit and tackled him. I've never been in a fight. That moment, when I threw someone into a chair and sternly explained that drugs are bad and can fuck

---

[6] Largely due to the fear of going crazy again.

you up was as close as I've ever come to one. I
really hate LSD, and eleven years later, I'm still
uncomfortable when people talk about it.

I don't blame the LSD, and perhaps he won't blame it as much
after reading this, but you should never forget the strong reactions
people around you will have to the content of your mistakes, long
after you've forgiven yourself.

Trinity must have known how madly infatuated Crow and I
were with her. We rarely said anything overt, we just showered her
with gifts and attention and dragged her out of her room, and
eventually she started partying with us. Crow hated me for being
talented at a bunch of media-related things, culminating in the
evening Trinity got trashed and started calling me a god after I
demonstrated that it was possible to briefly pull a large enough
flame off a lighter so it seems like it's coming from your hand.
Wonderful as this was for my ego, I waved it off because that was
definitely Not Okay Thinking. I resented Crow because he could
draw and she loved his gifts so much more than mine, and his and
her real names essentially marked them as soul mates. One night we
were all in my room, having a pretty good time, and though I
blamed the following on Crow for feeding her such strong drinks, it
was all our faults. Trinity was often suicidal, and neither Crow nor I
stopped and thought about what feeding a bunch of vodka and
orange juice to a hundred-pound girl with type II diabetes might
do to her. She eventually collapsed at the door, puking up some
viscous orange gunk. We rushed her to the shower, where I tried to
keep her awake. She became unresponsive so we called an ambulance. We stayed at the hospital until five in the morning, while
they pumped her stomach and stabilized her blood sugar. When I
discovered she would recover, I went home, so of course Crow got
to be the one hovering over her bed when she woke up.

She apologized profusely for this incident, but never thanked
me for keeping her awake and getting the dorm RD to call the ambulance. She was only eighteen, and I could have gone to jail, but
the police and the administration gave me a pass on it for doing the
right thing when it came to the point. I think she never thanked

me because she wasn't all that grateful to be alive. We all drifted apart after that. Crow and I tried to keep in touch, but there was a permanent underlying resentment in our relationship.

I wrote drunken emails to Trinity for years after that, and she got back to me sometimes. At one point, she told me some of the reasons for her markedly asocial tendencies. She had been sexually assaulted by a relative when she was eleven. After she told me this, she told her mother, and wrote to me to tell me that getting that story off her chest had been a huge emotional step for her. She went on to join the police force.

I looked for Trinity for years after I moved to New York, since we'd lost touch. She proved ungoogleable. She was good with computers before most of us knew what they were, and it occurred to me that she just kept herself off the grid, so I ended up going to Maine, finding a phone book, and copying out all the numbers of people with her last name in the Brewer area. I was about to call these numbers one by one when a friend of mine suggested I check the Maine court records, most of which were online.

I found her death certificate. She died in 2006, age 24. I don't know how. Her name was Robyn.

I called the number The Wrestler gave me and got his roommate. The Wrestler had tried to kill himself again and was back in the hospital.

Pocahontas picked up. She just said, "I'm sorry, I only made it to a level three . . . I gotta go. Goodbye."

I saw Other Thin Guy pass me on the road once while I was driving. I didn't have his contact information, so that was the last I saw of him.

A year later I saw Sirius in a parking lot. She said we couldn't be friends because it caused too many problems between her and her boyfriend, maybe husband by then. I guess I was creepier than I thought, but I think it's more because she was evil and her hubby was a jealous git.

I never saw Earth Mother again, though I expect she's all right. She went back to New Orleans after that week. Come to think of it, maybe she's not all right, but I haven't heard otherwise.

JD stopped having roommates after me. He still DJs around Downeast Maine, and I run into him now and then when I'm up there. Still chill as they come, and getting a few gray hairs in his dreads.

I haven't seen LA Queen since a year before this whole incident. Every time a new social network goes up she's on the list of three or four hundred people whose names I punch in, and she always accepts this digital re-friending, but never seems particularly enthusiastic about catching up. The last she knew me, I was going through my shell-of-a-man phase, and wasn't particularly good company, and nobody from Simon's Rock saw me at my best. I don't blame her, but I'm sad because she was good people, delusional alien royalty aside.

Jake's doing fine, living in Brooklyn not far from me. He gave up on the hallucinogens too. We're heterosexual life mates, so we argue a lot, but are basically family. His real family eventually forgave me, so I still keep in touch with them when I'm visiting Maine.

I lost touch with Duke, but Jun's a social worker in Maine, and we still hang out. I owe him a lot for how he helped me deal with all this over the next few years, though I've probably paid that back in whiskey by now.

And that's that.

Conclusions, Answers, Responses

I've had some complicated conversations about regrets with my friends, because of my opinion on them. I wrote a six-part anti-coming-of-age miniseries with Jake and his brother entitled "With Regrets,"[1] where we comically (and brilliantly, thank you very much) lament the failure of our generation to grow up. I used to abide by the usual "no regrets" mantra, but then a few things happened that I deeply regret. Then again, I like who I am, so that should mean I have no regrets, right?

My friend Viking Shaft put it together for me. I was looking at a recently returned bracelet after the protracted and violent end of my engagement, wondering what to do with it. I couldn't really bring myself to sell it or throw it away, and re-gifting it would be raping the concept of sentiment. So I asked Viking Shaft, and he said, without a pause, "Hang it on your wall. Some things you're not allowed to forget." That's exactly what I did. Liking myself isn't enough. I have to remember the unfixable mistakes, and force myself to hold on to the aches from the past. If it makes me sadder, all the better, as my unforgotten mistakes caution my actions emotionally, not just abstractly. Saying I have no regrets is an unforgivable disservice to all the people I've hurt in the past. I embrace my failures, and feel better for feeling worse sometimes.

That said, all my regrets have to do with things I did out of selfishness that hurt other people. The harmless ones I don't regret; I still do selfish things that annoy and offend people. I don't care so

---

[1] And yes, this title is registered with the WGA, so we'll sue if you steal it.

much about these. The really nasty things, whatever my excuses were at the time, I regret.

This episode was not one of those things. Yes, it hurt a lot of people, yes, it fucked up my life for years, but it was formative in who I am today, and at no point in the entire saga did I intend to do harm. That I did do so much harm says much of rats and men, but the lessons were practical, like "I personally shouldn't do more acid" and "don't do acid at high noon in Bar Harbor" and "get some shut eye before the 168-hour mark." There was no moment where I was rationalizing an action, that I absolutely knew would hurt someone, for my immediate personal gain. This all started because I wanted to share an amazing experience with my closest friend, and that, plus a lot of naiveté, can go either way.

The personal economic fallout was pretty minor, since I was in college, and not midway through a career and paying my own rent. It took a while to earn back everyone's trust, but when I did finally get back to college I burned through it like a good little paper-writing monkey.

The emotional toll, if billed in US dollars, would cover an EZ-Pass for the rest of my life. I will be paying it off forever.

Socially, I had to wrangle up a whole new set of friends, but I like these friends, so that's okay, and politically, I'm banned from public office, as are my children's children.

Narratively, it was like a reset button. All the regrets and angsty stories of my past became trivial. It was a new lease on life, albeit in a shitty cognitive neighborhood. It was an absolute low point, and having recovered from that, I can stiffen my ego and resolve when faced with new problems, because they're never as bad. The daily grind, bad days at work, relationship fallout and unemployment are all unpleasant, but are laughable hiccups as long as I still have some modest control over my mental faculties. The only things I fear are death and madness.[2]

I think of the brain differently these days. It's a default—if fading—misconception that there are conscious and unconscious trains of thought going on in the head, and the conscious mind

---

[2] And spiders.

uses about 10% of the brain's power, while the other 90% is all un-tapped potential in the form of Super You having its own, inaccessible conversations. People use this misinterpretation of MRI data and brain composition as an excuse to explain psychic powers and other nonsense. We all use 100% of our brains. The part of the brain we're aware of is all of what we can be aware of. Everything that happens in the brain has some affect on our conscious perception, we just don't know specifically which spark in the nether regions of our lizard brains made us not be able to remember someone's name. When you're at rest and furiously thinking to yourself, you're using a different part of your brain than you would if you were reading, watching TV, biking, or anything else. Accessing the old memories isn't digging into a lockbox; it's relinking your immediate connections to a pattern in your cortex not all that different from your knowledge of bus routes and the positions of the keys on your keyboard. When I'm not typing, I'm not thinking about hand position, and when I'm not trying to remember some childhood memory, I usually don't.

So there was no secret me I was accessing, no unconscious stream of thought or perceptive neurological doorway that opened and shut. There was only the furious rewiring of the same parts of my brain I normally use, triggered a little more haphazardly than usual.

I often say I couldn't have pursued programming as a career if I still did drugs. This is probably true, since weed was always immensely crippling for me. I would have weed hangovers for days, and while stoned, was unable to read or do much of anything besides clean and play video games. Whether or not this would have turned out to be true is academic, but it's definitely true that I wouldn't have become a programmer if I hadn't lost my mind, because the recovery process taught me my most valuable skill as a programmer: how to not think.

Programming requires the acceptance that you are entering meaningless symbols into a machine that's going to spit out other meaningless symbols, and this can be hard to accept.[3] It requires abandoning all hope of an answer for the existential "why?" in favor of shuffling boolean values ad infinitum. By no interpretation of the concept of understanding does a computer understand what you're telling it or what it's telling you.

On top of that, programming as an act is more often hindered than helped by thinking. Despite zero years of training in computer science, I've found I have an edge in debugging because I never look or ask for an explanation. Ninety percent of the bugs in a given program are tiny, one-line errors, and you just have to find that error. Holding the entire logical structure of a million lines of code in your mind is futile. The task is to find the references and connections and track them back until you hit the problem. If I get an error message, I copy it into Google, because someone somewhere has encountered and solved the problem, probably by tracking down the people who originally wrote the program. In seven years of programming, I've solved exactly two undocumented bugs via pure deductive reasoning.

If I'm busy, nary a coherent thought goes through my head, and if work is slow, I'm thinking about sex and food.

Philosophy is the exact opposite. Philosophy is the brain turned inward, deducing the nature and structure of each deduction and its composite thoughts and structures. Whether or not it's aware of and explicit about it, all philosophy is thought examining the mechanisms of thought and awareness. Awareness is largely superfluous in coding, while philosophy wouldn't exist without it. Coding is a world of extant and findable answers, while an answer in philosophy removes the question from the discipline.

---

[3] When I was teaching web design in Manhattan, the first serious hang-up for students was always the web form. The program I was teaching them made it very easy to set up a form, so when I had them design a mailing signup form, they usually did it within an hour. Then they almost invariably asked, "Why doesn't it do anything?" and I had to explain that it was just submitting pieces of information to itself, and they had to write something else to capture that information and store it somewhere. I could generally tell by the end of this lesson who was going to have a career in web design and who wasn't.

Both studies lead toward indecipherable gibberish in the eyes of non-practitioners. To me, the differences I've just described are illusory. Both are forms of hyper-abstraction, and lead toward seeing meaning as a name for a functionally useful operation of the brain, and it's this visceral experience of the notion of meaning as an operation, and not a thing, that is the defining change in how I used to think versus how I think now. Seeing things this way normalizes all pursuits, actions, and thoughts into essentially the same kind of reaction to a varying environment.

A final note on the similarity of supposedly different symbol structures and interpretations. I would estimate 99.9% of newcomers to hallucinogens, including me, suddenly realize *Alice in Wonderland* was about drugs. The elements seem to be in place: smoking hookahs, drinking potions, eating mushrooms, iffy spacetime, and intemperate feline ontology. Many ponder if Lewis Carroll, who started life as Charles Dodgson, did a few mushrooms himself. The truth is *Alice in Wonderland* is a parody of the mathematical theories being advanced at the time, and Carroll wasn't a fan of imaginary numbers and projective geometry, and Wonderland is his intentionally preposterous extrapolation of a world where his interpretation of the new math was true.

Since much of the math Carroll deplored turned out to be useful in the science that brought us the world as it is today, it's not far off to say that the abstractions of math present a model of the universe not unlike the one experienced when you abstract your own experience of yourself by wrenching your senses out of their standard model. I think Carroll would disagree with me, I don't think he ever tripped out, and I find it pleasantly ironic that he unintentionally created some common symbolic ground between theoretical mathematics and LSD.

On to questions.

What kind of drug-user were you before you went mad for three months?

I did a fair but not exhaustive amount of acid. I did shrooms a few times but only liked them the first time. I started hallucinogens fairly late for my demographic, so it was always an intellectual enterprise for me, something I thought I could master. If you go in like this, shrooms are a pain because they defy mental tricks. Give me the designer drugs any day.[4]

I did Ritalin like candy, and my favorite story about that was reading three hundred pages of the wrong book for an assignment. The book I was supposed to be reading was the one next to it on the shelf, and when I went for it, I missed by two inches.

I also smoked pot like it cured cancer.

Did you experience any mental "glitches" prior to this episode?

None. I was 99% mentally stable beforehand, and I've been 98% stable since. Outside this period, I've never been medicated for a mental issue. My doctors occasionally try to give me something for anxiety, but since I have a good social life, a healthy relationship, and a six-figure job, I tell them I'll call them when I think I need it.

Where do you stand in the drug war today?

I consider the "drug war," which is not a war, a means of incarcerating or killing immigrants and poor people. I support the legalization, taxation, and health awareness of all substances. This is one of those things that is so obvious I'm ashamed to be human when people debate it; the war on drugs just saps our economy and funds organized crime.

What made you write this story?

If I kept it to myself, it would just be a painful and terrifying memory. If I make it public, it becomes spectacle. Also, I want to stop working a day job, so anything I can say that people might buy gets said.

---

[4] Well, don't, but you know what I mean.

About how many hours/days did you go without sleeping?

About 14 days. I'm not clear about the exact point I fell asleep. I do know it beats the official world record, at least for people who didn't die from it.[5]

After all that you went through, are you still an advocate (maybe that's too strong of a word) of LSD and other hallucinogens?

I've been asked this question a lot, even before writing this. When I hear it from people like me who have done hallucinogens and stopped, it's usually to start the eternal dialogue we all have: was it worth it? Even before anybody does acid, they hear stories similar to mine, mostly apocryphal: every drug community apparently has the guy who thinks he's a tea pot standing on some corner, or the guy who thinks he's an orange who won't let you hug him because you'll squeeze his juice out. I've never met either of these guys, since even though they've lived in all the same places I have, they always leave six months before I get there. These are telephone whispers of the risks involved, and everybody who takes acid wonders what would have happened if they'd never come back.

I've finally figured out that when people who haven't taken acid ask me this, they're wondering about doing it themselves, and want some kind of blessing from me to allay their fears, since I describe it in equal terms of ecstasy and agony. This blessing I cannot give. Nor can I warn them away from it, because if I do try to instill fear,

---

[5] There's some contention over this. At the time this footnote is being written, Guinness credits Randy Gardner with the record at 264 hours and is no longer accepting applications, probably because of people like me. However, Guinness gives Maureen Weston the rocking-chair marathon record for rocking out for 449 hours, or more than 18 days, which presumably involved being awake, while the Australian National Sleep Research Project puts the record at 453 hours and 40 minutes. I made this brief foray into Wikipedia because it's worth noting that not everybody who stays awake for long periods completely loses it. Gardner was hallucinating and delusional near the end, but made a full recovery after one night of sleep.

that's all they'll think about if they ignore me and take it, and if I ease their anxiety, they may take it recklessly.

I reiterate Jun's quote: "Drugs are a revelation we're not ready for." I'm not an advocate of anything, except maybe a better educational system, atheism,[6] and being nice to people.[7] I cannot in good conscious recommend LSD to anyone, ever. Nor can I, with the same good conscious, tell anybody not to take it. One of the conclusions of *Acid Dreams* is that LSD is a nonspecific psychic enhancer. I think this is accurate, if incomplete. I think if you put your brain through its paces the hard way, you can achieve all the good things in LSD with less risk of losing your mind. But those paces are long, arduous paces that pretty much take over your life if you walk them, and who wants to do that when there's cheap beer in the world?

LSD is simply a substance that does something unique to you, along with penicillin and arsenic. It depends on what you want. I wanted LSD very badly for a while, now I never will again.

---

[6] I've been asked if being an atheist doesn't contradict my assertion that I don't believe in anything. The political and social debate invariably obscures the fundamental distinction between theistic and atheistic world views, so I'll clarify as succinctly as I can. Atheism does not mean, "I believe God does not exist." It is not a positive assertion. It is simply saying, "There is not enough evidence for the assertion that any god exists to justify basing actions on that assertion." I admit the outside possibility that a god may exist, but I am not an agnostic, as an agnostic claims, "Well, you have your model, I have my model, who knows?" I embrace that I have a model based on disprovable assertions, and that I could be wrong about anything at any moment if new evidence surfaced, and that my model is essentially a statistical assumption that may or may not reflect the true nature of reality, if such a thing even exists. Theistic assertions are not disprovable, and theism does not consider itself a model, it considers itself a reality based on an a priori hypothesis with no evidence. I admit the outside possibility that the universe was built yesterday by an infinite number of chipmunks, but since I don't have any evidence for that, I don't factor the possibility into my decisions.

[7] Because why is this so hard?

How do you know all of those memories were true if you said many of them might be fabricated?

I don't think any of them are fabricated. Some of them might be, and as time passes, everybody fabricates and alters memories. Witness testimony is the least reliable evidence, but I have slightly more trust in my memories of what happened during this period than a lot of the other things I purport to remember, because every moment was such an extreme experience.

Most of the factual events have multiple witnesses, if not police and medical reports. The actual physical things that happened that were out of the ordinary were the vanishing Rose-woman, the shooting star splitting, and locking myself in an unlockable bathroom. Since they were the only things that happened that were superphysically strange out of the three months of madness, and because they have plausible explanations, I assume they happened.

As far as the delusions go, I made a list of them shortly after I recovered, and they'll probably be the last things I remember when I go senile.

Would you say that you were happier when you were insane, or was it just different?

I had more extreme feelings, but they balanced out to the same average I have now. People are born with a baseline mood, and they hover around it their whole lives, barring extreme chemical or physical changes in the brain, temporary or otherwise. Emotionally, I had the same swings, they just swung faster and farther.

The difference was I had external meaning. Many people search for meaning and invariably end up disappointed or deluded, because there's no meaning to find. Everybody who has meaning creates it for themselves, and their desperation for it and the means by which they find it characterize their lives. Whether you seek it with words, gods, institution or protestation, there is no actual meaning Out There, there is only the meaning you create, because meaning is a name for the process of our brains with which we categorize and communicate.

I've slowly drifted from the Omar Khayyam poetic justification of life, or "we're all going to die, fuck it, let's get drunk," to the Lucretius poetic, or "everything is infinite randomness, life is awesome, let's get drunk and fuck." I don't need a reason to live, I just need access to booze and sex, and that's motivating enough.

However, I can understand why so many people give up booze and sex and all the other good things in life if they've let their search for meaning take over their minds to the point when they think they've found it. That's what happened to me when my reason left the building, and the thought that the universe cares about you trumps everything.[8] It's not that it made me happier, it just alleviated existential dread. And, frankly, I think alleviating existential dread is bad for humanity: if we really want immortality and rocket ships and all the possible pleasures of existence, we need hubris and dread. Monks be damned.

Do you think there is any merit to using psychedelics for any group/label of mentally ill people? Do you think, at the peak of this experience, LSD/psychedelic therapy could have been any use to you?

The short answer is there has been positive medical research in treating a variety of mental disorders. The research is either very old or very new, and as I am not a medical professional, all the information about this research comes to me second or third hand. LSD and psychedelic experiences in general will change you, for better or for worse, and there is nothing inherent in the experience that is therapeutic or traumatizing. What is inherently therapeutic is a room full of therapists, and if hallucinogens are taken under the careful guidance of medical personnel open to and trained in psychedelic therapy, or even a thoughtful and prudent person who knows what the drugs can do, I can only imagine the experience would be beneficial.

The long answer is this book, and I don't think the person who asked me this started at the beginning.

---

[8] Note, however, how many of my delusional escapades involved sex.

The next one is a two-parter:

A) *You seem to be implying that there's such a thing as OBJECTIVELY INSANE and it goes beyond being weird. Or, beyond abnormal. Or, beyond not behaving the way most people behave. That doesn't make sense to me, given the rest of what you've written. As someone who has lost their shit can you go into more detail on what you meant?*

I sort of thought this immensely long story would give the answer, but to be explicit, yes, there is such a thing as OBJECTIVELY INSANE. "Weird" and "abnormal" are purely relativistic judgments, thus have little bearing on the psychological and medical realities. You are insane when you've lost your ability to second guess, doubt, reason, and adapt your primary narrative to evidence, and instead are just finding ways to modify the evidence to mean something that will fit in your narrative. It's safe to say everybody does this to some degree, but once you do it on a word-by-word basis and knowledge of physical laws are no barrier to the process, you've lost your marbles. As I said, it's a scale, but there's definitely a dividing zone, past which you're nuts. The brain is still the same three pounds of flesh; it's going to work on the same principles no matter what it's doing. If it can't distinguish between dreams and reality when it's awake, it's broken, but not a fundamentally different thing.

Since so many people have rightly pointed out that we are witnessing a vast social explosion of people squeezing and ignoring facts in favor of their personal narratives, from the truthers to the birthers to entire demographics, parties, and nations saying things that are not even internally consistent, I've been trying hard to think of something that can I point at and say, "if you're doing this, you're crazy," at least for the purposes of average discourse, or non-linguistic philosophical discourse that comes in under three volumes. It's particularly hard because the waxing fanatics are blurring the lines, but here is my best shot:

I think I overuse the term "narrative" to cover my bases, when I sometimes mean "theme." My actual narrative of what happened was clearly crazy: I thought things that hadn't happened had, I thought people were other people who were dead, I thought I was specific people I wasn't. There was a thematic narrative as well, and that was also extremely complex and changing internally, but for any particular theme, it was not inherently different from an only slightly bipolar conspiracy theorist or a Mormon fundamentalist, or anyone fanatical about anything. Being a fanatic entails the exclusion of reason.

What's not in question[9] is the lingual level. If I say, "That's a car," you do not nod your head and think, "ah yes, that's a dragon." Let's say that every time I see a yellow car, you actually see what I would call a green dragon, and we've just adapted to different driving styles. If this has been going on your whole life, we both still see and communicate "car" without much issue. We share the reference point to a physical entity, and it's a relatively stable piece of communicable datum.

Now let's assume we both see an object descended from the Model-T, and not the offspring of a bat fucking an iguana in a wood stove.[10] Except now I'm secretly attaching the symbol of car to dragon. I did this by thinking transportation, some people rode dragons in myth, myth is real, myth is symbolism, all is myth, myth is now, dragon is powerful motion and transcendence, car is powerful motion and drive-thru, two out of three ain't bad, dragon and car are one, merely facets of the gem on the blind men's elephant's brow. Good. Now I've made two symbols—that I know are different—interchangeable. But I haven't lost the language or the knowledge that is classically bound up in those two symbols. So

---

[9] Unless you have a serious amount of time on your hands.

[10] I say natural selection demands that if you did this enough times, something would survive, and I bet that something would be a dragon. If there are any crazy people reading this right now, you have your mission.

now I freely mix the referenced qualities of cars and dragons.[11] So you can have a perfectly normal conversation with me about cars, since I recognize the actual physical properties of a car, but then I'll say, "Yeah, it hasn't been able to fly lately, I think it's hungry." You'll laugh nervously, then try to force what I just said into your car-referencing system, relating "fly" to speed, and "hungry" to oil, gas, or use, and above all try to avoid thinking that I actually believe my car is both a Honda and a thing that gets hungry and flies through the air, because that's crazy. Odds are you'll think you're behind on the slang, and you'll start telling everybody your car's "hungry" when it's low on gas, and can't "fly" because you haven't changed the oil, and that will all make perfect sense.

I'm tempted to believe this is how human culture mutates. If you go through this whole process very slowly, you have culture and language. Go through a little faster, you have philosophy and rhetoric. Go through at a canter, you've got politics, and if you break into a gallop, you're insane. The faster the process, the easier it is to get smaller, more literal symbols in the mix. Think about this sentence: "God is God but not God, God is everything, God is the water and the wave, the vision and its completion." Sunday morning, right? Now, trying to make Friday night before prom something worth confessing on Sunday: "Love is Love but not Love, Love is everything, Love is the water and the wave, the vision and its completion." Sweet. I've just demonstrated how the Bible can be used to get young atheists laid. Grab a short passage, replace God with Love, and say it to an insecure girl late at night. This can be done because Love and God are both huge, ancient symbols describing nothing in particular. Love, God, Earth, Hell, Heaven,

---

[11] Programmers can think of this as suddenly finding a lot of bad pointers. In fact, even though only ten percent of my audience got that joke as it was meant, the colloquial and literal uses of "pointer" also apply, so you're all thinking of something different. See? YOU'RE ALL MAD. But actually not, since the term "pointer" long ago lost any literal attachment to an object, so it has fewer definite qualities, and more metaphorical heft, without risk of madness. You can watch this process in action if you keep track of the public usage of the word "osmosis." Or "democratic" for that matter.

Hope, Faith, etc., are all big words people argue about, because by the process of insane osmosis[12] these words have merged with every other concept and thought process we have, and thus mean jack all. They're shortcuts between other, more literal concepts.

Now try this: "My car is my car but not my car, my car is everything, my car is the water and the wave, the vision and its completion." You say this, you're crazy, no matter how much you "love" your car. "Car" is a small literal concept, like pinky, femur, or table, that can't be randomly attached to other murky metaphors. Now imagine crazyland, where every word and concept is like Love or God.

B) A definition of crazy that I'm rather fond of is laughing when nobody else is laughing, or crying when nobody else is crying. Maybe all you mean is: a simply weird person learns how to behave in a not crazy way when it matters, which makes them not crazy. A crazy person can't figure out that this is key to their survival in society. Does this jive?

This is sophomoric diarrhea. Many people laugh when nobody else is laughing or cry when nobody else is crying; these are simply normal reactions to different information, or a perfectly normal difference in interpretation. Envision this scenario: a bar full of people watching the news, a report comes on about a man who died from an infected weasel bite. One of the people in the bar is Dave Barry, who rightly finds all things weasel-related funny, so he laughs. One of the other people is the guy's widow, and she bursts into tears. Even if you say this is an exception and not indicative of a lifelong habit, a person who laughs when nobody else is laughing is Andy Kaufman, or anyone who gets an obscure pun because of rare knowledge, and a person who cries when nobody else is crying is half the depressed people I know. You may say that if the widow laughed, she'd be crazy, and that's the distinction because she's reacting to a situation atypically, but it could just be an effective coping mechanism, or she could be a psychopath, and a psychopath isn't necessarily crazy. We could play this game all night, reposition-

---

[12] Choke on it, grammar nazis.

ing the situation, but we won't get anywhere. This is a ridiculous definition.

A truly crazy person can survive just fine in society, and—under the right circumstances—can do better than a "weird" person, or run a country. I'm submitting that crazy in the way I was crazy is not a social definition, it was a severe chemical lapse in my brain's ability to do its job. I've heard people say, "If everybody was crazy, the sane ones would seem crazy." Also not true. If everybody was crazy, civilization would collapse overnight. You may have the thoughts and dreams of a god, but you have the practical living skills of a retarded puppy.

This next bit is not a question, but needs to be addressed.

The guy had one hell of a bad trip but maybe it was because he simply wasn't good enough. Such things are possible. Draw the attention of the Eye, and it might decide you unworthy.

Might be fun to try sometime, going crazy. It'll be on my bucket list.

I dismissed this comment until I realized he'd said some extremely dangerous and stupid things:

". . . maybe it was because he simply wasn't good enough."

This is something that could lead people to believe that they need to train harder, or be "better" at doing drugs, or if they're bipolar, maybe they just weren't good enough last time they went off their meds, but they've learned something and now they'll be okay. I fervently want to believe I could navigate through madness again, but the winning bid is chemical, not cognitive. It doesn't matter how "strong" your mind is if your dopamine levels are off. I can't stress strongly enough to people with either diagnosed or possibly pending mental issues that you shouldn't listen to anyone who says things like this.

"Draw the attention of the Eye, and it might decide you unworthy."

This is precisely the kind of thinking you want to avoid while tripping, and in general. This is an appeal to the unexamined, semi-natural force the neo-hippies and pseudo-intellectuals bring up to suggest some connection with the big Out There that they've touched while high. It's non-religious idol worship, whatever name it takes. I'm not speaking to the religious nor the spiritual, neither of whom can be convinced, I'm speaking to the rational, thinking people experimenting with alternative perspectives: there is no "Eye," judging you, there is nothing out there to which you must prove yourself, and there are no "worthy" or "unworthy" notes being written on the big book in the sky. You have nothing to prove to anybody, and don't let anyone tell you otherwise.

"Might be fun to try sometime, going crazy."

If I have in any way made being crazy sound fun, I have erred. You cannot have fun when everything is important. I recently saw the documentary *Jesus Camp*, and there's a sad scene where a young girl talks about dancing. She says, "When I dance, I really have to be sure that it's God, because people will notice when I'm dancing for the flesh." When everything means something, nothing is fun. Everything is important and vital to the nature of the universe. Being crazy can be, if you're lucky, existentially satisfying, and if you're willing to sacrifice your real life for a temporary and not necessarily gratifying thrill, I still suggest you don't do it.

People who say things like this are fools. Do not listen to them, and if you are going to do drugs, do them with someone else.

Did you see Inception *or* Black Swan? *(I'm wondering because they are both psychological thrillers and I've read of your aversion to them.)*

I've gotten a few of these questions, mostly relating to the two movies mentioned. I did see both of these movies, and I suppose they are "psychological thrillers," but not the kind that freak me out. Both of them broach altered perceptions, but not accurately enough to trigger fear, at least for me. The most accurate things for me have been *The Invisibles* graphic novels, *The Last Temptation of Christ*, and the movie *Special*.[13] These were all media experiences that I had to take in parts, because they were too close. Others in-

---

[13] Aside from the shitty ending.

clude *The Caveman's Valentine* (movie), *Soon I Will Be Invincible* (book), and *Donnie Darko* (movie). Although I enjoyed both movies, *Black Swan* was eye candy and *Inception* was a study in film theory.

Were you on "kiddy-crack" or other uppers while you couldn't sleep?

Nope. It was acid initially, then stress keeping me awake.

People . . . actually seek out other people's banal psychedelic "revelations"? I mean, we all think we experience something deep and revelatory when we're tripping on whatever it is that we're tripping on, but in the cold light of day it's pretty obvious to most of us that while those "revelations" may feel deeply personal and significant, what they actually are is clichéd and utterly boring.

I both agree and disagree with this. Telling somebody "everything is one" is dismissible, but experiencing it is life-altering. The mystic experience, common to nearly all religions past and present, has never changed, and it is, sadly, not possible to describe. I've done the best I can here, but it's not enough. The last time I checked up on the science, it has to do with getting a particular kind of wave going in your brain (not a metaphorical wave, a wave you can read on an EEG) which triggers some glands and chemicals that alter your perceptions of time and identity. There's nothing magical about it; it's just a moment of experience devoid of symbolic cognition. Coming back and describing it is impossible, because it's a moment when your awareness is focused solely on the experience of its own existence. Everybody has an indescribable personal experience of existence every day in every single thing they do, they just don't focus on the fact of it. Focusing on the fact of it is the mystic experience. You can have it on tap with a little practice.

Coming back and trying to explain that existence alone is enough will lead to the clichés like "everything is one" and "all is illusion," and there's no getting around that. There are also deeper places to go in meditation and drug experience, but even the very first level of this exploration is indescribable, and it gets more pointless from there.

People who have not had these experiences don't need to explain themselves, but it's worth knowing that your personal experience of reality is not the experience of a "real" thing. It's the chemistry of your naturally selected brain structure, and the common world to which we ascribe abstract patterns and meanings is not the only one out there to experience. If you come back from such an experience and think, "Oh well, I wasn't really in the Christian heaven," and dismiss it, you've missed the point, and haven't had a revelation at all. If you come back and think, "Wow, my brain, on the most fundamental level, doesn't actually have to work the way I always thought it would," then you've had a revelation. It's not an experience you can share, but it's something to think about.

Before and Now

My nihilist, atheist, empirical, almost reductionist mindset grates on even the most skeptical. The fundamental disconnect is between believing things happen for a reason and believing nothing happens for a reason. I fall in the latter camp because I don't even believe that there can be an objective concept of reason. Given this, people have asked if I would have interpreted my experience differently if I'd come to it with a more spiritual worldview.

But I did come to the experience with exactly that. Prior to all this, I was experimenting with hallucinogens in a Fritjof Capra sort of way. I felt an energy and a flow to the universe, I felt I was on the cusp of a spiritual awakening, and I sought a holistic truth independent of human experience and thought. I was an avid proponent of free will and the emergent nature of consciousness, and threaded quantum physics, relativity, eastern and western philosophy together to make arguments for the concept of consciousness as both an integral focal point for reality and as an autonomous guiding force in the nature of being human. I wrote several terrible screenplays trying to artistically demonstrate the necessity and possibility of not existing in a universe of inexorably unfolding physical processes.

What changed for me was experiencing the sort of spiritually satisfying world that the human mind seems so predisposed to desire. The two states of bliss known to the human mind are the elimination of ego and the total fulfillment of the ego. I had both, by turns, in excess, and achieving that kind of fulfillment so completely while in psychedelic and psychotic states demonstrated to me that they are possible and that there is no underlying, non-mental architecture in achieving them.

There are theories floating around that the modern human mind is somehow broken, and there are various diets or drugs or pursuits that can fix it. It's the fallen-from-grace model, known best in the West as being expelled from the Garden of Eden. I think this comes from the false assumptions that the mind is in a constant state and that radically altered states can be thought of as a fuller potential, and from the ennui that comes from not having to fight for survival as avidly as we once did.

In response to the first assumption, the mind achieves wildly different states all the time, from total unconsciousness and non-experience to dream states to happiness and despair. I've been depressed and euphoric and interpreted the world accordingly, and my life changed drastically for the better when I started eating right and sleeping on a schedule. Look into a mirror too long and you can achieve a dissociative state. Nearly all computer programmers eventually experience a moment upon waking when they perceive the universe as code. The mind is a complex tool for survival, and our experience of having one takes many different flavors on daily basis.

The idea that drugs and radically altered states express a higher potential is a bit like saying humans are the pinnacle of evolution. Evolution has no pinnacle, and an altered state of mind is just that. It's not better or worse: it's different. I think contrast in general is an excellent experience for broadening the mind and making it more able to be further broadened, and if that's what you want, extreme brain alteration is part of it. But extreme and continuing contrast is also the thing that gradually instills a sense of the arbitrariness of interpretation and meaning. A popular altered state of mind that lacks contrast is fanatical guru, and their universal cry is "everybody should shuck the rest of the world and listen to the thoughts in my head." Exploring one's own mind excessively is not pursuing universal consciousness. It's narcissism.

I've had a great deal of contrast in my life. I've lived in several states, visited Europe and South America, and had homes in various coastal suburbs and rural areas before settling in the secular stronghold of New York City. Every experience and encounter with people who'd lived in a different setting introduced me to a different way of living, and demonstrated that my preconceptions about life were not necessarily the best or only approach. Since I was happy and comfortable, with no worse than average teenage depression, throughout this process, I didn't feel the need to protect myself against these cultural and idealogical intrusions. Instead I learned how arbitrary many of my cultural assumptions really were, and dispensed with them as best I could. At the same time, I began picking out things that were universal in people whose culture or outlook seemed totally alien, and found that the whole process and state of alienation could be short-circuited by appealing to empathy, shared knowledge, and most people's desire to talk about themselves. I was stripped of any notions of stability, patriotism, or belonging to any abstract, human-designed group, and I ended up with a strong sense of belonging to an interesting species.

With mind-altering substances, I achieved even more profound contrast, and it had similar benefits and drawbacks to my worldview. When I harp on my concept of a fundamentally uncaring and godless universe of physical processes, people often assume I'm an angry and empty person who feels betrayed by his own birth. I'm not. The experiences that showed me my means of perceiving and believing weren't necessarily the best or only means stripped me of any hope of existential certainty, but allowed me to see the universe and all my experience of it as an ever-changing flux of strange beauty. The experience of a single instant still fascinates me, as does recalling a memory, blinking, waking up and falling asleep. The knowledge that we don't really know how the universe works, or even how to communicate or explain the nature of our immediate experience, leaves a vast unexplored territory for the curious person. Accepting that your consciousness is the you that you care so much for, and the chemical construction of your brain, and composed of the same vibrating energy as all physical things is more mindblowing and elegant than the thought that that vibrating energy has some kind of guiding force behind it with which we can shake hands in Nirvana.

And though I lost the kind of faith that sustains many people, I discovered the capacity for my mind to feel new and extreme emotions, and be in new and extreme states. Knowing that those things are in some sense still in my head, and to some degree knowing how they work, gives me a significant mental arsenal with which to approach the rest of my life. As damaged as I had to be for a long time, I wouldn't trade my mind now to take those years back.

I've been told that maybe I "just wasn't ready for the world beyond." This is certainly true in the sense that I wasn't ready to eliminate my entire interpretation of reality and immediately follow up with a psychotic break, and I admit this could be true in the sense that higher beings turned me away from the party, but I admit it in the same way I admit that maybe God is a 6' 4", well-muscled caucasian with a harp fixation. I don't find it necessary to name the unknown quantities of my experience to validate it.

There is at least one view I have that is generally shared by everyone who has an experience of this scale: the process of consumption and achievement so treasured by modern western culture is the very smallest part of the experience of life. It's odd to me that in America—a country that treasures individuality so highly and fears socialism so pathologically—the encouraged values are totally external, only valuable to the continuation of the social and economic structure of the country. As Graham Hancock points out in *DMT: The Spirit Molecule*, the only valued frame of mind in western culture is alert, problem-solving consciousness, since that's what you want for business and production. Anything that detracts from that state of mind is frowned upon, if not vigorously persecuted and prosecuted.[1] Though I reject the thought that our brains are somehow physically and artificially limited due to the modern world, our relationship to our own culture, our internal lives, and the

---

[1] This is not a conspiracy. In the case of LSD, the effects on oneself and others can be terrifying, especially if you don't know what's happening. Combine the sudden burst of these substances with an anti-establishment movement a lot of people are already afraid of, plus an establishment that, like all establishments, will jump on the chance to use fear to keep itself established, and the political outcome is obvious.

world we live in is badly broken; as Sidney Cohen says, "Something must be wrong with a society from which so many wish to escape." After two centuries of the pursuit of happiness, the fifties touted itself as the end of the chase, and when it became obvious that it wasn't, a reaction was inevitable. None of this is something I learned from a psychedelic experience, it's something I learned by having a thorough, non-indoctrinating education before I ever touched a drug, so it's never been connected to a spiritual revelation or altered state.

I don't consider this a spiritual versus material world. More specifically, I don't believe there's a distinction between experiences "out there" and "in here." The oddness and mystery of the nature of the universe and the nature of consciousness are one and the same. The mystery of what we experience on LSD or DMT or during a psychotic episode is not categorically different from the mystery of what we experience every day. In a simple example of how weird the supposedly ordinary world is, the light hitting our optic nerves after traversing the biological lens is upside down, patchy, and about twenty percent of what we think it is. Our brain constructs a rich visual landscape out of cognitive correction and guesswork. It's hard to believe because we only see the rich visual landscape.

The dissolution of the ego and the feeling of oneness is a remarkable alternative to the normal western experience, and I look forward to a more balanced global awareness that takes into account the inescapable fact that we are part of the world, and not above it. This is not a call to drugs: people have been eliminating their egos for thousands of years, with and without chemical assistance. In fact, over the years I've found that just trying to experience all of your senses simultaneously and completely is both nearly impossible and one of the quicker routes to no-mind, and I do it on my commute daily. However, I won't condemn the ego either. It is the single most powerful survival mechanism ever produced by nature. It is the coordinated appeal to the continuation of the self, and it does not need to be sublimated to make way for the understanding that the self is also part of the world. Alienation is not a physical deformity of the mind, it's a byproduct of culture, an illusion that can be eliminated with existential humility as quickly as it can be eliminated by transcendental experience.

In *Breaking Open the Head*, Daniel Pinchbeck, dissatisfied with being a nihilistic New Yorker, embarks on an intense psychedelic journey, has a spiritual awakening, and comes to believe in a consciousness binding all things, and beings above us, evolving with us. I had the opposite experience: I started with a palpable feeling of spiritual truth that was completely stripped away, and now I'm a nihilistic New Yorker. The difference for me is that I don't find a purposeless, meaningless universe unsettling: the core mystical awakening is in the experience of being, and even a laymen's exploration of modern science reveals that the universe is an extremely strange place that we don't really understand. The quest for spiritual truth becomes a need when people project the banality and frustrations of their internal worlds and see the universe as boring and faulty. A spiritual awakening is primarily breaking the mind out of that interpretative trap, which is enough for me. Somehow fitting visions and feelings into a framework with beings and consciousnesses and unknown forces that care is superfluous. I find such attempts less revelations than they are representations of a longing to be loved. All of my altered experience, psychedelic and otherwise, has left me with the lesson that it is far more important to love than to be loved.

Furthermore, the concept that Western thought is a left-brained abomination that tipped us out of Eden is naive.[2] The his-

---

[2] Especially when prevalent right-hand dominance is presented as evidence of said abomination. I'm sure I could write fluidly with my left hand if I practiced, just as many left-handed people were forced to write with their right hands and ended up being able to do both. As a bass player, I can attest my left hand is doing much more complex and dextrous things than my right when I perform. Is that because my right brain is better suited to the creative complexities of the neck over the rhythmic qualities of the right hand's job? I doubt it, since the game-changing guitar player of the modern era was Jimi Hendrix, a lefty who restrung his guitar so he could play the neck with his right hand. There are obviously neurological differences between truly left-handed people and truly right-handed people, but we're all using both sides all the time.

tory of technology, the world we live in, and the state of mind for the average First World inhabitant is not the work of half a brain, nor has it preempted the possibility of feeling connected. The processes of greed and fear have always been at work, we've just created a world where they can potentially do more harm. We're not living in an unnatural world: all of civilization emerged from nature as naturally as any tree. Romanticizing the awesome power of nature and claiming it has a greater, somehow more valid role in the universe than we do overlooks the fact that the vast bulk of the universe that is actually matter is composed of dust and burning gas.

It doesn't take a disembodied spirit world of otherness to connect the universe. The replicating patterns of waves, DNA, symbolism, consciousness, ecosystems, society, neurosis, psychosis, mathematics, and any other system that exists exhibit similarities in their motion of energy transference if you admit the possibility that our grasp of the concept of an atom is as much a function of conscious confabulation as our grasp of the concept of morality. Both are patterns we name in an attempt to make sense of how the world works, functional lines of demarcation we apply to the energy of the cosmos.

Every few years I reread *How the Mind Works* by Steven Pinker, possibly the least humbly titled book I own. It's a description of the brain as a computational response machine, and he breaks down various functions of thinking in a strictly evolutionary model that's hard to argue with. Near the end, he points out that many of the greatest minds of history have been working on mysteries like consciousness for millennia with no progress, and suggests that we're no more equipped to solve them than a rat is equipped to learn calculus:

> Given that the mind is a product of natural selection, it should not have the miraculous ability to commune with all truths; it should have a mere ability to solve problems that are sufficiently similar to the mundane survival challenges of our ancestors. According to the saying, if you give a boy a hammer, the whole world becomes a nail. If you

give a species an elementary grasp of mechanics, biology, and psychology, the whole world becomes a machine, a jungle, and a society. I will suggest that religion and philosophy are in part the application of mental tools to problems they were not designed to solve.

Madness and psychedelics taught me, above all else, that consciousness is more profoundly strange than I could have imagined, and it remains inexplicable. Though the functioning of my thought is no longer a mystery, the question of what it is to exist and think at all remains unanswered. The qualitative nature of these experiences is indescribable in the language we have now, partly because it is impossible to understand it when you're not experiencing it, anymore than you understand the waking, sober world when you're dreaming. Even if I saw, with absolute clarity, the inarguable solution to all questions of being, I would have no way of knowing, despite remembering the moment. However, even if we can't dissect it with the tools at our disposal, as Pinker says, we are living it for the duration of our lives, and the word-resistant absoluteness of being a mind that Is satisfies me most of the time. We build our symbols to communicate and extrapolate, and though the rudimentary transactions between the synapse and the thought cannot be described, they can be experienced.

There has been a slow resurgence of psychedelic research in the last few years. The disastrous ending for mind-altering drugs in the 60's came about in part because one side thought the experience was nothing but good and the other thought it was nothing but bad. As Hoffman says about LSD, it's no more good or bad than a knife. The power of the experience tends to send people reeling toward one pole or the other, believing it's all grace or damnation, but it's neither. It's a neutral possibility that can take either side or none at all, and I think it's done the world more good than harm.

I had a stoned conversation with Jun in 1998, when I was couch surfing after the end of a relationship upon which my living situation depended, and he mentioned an early report on LSD by two authors. It ended with one of the authors saying nobody should do it, and the other saying everybody should do it. This conversation took place at almost the exact midpoint between my first and last experiences with acid. After mentioning this story offhand, I decided to track this report down, and after some research, I surmised that Jun was probably talking about the report *LSD* by Richard Alpert and Sidney Cohen. Incredibly, I managed to get a used first edition of the report, printed in 1966, the year the hammer came down on LSD and drugs in general.

The authors, after both having used LSD in the past, embarked on this report with the same opposed views with which they finished it, and I think everyone who reads the book will maintain the opinion with which they started. The views were not as mutually exclusive as I'd expected: Cohen suggests caution with LSD and a neurological interpretation of its effects, while Alpert sees LSD as transcendence, revolution, and universal spiritualism. There are agreements, and my favorite is this one:

> [Meher Baba] has suggested that while LSD and the other psychedelics may start one on the spiritual journey, or be of therapeutic value, their value as a way to the highest levels of consciousness is illusory.

My story is an inherently cautionary tale, but consider the story of the father of LSD: In 1943, at age 37, Albert Hoffman was working in his and lab when he had the first acid trip in history, which was two hours of mild disorientation and pretty colors. After deciding that the experience was probably caused by the LSD-25 he was working with at the time, he experimented on himself to verify the effects, and took 0.25 mg orally. His experience sounds similar to my first acid trip:

> Every exertion of my will, every attempt to put an end to the disintegration of the outer world and the dissolution of my ego, seemed to be wasted effort. A demon had invaded me, had taken possession of my body, mind, and soul. I jumped up

and screamed, trying to free myself from him, but then sank down again and lay helpless on the sofa. The substance, with which I had wanted to experiment, had vanquished me. It was the demon that scornfully triumphed over my will. I was seized by the dreadful fear of going insane. I was taken to another world, another place, another time. My body seemed to be without sensation, lifeless, strange. Was I dying? Was this the transition? At times I believed myself to be outside my body, and then perceived clearly, as an outside observer, the complete tragedy of my situation. I had not even taken leave of my family (my wife, with our three children, had traveled that day to visit her parents in Lucerne). Would they ever understand that I had not experimented thoughtlessly, irresponsibly, but rather with the utmost caution, and that such a result was in no way foreseeable?

Unlike me, he had nobody around him familiar with the effects of psychedelic substances, and he had just taken the most powerful one in existence. But he came out okay, and experimented with smaller doses thereafter, throughout his life, as well with other psychedelic substances. He approached all his experiences with the mind of a scientist, and though he was changed, he didn't lose his mind or follow Leary and Kesey in trying to rewrite society and spiritualism overnight. He continued to make discoveries about psychedelic substances as a chemist. He took LSD for the last time when he was 97, and lived to be 102, whereupon he died a gentleman, a scholar, and an unrepentant square.

Although you can take my story as a particularly urgent warning against drug use, I would rather you take it as a warning against being stupid, and remain open to the uncharted territories of existing.

Epilogue

Before, during, and as recently as five minutes ago, I've read up on psychiatric and otherwise academic studies of hallucinogenic experience, and I've been constantly disappointed. First and foremost, they tend to be boring. They are reports of the linguistically sensible communications from the altered state. I can't claim I've done better. All I've tried to do is communicate the subjective experience of losing my mind. The failure of the psychiatric investigations is in their attempts to codify the half-sensible trip reports of subjects into a preexisting framework of meaning. The most recent one I've read talks at length about psychedelic experiences rooted in experiences from the womb. I would suggest that this is not a recollection of pre-birth experience, but an attempt to encode universal experiences in near-Freudian terms. There are notable commonalities in non-sane experience, but there isn't external meaning or semantic structure inherent to it: there are only repetitions of the natural structure of the brain, and the common language for expressing that structure. Literal interpretation of reports of reliving birth, traveling to other dimensions and through time, leaving the body, meeting spirits, and the like, seems to discount the existence of the imagination. Losing the ability to distinguish between autonomous exterior systems and internal systems of expectation and hypothetical constructs naturally leads to reports of unlikely experiences.

The nature of the psychotic experience is to see the mechanism of symbolism unhinged. The psychedelic experience is similar, but still connected to the doorframe. The risk of the psychedelic experience is to see the mechanism at work, but retain the need to make it meaningful, when by its nature it is demonstrating the lack of meaning in everyday experience. The risk of a psychotic experience is essentially the same, but with less effort. Taking the commonalities of psychically altered experience and applying a semantic, symbolic map to them is missing the point entirely. The lesson is that the map is an illusion.

I specifically wanted to convey the way I thought during all of this, and how that means of thinking came about. A trip that doesn't go out of control leads to brief descriptions of the is-versus-isn't nature of everything perceived, and the hint of some great revelation. There isn't one. It's your brain on acid. The great revelation is madness, and the goal is to tap the deeper and weirder expressions of your consciousness without falling in.

After speaking to Jun, I would be remiss in pointing out a couple of things. Yes, I do argue that the drugs didn't help me get cured, but it's important to note I didn't jump off any piers or buildings once I was medicated. I did steal a car, sure, but I actually thought I was being directed to steal a car; the drugs made me supremely biddable, which is important when your autonomous direction is telling you to drive to San Francisco and tame alien queens. I was also able to make a complete recovery because I had no underlying chronic mental illnesses. If you do have such an illness, please do not stop taking your meds and expose yourself to complex social environments. I'm sorry to say that severe bipolar disorder is not going to go away, nor will persistent schizophrenia. I didn't stop taking my drugs until long after I recovered, and then I was carefully weaned from them under the supervision of three separate doctors.

I've mentioned many things good and bad about the psychiatric profession. If held parallel to the rest of the medical profession, psychiatry is making progress, but has yet to find its germ theory. It will be many years before the brain is cracked, and until then, they're doing the best they can. I put drug manufacturers right next to oil and tobacco companies in terms of diabolical evilness, but the innovators and prescribers of these drugs are trying to help people, with some results. Drugs are ubiquitously over-prescribed these days, because drug companies can profit by expanding the hazy demarcation between functional and non-functional on the continuum of mental problems. Everybody has psychotic thoughts once in a while; non-crazy people call it creativity. Everybody has mood swings; if those swings go between suicidal depression and psychotic mania, it's bipolar disorder. Since illnesses and personality quirks are not fundamentally different operations of the brain, the unprincipled can blur the distinctions to profit from the untrained. Everybody on Earth has a variation of ADD, especially when growing up. It can be so severe the person cannot function, but I know a number of pretty bad, unmedicated cases, myself included, and we're all programmers, musicians, and artists. The mind oscillates between neurotic reflection, which spirals inward, and psychotic, nearly random connections, which create new patterns and loops of thinking. Either of these operations can go too far, and the trick to enjoying good mental health is, by whatever means, finding a stable speed and breadth for these oscillations. You can't stop them and have a single, perfectly rational train of thought, because your brain is a rushing river and your control over it is not the control of the Earth or a god, it's the control of a small team of civil engineers.

I cannot overstate this: I am not a doctor. I have no training or license; I have a handful of mediocre psych classes from a school I left nine years ago. At best, I am a dilettante armchair scholar, and any advice I may have appeared to have given should not, under any circumstances, be construed as something that could take the place of professional consultation. When I needed details about the medical parts of this story, I went to medical professionals. This is just a story, and to quote my brother, "I am not special and so is everyone else."

Ultimately, LSD showed me a window into the universe I'm glad to have seen, even if it also shoved me out of that window. I am happier, more productive, and definitely much better paid since I quit drugs, but I firmly support their legalization. In fact, I think there should be mandatory joint a day for everyone with a job except me. But every drug is a remixing of the mind that can be achieved without the drug. The spiritual revelations that tell people to be nice to one another and live in harmony were unnecessary for me because I always thought that: at first just because I was nice to people and wanted them to be nice to me, now because a meaningless and unknowable universe all but demands that conscious beings care for one another as we traverse the space between mysteries. Only total ignorance of all flavors of knowledge, or an ingrained submissiveness to authority and alienation, could lead a person to think the universe is not a motion of energy that includes us all, whether they simply know it, or simply feel it.

I say I miss drugs, but I've realized over the years that the reason I haven't done them in so long is not because I can't do them, or that I fear them. It's because I don't need them.

Appendix A: Other People's Stories

After posting the early version of this book on my blog, I received a number of emails from people who had gone through similar experiences. I was surprised how many others had had psychotic breaks, drug-induced or otherwise, and just hadn't told their stories. It was also interesting how many of these people had delusions similar to mine. The Jesus and popular media delusions made perfect sense, but there were other, more subtle commonalities that struck me. Just as important were the stories sent by people who had seen someone else go crazy, and hadn't understood what was happening. I also got a lot of feedback from people on other points on the experiential and observational planes of drug experiences.

Here are a few:

A decade or so ago I dated a woman who had a psychotic episode something like this. Watching her lose her sanity, over the span of just a few hours, was a singularly terrifying experience. Her body was still there, her voice was still there, and her personality was in there somewhere, but *she* wasn't there anymore, and the new program running in her head was not something you could relate to as a fellow human being.

It was like her pattern-recognition system had stuck on full throttle, and she had no way of filtering anything out. The whole world around her was full of messages and meanings, patterns, hidden identities, instructions from the divine; every thought sent her off in a new direction with full confidence, seemingly unaware that she had been just as confident about something totally different a moment ago. She kept looping back through similar chains of delusions, but she couldn't sustain any plan or idea for more than a few minutes before something new distracted her.

Ha ha, drug humor, drug experience, whatever. Once you know the cliché, what more is there, right?

Once I experienced some of these things myself, though, I found these things—both stories and depictions—far less boring (well depictions if well done; otherwise frustrating). A little like travel in that way. Because from that point on, what started to happen is that I would catch little moments of "truth"—not in terms of some kind of universal revelation but in authenticity of experience. I'm recognizing a moment. On top of this, a number of these stories are tremendous first hand accounts of endless terror and incalculable joy; I'd have to have some kind of heart of stone not to be moved by them. Which is why I'll never understand the utterly dismissive attitude some people have toward experiences that may look outwardly idiotic because they look outwardly idiotic. It strikes me as extremely and unnecessarily self-conscious and insecure. The experience is real enough, and it's the experience I'm interested in.

Over 10 years ago I worked in a transitional housing for the chronically mentally ill. The majority of my clients had a history of some sort of psychotic disorder—schizophrenia, bi-polar with psychotic features, major depression with psychotic features, schizoaffective disorder. For the most part, they didn't share what was going on in their heads and most were sufficiently medicated so that their positive symptoms were pretty much in check—for example, they might hear voices, but they knew that the voices weren't real. One time though, I observed one of the more together client's descent into delusional psychosis. It was very unsettling.

She was a woman in her fifties. She had spent the majority of her life working as a nurse. She was a lovely person to talk to—intelligent, thoughtful and pleasant to be around. She was, however, suffering some pretty dramatic side effects from her medications. She swayed from side to side constantly and shuffled when she walked. She had a very hard time waking up in the morning and had very little energy to do much of anything during the day. Needless to say, she was frustrated and depressed about the side effects of the meds.

The staff felt bad for her—here was this seemingly perfectly rational woman who was so overmedicated that she couldn't even function. How could she get reintegrated into the community if she had no energy to do anything and had such dramatic uncontrollable body movements? Hospitals frequently discharged people to us who were completely overmedicated and this seemed to be a textbook case of it. We advocated to her doctors to change her medications and asked them to discontinue the antipsychotic she was on.

For the first week she seemed great—brighter, more energetic, less of the swaying and shuffling. Then, she came to me saying that she needed some emotional support. She was plagued with guilt about the death of a dear friend. Okay, I said, let's talk.

Out came this very elaborate delusional system involving her being part of a medical rescue team who worked with/against the Hells Angels. The Hells Angels (in her delusional system they ran everything and were in the highest branches of the government) would break into people's houses and hang them; her rescue team would come along shortly and revive them. They had fucked up with her friend, she said—they got to his home too late and were unable to revive him. His death was all her fault.

Fuck. This belief system was firm and all-encompassing; no amount of "reality testing" could make a dent in her delusions. She was terrified of the Hells Angels, told me that they were going to track her down and hang her—she was really suffering. We called the doctor and she went back on the antipsychotic medication, albeit at a lower dose.

It stayed with me for a few days like a mild case of the flu. I felt a little uncertain about my own reality.

I think going crazy must be easier for religious types—or at least, more socially acceptable. You can have totally screwed up, unsupportable theories about the world, and if it fits the pattern similar crazies have laid down before you, it's cool. You're a shaman, or a prophet. It's tougher when the core of your worldview is physics and logic.

My only really bad experience was actually with nitrous oxide and weed. Nitrous alone would start to do it, but apparently it needed something else to amplify the effect. Fortunately it was (objectively) very brief, but seriously damaging nonetheless. I understand the PTSD, and the fear that you're going to slip back into that place, and the nagging thoughts that maybe none of it is real. (And on the subject of TV shows and such, I came as close as I've ever been to an anxiety attack when I watched Inception.)

The harmonic thing really fits with my experience. I remember that everything was a complex waveform, and that I could imagine a Fourier series representing the universe. All of the waveforms eventually made their zero-crossing at the same point, and that was my singularity. The complexity of their sum grew again as I moved away from that point, but I knew there would be other minima to come and that no matter how complex and real the universe seemed between those minima, I would get there and it would condense and I would again have a moment where it was all visible and understandable to me. I don't dare do nitrous again—I tried a couple of hits long after that with no other drugs in my system and I was immediately sliding right toward that singularity. The pattern's established in my brain, and even totally sober I can't completely shake the idea that my theories were right.

My fear of death increased a hundredfold after that incident. I get that part. I don't think I need to elaborate. I'm pretty sure it's enough to just point at it and say "yeah, that."

Doing psychedelics is like sightseeing in a beautiful place where you've heard rumors that there may be an unimaginably deep chasm somewhere nearby, but you're not sure because many of your companions insist it's just a rumor.

So at first, it's all pretty safe. You just don't go too close to where you think that edge might be. But over time, you get more brash. You keep looking for that edge, because the view is better there, of course. But it's a weird edge, enshrouded in mist. It takes very skilled, experienced footwork to actually find it.

Most of us [. . .] just find a spot where the view is good enough. But some of us don't. And, assuming youth, recklessness, lack of respect for the "reality" of the situation, that means we eventually go too far, we fall off, often without realizing . . . because first we get caught in an updraft. We're flying, we think . . . but then we fall.

And it can be a very long, incomprehensibly deep fall.

But it usually doesn't kill us (drive us mad). It just shakes us the fuck up, smacks us around, it wounds us. Sometimes deeply. To the extent that what we're left with is something approaching post-traumatic-stress-syndrome—a wound that takes a long time to heal, assuming it can ever be fully healed.

At least, that's how it was for me.

My happy ending goes something like this. It took more than a year before I'd really shaken the "shaking" I'd taken, the deep, gnawing, almost Lovecraftian existential dread I was haunted by in the aftermath of my "bad fall." But I did get over it to the extent that I was eventually doing psychedelics again, but I was wiser now, I was more cautious now. I now knew for sure that there was an edge and no, I couldn't tell you exactly where it was, but I could always sense it when I was getting close . . . so I learned to stop right there, close to the edge, not over it. And over time, I kept edging closer such that, eventually, I was getting right to it. I had the footwork figured out. I could even catch the updrafts and float around a bit . . . without going over.

Another supposed master of the universe here from 2005.

Nowhere near your reaction, of course. But everything you said about your experience rings true. I thought about writing about my experience, but it's hard to put into words when you realize that it just sounds like a fantasy story and thinking most people can't even dream of relating. My thoughts still linger in the background.

I'll never really forget the feeling. Unrestricted access to self-esteem, confidence and a feeling of possibility/discovery. Enlightenment. Even the memory of it is like being able to tap it for an instant . . . but it's a deadly emotion. And can unlock actions that society deems disturbing.

It's kind of a shame because I've tried to block it out so much that now when I think about it I can barely remember more than a few details. It's happened to me three times so they blend together. The last time wasn't even caused by drugs. That's when I realized that the mind is not a static thing when it comes to traumatic experiences. It doesn't just repair itself . . . it adapts.

I perhaps tasted a bit of this insanity last New Year's Eve. I ate 11.6 grams dried mushrooms last November. It was my first experience with such a dose, and needless to say, I underestimated the extent of the effects. Fast-forward a month to New Year's Eve, when I took an eighth. I stupidly decided to drink, and at some point, something snapped. I had what I can only describe as a flashback, during which I left the room I was in and visually and emotionally experienced the feeling of being lost in endless loops on a heroic dose. I came out of the stupor with my friends looking worried. Throughout the night I began to question my sanity, question reality, and decided that my entire life had been a "coma-dream," and that the real me was lying in a hospital bed in the real universe. Unlike you, my series of delusions lasted only as long as the mushrooms did, but I ended up going to my dad (whom I also thought was God, and asked him if that was the case) and begging for help. Stripped naked in his bed, etc, etc.

In my psychedelic days I did get to a point where belief started to take over in this pernicious way. There were a few months in which I quietly "believed" in strong solipsism (e.g., that I was the only existing consciousness and I was dreaming the world) or, alternatively, that I could somehow help bring about an end of suffering in the world by getting rid of all of my possessions and wandering homelessly. I also sometimes "believed" that certain people in my life were real (as consciousnesses), but we were trapped in this dream-world together, and we were all half-consciously and secretly signaling to one another in some kind of half-remembered, ancient code that we needed to remember that this is a dream and learn how to wake up from it. Oh, and I also sometimes thought of myself as a sort of prophet that could "wake" other people up and turn them onto this ancient wisdom I was in the processes of "remembering."

Fortunately, I also got sleep and remained interested enough in my classes to keep me from becoming completely untethered. Eventually, I had my first full-blown panic attack on the most heroic dose I've ever done (I was convinced I'd truly lost my mind and would never get it back), and that was pretty much the end of my psychedelic detour away from reality.

Looking back, I guess I characterize that period as a drug-induced manic episode, not a psychosis. But, yes, belief had absolutely everything to do with it.

If I achieve nothing else in the next forty years and look back from my death bed, this letter will have been enough:

As a twenty-year-old college student (biochemistry major), atheist, **programmer, and an infrequent, low-dose 'cid user, your story has given me a much more sobering perspective on the use of this drug.**

Your description of madness being the lack of the ability to second-guess is especially sobering, considering that I've been dabbling in the world of UFOs and 2012. After a period of sober reflection I've come to realize that I've been testing the waters of conspiracy too frequently, and that I should spend my time doing more productive things, such as memorizing all twenty amino acids for my biochemistry exam next week. I still like to read about what people have to say, even if I know they are bat shit insane, because while it is not in tune with reality, it **still retains its entertainment value, and it is not all that different from a Stephen King novel. I must always remember to treat it as such. Your story has caused me to reflect on my capacity to be a skeptic, and to concentrate on my short-term goals in life.**

Even after reading your story, at this point in time (things could change) I will still continue trying out acid, but I will do so with much more caution and respect than I previously had.

Appendix B: Medical Reports

The following reports are unaltered except for the names of the staff, which are removed, and various tracking numbers and unchanging headers, which add nothing, and one typo in which the doctor, in reference to me, says, "His fund of knowledge appears to be god." I couldn't let that one go. Many thanks to Ashleigh for typing these up for me.

PSYCHIATRIC ADMISSION HISTORY

PT NAME: HUNT WELCH, PETER
SEX: M
MR#: 1005040
FIN#: 38864377
ADMIT DATE: 08/24/2000
DOB: 02/28/1980
DOS: 08/24/2000
SITE OF SVC: 3SOU

IDENTIFYING INFORMATION: This is the first psychiatric hospitalization for this 20-year-old single Caucasian male from Bar Harbor. Currently, he is a UMO
student with no record prior psychiatric history who
was admitted on an involuntary basis and transferred
from MDI because of confusion and disorganized behavior. He was seen and the records were reviewed.

CHIEF COMPLAINT: Strychnine and acid.

HISTORY OF PRESENTING ILLNESS: The patient was a
fairly poor historian, appearing unable to provide a
coherent description of the events preceding his current hospitalization. In a rather vague and disorganized manner, he acknowledged the presence of persecutory concerns. He spoke about his mother following
him around because I tried to eat her. He reported
unusual experiences like having seen the earth and
the bottom of the sea. He stated that almost continuously he is able to see around him many of his
friends. He denied perceptual disturbances, even
though he appeared to respond to internal stimuli. He
acknowledged the presence of thought broadcasting but
denied thought insertion or withdrawal. He also denied any ideas of reference. He stated that he has
been running around, quite anxious and distraught
because of the recent breakup with his friend. He
could not come up with any other psychosocial stressors. He just talked about feeling perfectly well.

When his mother asked to provide further details, she explained that she has not had overall much contact with him in the last three years since he went to college. She lost track of him in the previous two weeks when he left town and went to Massachusetts to stay with some friends in Great Barrington. Quite recently, he came back to Bar Harbor. Reportedly, in the last two days, he has been displaying markedly abnormal behavior with confusion, illogical statements, and appearing disoriented and as if walking in a daze. The family became aware of his LSD use as recently as two days prior to the admission and probably in significant amounts. The patient went to the emergency room at MDI yesterday, but bolted out before any assistance could be provided. Today he was taken back to the same emergency room and cleared medically. Reportedly, the toxicology screen revealed only the presence of _____*. In the emergency room, he reported concerns that he might have killed a buddy of his and that he could take a friend's soul from his body. He also reported his ability to be in contact with God. He was sent to Acadia on blue paper for further psychiatric evaluation and treatment. Mother also explained that possible precipitants could be the family's high expectation from an academic standpoint and the recent completed suicide of a friend of his.

PAST PSYCHIATRIC HISTORY: According to the patient's mother, when he was 6 years old, he had a psychiatric evaluation due to depression and anxiety. He participated in family therapy and improved. As a teenager, mother remembers him as having been on and off depressed but never to the point of requiring treatment.

PAST MEDICAL HISTORY: Tonsillectomy; history of multiple sinus infections.

MEDICATIONS: ?Valium [sic] 10 mg t.i.d.

ALLERGIES: Dust, pollen, and cats and dogs

ALCOHOL AND DRUG HISTORY: The patient's reporting was
rather unreliable. Initially he denied any alcohol or
drug use. Later on, he admitted having had LSD on
several occasions. He described his trips as traveling the world and touching things. He also acknowledged the use of heroin, crack cocaine, mushrooms,
ecstasy, and speed, but he was not able to provide
more details. He reported at one time having had to
go through detoxification. He also described daily
ingestion of a glass of wine and occasionally the use
of beer and hard liquors. Questionable history of
blackouts and alcohol withdrawal seizures.

MENTAL STATUS EXAMINATION: He appeared as a disheveled, withdrawn, guarded, and underweight young Caucasian male. He had very poor eye contact. Minimal
cooperation with the interview. Significant psychomotor retardation to the point of near catatonia. For
prolonged periods of time during the interview, he
would remain almost motionless with closed eyes. When
moving, he would do it extremely slowly. Speech was
spontaneous, fluent, hypophonic, and monotone without
much inflection and minimal emotional content. Mood
was detached and affect flat. Thought processes were
with significant circumstantiality, tangentiality,
and looseness of associations. At times, positive
thought blocking. Thought content was with vague delusions of persecution. Positive visual and auditory
hallucinations. Denying, in an inconsistent manner,
suicidal and homicidal thoughts or plans. Cognition
was difficult to assess because of poor compliance.
He appeared alert and oriented to person and place
but not to time. When asked the date, he initially
replied, February 28, 1980, and then later on January
1, 2001. Capacity to focus, sustain, and shift attention, as well as the ability to present events of the
recent days in a sequential manner, were impaired.
Insight and judgment were quite poor.

DIAGNOSES:
AXIS I:
1. Psychosis, NOS [not otherwise specified].
2. Rule out substance-induced delirium, probably due to LSD [lysergic acid diethylamide].
3. Rule out substance-induced psychosis.
4. Rule out schizophrenia.
5. Rule out schizoaffective disorder.
6. LSD [lysergic acid diethylamide], heroin, cocaine, mushrooms, ecstasy, and amphetamine abuse.
AXIS II: 1. Deferred.
AXIS III: Status post tonsillectomy; history of multiple sinus infections
AXIS IV: Psychosocial stressors: Severe - Suicide of friend, recent relationship breakup, and family arguments.
AXIS V: Global Assessment of Functioning: Current: 15.

PLAN: Admit the patient to 3-South. Monitor for psychosis and cognitive difficulties. Physical exam and labs. Start Risperdal 1.5 mg twice a day and Thorazine 100 mg q.i.d. p.r.n. to help with agitation, irritability, and explosive behavior. Initiate a Valium protocol. State multivitamins one q.d. and thiamine 100 mg q.d. Involve in the milieu. Obtain more information from family.

THIS REPORT IS STRICTLY CONFIDENTIAL.
Redisclosure is prohibited by law.

CC/DMT
D: 08/24/2000
T: 08/24/2000 20:32

NOTE: This information has been disclosed to you from records whose confidentiality is protected by federal law. Federal regulations

(42CFR part 2) prohibit you from making any further
  disclosure of it without the specific written consent of the person to whom it pertains or
as otherwise permitted by such regulations. A general
  authorization for the release of medical or other
  information is NOT sufficient for this
purpose.

MEDICAL HISTORY ' PHYSICAL/ADMISSION ASSESSMENT

PT NAME: HUNT WELCH, PETER
SEX:M
ADMIT DATE: 08/24/2000
DOB: 02/28/1980
DOS: 08/24/2000
SITE OF SVC: 3SOU

SOURCE OF INFORMATION: The patient who is an extremely unreliable historian, due to his psychotic
state.

REASON FOR ADMISSION: This 20-year- old, young man
was transferred from MDI hospital. He had been recently evaluated at MDI for psychotic symptoms. Over
the last few days, he stole his mother's car, and
ended up at the Southwest Harbor Police Station. He
then told the police that he had killed someone. His
urine at the emergency room at MDI hospital was positive for marijuana. According to a friend of his he
did take 6 or 7 hits of LSD on August 21, 2000.

AGE: 20

HANDEDNESS: He is ambidextrous.

ALLERGIES: Allergies to dust, pollen, cats, and dogs.

PAST MEDICAL HISTORY: He denies any recent exposure
to infectious process, but states that he was exposed
to HIV when he was 18 years old. He states that a
friend of his was cutting himself, that he wanted his
friend to stop cutting himself, and that he licked
his friends blood. When asked if this person had HIV,
he said he thought so. He has a history of a head
injury. He states he was dropped when he was little.
He tripped and fell onto a concrete floor at the age
of 4 and lost consciousness. He is unable to give me
any other medical history.

CHILDHOOD ILLNESSES/IMMUNIZATIONS: He did say he had a tetanus booster in the last 10 years.

HOSPITALIZATIONS: None

SURGERIES: Tonsillectomy at age 7, appendectomy at age 8.

FAMILY HISTORY: He is unable to give me his mother or father's ages. When asked how old they were, he told me 150. According to him they are both alive and well, but he has a brother age 25, a brother age 14, and a sister age 21 with no health problems.

SOCIAL HISTORY: He has been living at _____ Street in Bar Harbor. He attended MDI High School, but left after his sophomore year. He has worked in the Bar Harbor area as a waiter, dishwasher, tennis instructor, and a bartender. He states he also has taught math and English. Drug, Alcohol, and Tobacco Use: It is reported that he had 6 to 7 hits of LSD on August 21, 2000. He has used IV heroin, mushrooms, ecstasy and speed, also marijuana. He is single.

CURRENT MEDICATIONS: He has been on the Valium protocol of Risperdal 1.5 mg p.o. b.i.d and Thorazine 100 mg p.o. t.i.d.

REVIEW OF SYSTEMS: Is extremely limited. He is unable to answer questions, so I will only provide positive review that he was able to tell me. He states he did have a head injury at the age of 4 with loss of consciousness. He states that he has excessive stomach acid, that he lost approximately 30-40 pounds since the beginning of the summer. He has used IV drugs. When asked about blood transfusion, he states he was transfused 2 weeks ago (question reliability of this information). When asked about sexual activity, he does not discuss whether he prefers males or females,

but states that he has used condoms, and he has been
sexually active.

PHYSICAL EXAMINATION: General: This is a very emaci-
ated, 20-year-old who is awakened for the physical.
He is somewhat sedated. He is very spacey. He appears
to be responding to internal stimuli and stares. No
eye contact. He is cooperative. He has been making
inappropriate hypersexual comments, so much of this
physical examination is also limited, due to that
fact. Height is 5 feet 8 inches. Weight is 123-1/4
pounds. Temperature is 37, pulse 60, respirations 16,
blood pressure 108/80. Head: Normocephalic. No lesions or tenderness. Skin: there is some slight facial acne. The patient appears to have a tinea infection of his arms, back, and chest. He has several
concentric erythematous lesions with central clearing. Eyes: Pupils are equal, round, and reactive to
light and accommodation. EOMs are intact. Peripheral
vision is in tact by confrontation. Disc margins are
clear. Ears: TMs are pearly gray. Weber is midline.
Rinne testing is AC greater than BC bilaterally. Nose
and Sinuses: Clear. There is no sinus tenderness.
Mouth and Dental: Uvula deviates to the right on
phonation. He has an asymmetric posterior palate. No
tonsillar enlargement or exudate. Neck and Nodes: No
thyromegaly or lymphadenopathy. Chest: Clear to aus-
cultation. No rales, rhonchi or wheezes. Cardiovascu-
lar: Regular rate and rhythm. The patient is somewhat
bradycardic with a rate of about 56 to 60, but rate
is regular. No murmur, run, or gallop. Lymphatics:
There is no axillary or inguinal lymphadenopathy.
Breasts: No nipple discharge, tenderness, or masses.
Abdomen: Scaphoid. Nontender. Hypoactive bowel
sounds. No palpable masses or organomegaly. No CVA
tenderness. Genitalia: Deferred, due to patient's
current psychotic state. Rectal: Deferred, due to
patient's age and lack of symptoms. Extremities: The
patient has several concentric erythematous lesions
that have central clearing. He states that they do

not itch. He has the lesions on his arms, chest, and back. Pedal pulses are full and equal. The patient has full active range of motion. Back: The patient has pronounced curvature or the spine. When asked if he has been diagnosed with scoliosis, he says yes. No paraspinal tenderness.

NEUROLOGICAL EXAMINATION: The patient is not oriented to time, place, person, or situation. He appears to be responding to internal stimuli. He hesitates for several moments before being able to answer questions. He has trouble retrieving information. Cranial Nerves I-XII are intact. Cranial Nerve I: The patient is able to detect peppermint. Cranial Nerves II, III, IV, and VI: See eye examination. Cranial Nerve V: Facial sensation and jaw strength are intact. Cranial Nerve VII: Facial movements are symmetrical. Cranial Nerve VIII: Auditory acuity is intact. Cranial Nerves IX and X: Swallow reflex is intact. Cranial Nerve XI: Symmetrical shoulder shrug. Cranial Nerve XII: Tongue is midline. The patient articulates well. Sensory Examination: Intact to touch, pinprick, and vibration in all extremities. Motor Examination: Gait is within normal limits. The patient has 5/5 muscle strength against resistance. He has reduced muscle bulk in all extremities secondary to muscle wasting. No abnormal movements, tics, or tremors. Cerebellar Examination: Romberg is negative. He is able to tandem gait walk. He performs rapid alternating movements of fingers very slowly. Deep Tendon Reflexes: Are all 2+ and symmetrical. Babinski Reflex: Toes are down going bilaterally.

ASSESSMENT/PLAN:
1.   Psychosis, question origin, question drug-induced psychosis.

        Plan: Refer to Dr. _____ for individual and group psychotherapy, and pharmacological intervention.

2.   History of intravenous drug use, as well as question of unsafe sexual practice. Have ordered hepatitis 2 panel, HIV testing with posttest counseling, a urine for GC and Chlamydia and RPR, and we will follow as needed.
3.   Weight loss. Have ordered a dietary consult, 8 ounces of Boost p.r.n. if patient eats less than 50% of his meals, and weekly weights.
4.   Tinea infection. Lotrimin cream, apply topically b.i.d.x7 days to lesions.
5.   Scoliosis. The patient needs to be established with a primary care provider following discharge.
6.   Psychosocial stressors. It is unclear about this young man's support network and lifestyle. Question if family is supportive. He also appears to be involved with peers who also are drug abusers. Plan: Refer to clinician.

THIS REPORT IS STRICTLY CONFIDENTIAL.
Redisclosure is prohibited by law.

NOTE: This information has been disclosed to you from records whose confidentiality is protected by federal law. Federal regulations
(42CFR part 2) prohibit you from making any further disclosure of it without the specific written consent of the person to whom it pertains,
or as otherwise permitted by such regulations. A general authorization for the release of medical or other information is NOT sufficient for
this purpose.

INPATIENT PROGRESS NOTE

PT NAME: HUNT WELCH, PETER
SEX: M
ADMIT DATE: 08/24/2000
DOB: 02/28/1980
DOS: 08/25/2000
SITE OF SVC: 3SOU

The patient came to doctor's group. He was distant,
detached, at times intrusive. Appearing disoriented
to time and situation. Not reacting when I explained
that he took another patient's belongings. Unchanged
loosening of associations and thought blocking. Vague
persecutory ideas. Possible perceptual disturbances.
Compliant with medications. Labs refused by the patient.

PLAN: Order MRI due to recent onset of confusion and
psychosis. Increase Risperdal to 2.5 twice a day.
Discontinue Valium protocol and start Ativan 1mg
q.i.d. p.r.n. A 24-hour recertification was filled
out. Monitor for psychosis and behavioral dyscontrol.
Engage gradually in the milieu.

THIS REPORT IS STRICTLY CONFIDENTIAL.
Redisclosure is prohibited by law.

D: 08/25/2000
T: 08/25/2000 14:04

INPATIENT PROGRESS NOTE

PT NAME: HUNT WELCH, PETER
SEX: M
ADMIT DATE: 08/24/2000
DOB: 02/28/1980
DOS: 08/28/2000
SITE OF SVC: 3SOU

The patient came to doctor's group. He was more
friendly and cooperative. Appearing oriented to place
and time as well as to person. Thought processes remaining tangential and loose. He expressed his concerns about taking away joy from people. Vague persecutory and referential thoughts. Maintaining good behavioral control. Compliant with his medications.
Normal CBC, CMP, and TSH reflex.

PLAN: Continue to closely monitor for psychosis. No
medication changes for now. Engage in milieu. Family
meeting coming up today.

THIS REPORT IS STRICTLY CONFIDENTIAL.
Redisclosure is prohibited by law.

D: 08/28/2000
T: 08/28/2000 17:12

INPATIENT PROGRESS NOTE

PT NAME: HUNT WELCH, PETER
SEX: M
ADMIT DATE: 08/24/2000
DOB: 02/28/1980
DOS: 08/29/2000
SITE OF SVC: 3SOU

He came to Doctor's Group. Significant improvement in
his psychotic condition. Less evidence of persecutory
and referential ideas. Alert and oriented to all dimensions. Speech is spontaneous, fluent, and focused.
Affect is euthymic. The patient is compliant with
medications and becoming quite active in the milieu.

PLAN: Increase to level 2. Continue with the current
medications. Pursue MRI and EEG. Engage in the milieu.

THIS REPORT IS STRICTLY CONFIDENTIAL.
Redisclosure is prohibited by law.

D: 08/29/2000
T: 08/29/2000 17:25

INPATIENT PROGRESS NOTE

PT NAME: HUNT WELCH, PETER
SEX: M
ADMIT DATE: 08/24/2000
DOB: 02/28/1980
DOS: 08/30/2000
SITE OF SVC: 3SOU

The patient was seen in doctor's group. He was pleasant and easily engaged. Good eye contact. Appropriate
interaction. He was stating that he feels much better. Sleep and appetite normalizing. Thought process
is much better organized and focused, given though at
times long lags and circumstantiality is present.
Thought processes do not show any evidence of overt
delusions. He denied perceptual disturbances.

PLAN: No medication changes. Pursue MRI and EEG. Engage in the milieu.

THIS REPORT IS STRICTLY CONFIDENTIAL.
Redisclosure is prohibited by law.

D: 08/30/2000
T: 08/30/2000 17:54

INPATIENT PROGRESS NOTE

PT NAME: HUNT WELCH, PETER
SEX: M
ADMIT DATE: 08/24/2000
DOB: 02/28/1980
DOS: 08/31/2000
SITE OF SVC: 3SOU

He was seen in Doctor's Group. He is continuing to improve in his cognition and psychosis. Minimal referential thinking. Thought process is quite logical and goal directed. Appearing to minimize the whole experience, and especially the use of street drugs. Wondering about discharge and his return to school. Appropriate and active in the milieu. Compliant with his medications and denying side effects.

PLAN: Continue with the current psychotropics. May go tonight on a pass with his parents. Also encourage a weekend pass and target discharge for the beginning of next week.

THIS REPORT IS STRICTLY CONFIDENTIAL.
Redisclosure is prohibited by law.

D: 08/31/2000
T: 08/31/2000 18:04

INPATIENT PROGRESS NOTE

PT NAME: HUNT WELCH, PETER
SEX: M
ADMIT DATE: 08/24/2000
DOB: 02/28/1980
DOS: 09/01/2000
SITE OF SVC: 3SOU

He was seen in Doctor's Group and on a one-to-one basis. Quite friendly and engaging. Making attempts to
integrate his unusual perceptual disturbances. No
evidence for overt delusional thinking. Denying suicidal or homicidal thoughts or plans. Cognitively intact.

PLAN: Continue with the current psychotropics. Weekend pass discussed with team and approved. Engage in
milieu and group therapy.

THIS REPORT IS STRICTLY CONFIDENTIAL.
Redisclosure is prohibited by law.

D: 09/01/2000
T: 09/01/2000 22:03

INPATIENT PROGRESS NOTE

PT NAME: HUNT WELCH, PETER
SEX: M
ADMIT DATE: 08/24/2000
DOB: 02/28/1980
DOS: 09/05/2000
SITE OF SVC: 3SOU

He was seen on a one-to-one basis on two occasions.
He explained that the weekend pass with his parents
went well. He was wondering about a discharge today.
A report stated that upon return from the pass, he
looked distractible, confused, and forgetful. At one
point, he left the water running in the bathroom. He
did not seem to remember the names of the patients
and staff. During the meeting, he appeared withdrawn
and initially hard to engage. Thought processes were
circumstantial and tangential. He would perseverate
on certain themes, especially related to the positive
experience having been on LSD. Even though he was
alert and oriented to person and place, he seemed to
have difficulty with the exact time frame. Later in
the morning, he was sent to Eastern Maine Medical
Center for an EEG. Afterwards, he eloped, taking one
of the cars from valet parking. He was brought back
in the afternoon by the police. He admitted having
used some marijuana and having gone to some classes
and to see his ethics teacher. At that time, he was
quite withdrawn, anxious, irritable, avoiding eye
contact, and appearing even more disorganized in his
thinking and behaviors.

PLAN: Pursue results of the EEG. Check a toxicology
screen, particularly for LSD. Order a prolactin level
to monitor compliance with Risperdal. Restrict the
patient to the unit for now and consider him an
elopement risk. Postpone scheduled discharge for now.

THIS REPORT IS STRICTLY CONFIDENTIAL.

Redisclosure is prohibited by law.

INPATIENT PROGRESS NOTE

PT NAME: HUNT WELCH, PETER
SEX: M
ADMIT DATE: 08/24/2000
DOB: 02/28/1980
DOS: 09/06/2000
SITE OF SVC: 3SOU

The patient was seen in the presence of the clinician. Looking withdrawn, anxious, subdued, with
avoidant eye contact. Speech hypophonic and with decreased productivity. Mood detached and affect anxious, labile. Thought processes remaining circumstantial and at times tangential. The patient having a
hard time remembering and putting the details of yesterday in perspective. Hard to engage on the unit.
Responding well to redirection.

PLAN: Pursue results of the toxicology screen, Prolactin level, EEG testing. No change in the dose of
Risperdal. Engage in the milieu.

THIS REPORT IS STRICTLY CONFIDENTIAL.
Redisclosure is prohibited by law.

D: 09/06/2000
T: 09/07/2000 12:18

INPATIENT PROGRESS NOTE

PT NAME: HUNT WELCH, PETER
SEX: M
ADMIT DATE: 08/24/2000
DOB: 02/28/1980
DOS: 09/07/2000
SITE OF SVC: 3SOU

The patient was seen in doctor's group. Somewhat more
friendly and talkative. Still moving around in a slow
manner. At times long lags before his answers. Affect
inappropriate. Thought processes with tangential elements. No clear-cut delusions. Denying perceptual
disturbances. Still quite unable to put into perspective the recent experience. Prolactin level is mildly
elevated to 29.3. EEG still not available

PLAN: Continue with the current psychotropics. Monitor for psychosis and cognitive difficulties.

THIS REPORT IS STRICTLY CONFIDENTIAL.
Redisclosure is prohibited by law.

D: 09/07/2000
T: 09/07/2000 21:33

INPATIENT PROGRESS NOTE

PT NAME: HUNT WELCH, PETER
SEX: M
ADMIT DATE: 08/24/2000
DOB: 02/28/1980
DOS: 09/08/2000
SITE OF SVC: 3SOU

He was seen in Doctor's Group and during a family meeting. More verbal, talkative, and engaging. Making the strong case that he feels much better and ready to go soon. Stating of the strong support he received at the university during his recent trip there. Stating his understanding about the need to maintain sobriety. Thought processes are somewhat more organized and focused, even though at times, circumstantial comments are present. He denies perceptual disturbances. Cognitively, he still had some time figuring out the exact date, but otherwise, no gross abnormalities were seen.

PLAN: Pursue special urine toxicology screen for hallucinogens. The results of EEG testing are not available. No change in the psychotropics.

THIS REPORT IS STRICTLY CONFIDENTIAL.
Redisclosure is prohibited by law.

D: 09/08/2000
T: 09/08/2000 17:14

INPATIENT PROGRESS NOTE

PT NAME: HUNT WELCH, PETER
SEX: M
ADMIT DATE: 08/24/2000
DOB: 02/28/1980
DOS: 09/11/2000
SITE OF SVC: 3SOU

This patient was seen in doctors' group appearing
very pleasant but withdrawn and anxious. He is in-
sisting on being discharged soon since I am doing
perfectly well. Improved grooming and eye contact. No
psychomotor agitation or retardation. Thought process
is linear and Goal directed. Occasional circumstantiality. No evidence for overt delusional elements. He
denied perceptual disturbances. Cognitively at baseline.

Interpretation of the EEG became available. It showed
the presence of left temporal intermittent theta
waves. The case was discussed with Dr. _____,
who stated the importance of reviewing the clinical
situation and the need for repeat EEG after at least
two or three months of sobriety.

PLAN: No change in medication regiment. Continued in-
volvement in the milieu. If condition continues to
improve, discharge by Wednesday.

THIS REPORT IS STRICTLY CONFIDENTIAL.
Redisclosure is prohibited by law.

D: 09/11/2000
T: 09/11/2000 19:17

INPATIENT PROGRESS NOTE

PT NAME: HUNT WELCH, PETER
SEX: M
ADMIT DATE: 08/24/2000
DOB: 02/28/1980
DOS: 09/13/2000
SITE OF SVC: 3SOU

He was seen in Doctor's Group. He was looking relaxed
and friendly. He had a good pass yesterday at the
university. He was able to see some friends and got
to one course. Feeling safe. Stating that his thinking is much clearer and efficient. Denying perceptual
disturbances. Thought processes are overall logical
and linear. No suicidality.

PLAN: Discharge the patient as scheduled. Follow up
through the university.

THIS REPORT IS STRICTLY CONFIDENTIAL.
Redisclosure is prohibited by law.

D: 09/13/2000
T: 09/13/2000 21:26

DISCHARGE SUMMARY

PT NAME: HUNT WELCH, PETER
SEX: M
ADMIT DATE: 08/24/2000
DOB: 02/28/1980
DISCH DATE:09/13/2000
ATT: _____
DICTATED BY: _____
DOS: 09/13/2000
SITE OF SVC: 3SOU

IDENTIFYING INFORMATION: Peter Hunt Welch is a 20-
year-old single Caucasian male who was residing in
Bar Harbor, Maine this summer. He is a University of
Maine at Orono student with no prior psychiatric history, who was admitted to the Acadia Hospital on an
involuntary basis due to an acute level of confusion
and disorganization, both behaviorally and cognitively. He was evaluated at MDI and was transferred
from that facility due to psychosis, impulsive
thoughts, delusions, and disorientation. He was felt
to be a risk to himself and others due to his high
level of disorganization and disorientation and impulsivity. He did not know where he was. He believed
that he had murdered his friend by _sucking out his
soul._ The patient was also reporting, upon admission, that he could see, smell, hear and touch God,
She has an acid smokey smell. At the time of admission, the patient's history was somewhat questionable, as he appeared rather unreliable. He initially
denied any alcohol or drug use, but later admitted
having had LSD on several occasions. He also acknowledged the use of heroin, crack cocaine, mushrooms,
ecstasy, speed, etc. Just prior to his admission to
Acadia Hospital, he had been displaying markedly abnormal behavior with confusions, illogical statements, and appearing disoriented, and as if _walking
in a daze._

TREATMENT SUMMARY/COURSE OF TREATMENT Condition At
Admission: Upon admission, Peter presented as a disheveled, withdrawn, guarded, and underweight young
Caucasian male. He had very poor eye contact, minimal
cooperation with the interview. There was significant
psychomotor retardation to the point of near catatonia. For prolonged periods of time during the interview, he would remain almost motionless with closed
eyes. When moving, he would do it extremely slowly.
His speech was spontaneous, fluent, hypophonic, and
monotone, without much inflection and minimal emotional content. His mood was detached, and affect
flat. Thought processes were with significant circumstantiality, tangentiality, and loosening of associations. At times, he was positive for thought blocking. His thought content was with vague delusions of
persecution. He had positive visual and auditory hallucinations. He denied in an inconsistent manner suicidal and homicidal thoughts or plans. His cognition
was difficult to assess because of poor compliance.
He appeared alert and oriented to person and place,
but not to time . when asked the date, he initially
replied_February 28, 1980,_ and then later on, _Janu-
ary 1, 2000._ capacity to focus, sustain and shift
attention, as well as the ability to present events
of the recent days in a sequential manner, were severely impaired. His insight and judgment were quite
poor.

Problems Addressed: During the patient's hospitalization, specific problems addressed included his psychosis and chemical dependency.

Treat Progress or Lack Thereof: Peter was admitted to
3 South, a locked inpatient psychiatric unit, where
he participated in individual, family, group, and milieu therapy. He was monitored for psychosis and cognitive difficulties. He had complete physical exam
and labs. He was started on Risperdal upon admission
at 1.5 mg b.i.d. an Thorazine 100 mg q.i.d. p.r.n. to

help with agitation, irritability, and explosive behavior. We initiated a Valium protocol and started on
multivitamins 1.q.d and thiamine 100mg q.d. During
the initial days of his hospitalization, the patient
remained very disorganized, agitated, pacing, going
into other patients' rooms, and attempting to leave
the unit several times. He was quite distant and detached. He appeared to be disoriented to time and
situation. There was unchanged loosening of associations and thought blocking. There was vague persecutory ideas and possible perceptual disturbances. He
initially reused to do any labs. An MRI was ordered
due to the onset of confusion and psychosis. Due his
significant confusion and disorganization, his
Risperdal was increased to 2.5 mg q.d. because of his
agitation, he was started on Ativan 1 mg q.i.d.
p.r.n. By August 28, 2000, the patient was beginning
to be more friendly and cooperative. He appeared to
be more oriented to time and place, as well as person. He continued, though, to have tangential and
loose thought processes, as well as vague persecutory
and referential thoughts. He began being more focused
in conversation, and his behavior was less intrusive.
There appeared to be significant improvement in his
psychotic condition, less evidence for persecutory
and referential ideas. He was alert and oriented, and
his speech was becoming more spontaneous, fluent, and
focused. His affect was becoming more euthymic. His
sleep and appetite began normalizing, and by August
30, 2000, his thought processes did not exhibit any
evidence of overt delusions, and he was denying any
perceptual disturbances. His cognition and psychosis
appeared to continually improve, with minimal referential thinking. The difficulty was that Peter appeared to minimize his whole experience, especially
the use of street drugs. He was quite focused on discharge, and wanting to return to school otherwise, he
was quite appropriate and active in the milieu. He
was compliant with his medications and was denying
any side effects. We began initiating therapeutic

passes with his parents in order to allow him to test
his skills in a less restrictive environment with the
target discharge for September 5, 2000, after his
sleep-deprived EEG. However, the patient did go on a
pass on Monday, September 4, 2000, when staff reported upon his return he appeared much more disorganized and confused. The patent reported on his return that he _had a beautiful day, went for a sail,
saw an old girlfriend, played piano, went to France._
It was also noted that later in the shift his behavior became even more erratic; for example, taking
peers' belongings, picking up staffs' check boards
and starting to complete them. The patient was questioned as to what he may have _taken_on pass, and at
first he laughed, saing_heroin,_ but then later denied it. He appeared to be very lethargic with no
change in his pupils. His pulse at 2130 on September
4, 2000, was 72. No specific physical complaints. Dr.
_____ ordered a urine and serum drug screen. We
discussed withholding his discharge a few days due to
his decompensation. He left for his EEG, and we were
notified later that morning that he had eloped. Involuntary hospitalization process was initiated. Apparently, during the patient's leave, he allegedly
took a car from the valet parking area at Easter Main
Medical Center and drove to the University of Main at
Orono, where he is a student. He was picked up by the
police and returned to Acadia Hospital. At that time,
he continued to present as very confused and disorganized. He did acknowledge at that time that he did
smoke marijuana when he was out on an absence without
leave, but then later retracted that, denying that he
had. Throughout his stay, he exhibited little, to no,
insight into the extent and severity of his drug use.
He tended to talk about his drug experiences in a
somewhat positive manner. After his return, he patient continued to look withdrawn and anxious, subdued, and had avoidant eye contact. His speech was
hypophonic with decreased productivity. His mood
again appeared detached, and his affect was anxious

and labile. His thought processes were remaining circumstantial and, at times, tangential. The patient
again began to start clearing cognitively. He was
less confused and disorganized. He attempted to rationalize his behavior and thought processes, especially related to his comments that appeared to be
somewhat confused and disorganized. He began talking
more about understanding the need to maintain sobriety. His thought processes were somewhat more organized and focused, even tough at times circumstantial
comments were present. He would deny any perceptual
disturbances. There were no gross abnormalities. We
pursued a special urine toxicology screen for hallucinogens because of a concern that he may have re-
lapsed. His grooming began to improve, as well as his
eye contact. There was no psychomotor agitation or
retardation noted by discharge. His thought process
was more linear and goal directed, although occasional circumstantiality continued. There was no
overt delusional thinking, and he denied any perceptual disturbances. Overall, by discharge the patient
was less disorganized and confused. He was able to
uphold a long-term conversation and maintained focus
without any loosening of associations. He exhibited
more insight into the need to maintain sobriety. He
was denying any depression or anxiety. He was also
denying any thoughts of self-harm or harm to others.

PHYSICAL FINDINGS: During Peter's hospitalization, he
had a medical history and physical assessment with
_____, APRN, on August 24, 2000. The patient re-
ported allergies to dust, pollen, cats, and dogs.
Upon admission, the patient reported a history of intravenous drug use, as well as a question of unsafe
sexual practices. Hepatitis 2 panel was ordered, as
well as HIV testing, with post testing counseling; a
urine for GC and Chlamydia, and RPR, with followup as
needed. The patient was ordered a dietary consul due
to significant weight loss. Boost 8 ounces as needed
was ordered if the patient ate less than 50% of his

meals. He had tinea infection and was ordered Lotrimin cream which was to be applied topically b.i.d.
x7 days to his lesions. The patient also has scoliosis and needed to be established with a primary care
provider following discharge. No other significant
findings were obtained during this hospitalization.

SUMMARY OF LABORATORIES: The patient had a hematol-
ogy, which was within normal limits. A routine chemistry was within normal limits, as well as his TSH. A
microbiology RPR was nonreactive. His toxicology was
positive for nicotine. His microbiology STD was negative. His urine drug was normal. Serum drug was also
normal. Hallucinogen panel was sent out of state, but
the results were still pending at discharge. He was
HIV tested negative. His protein, enzyme, hormone,
Prolactin level was 29.3, although this did not require any medical followup as it was related to his
Risperdal.

OTHER DIAGNOSTIC TESTS: The patient had an MRI, which
was essentially negative. His cranial CT, there were
2 minute punctuate high T2 signal foci in the left
high parietal white matter, given their morphology,
small number and small size, it was believed that
they were incidental, benign, and not clinically significant. Please refer to the dictated report for
more in-depth information. The patient also had an
EEG during his hospitalization. The impression was
that it was an abnormal awakened sleep EEG for the
patient's age. The presence of left temporal beta activity intermittently, while not consistent with an
epileptiform process, may be suggestive of such. A
24-hour ambulatory EEG would help to further clarify
the significance of these discharges. The case was
discussed with Dr. _____, who stated the importance of reviewing the clinical situation and the
need for a repeat EEG after at least 2 to 3 months of
sobriety. Please refer to the dictated report for
more in-depth information.

CONSULTANTS' REPORTS: During the patient's hospitalization, he had a Occupational Therapy screening that
indicated his ACL was 5.0, on August 29, 2000. This
would be indicative of him having some difficulty at
home and work secondary to his inability to antici-
pate and avoid errors. He would most likely use a
trial and error approach, and may not always be successful. He does have the ability to transfer skills
from one setting to another, but may need assistance
to transfer skills to a new setting. He has minimal
difficulties with concentration and attention span.
He is able to comprehend verbal and written direc-
tions. Impairments are in memory and problem solving,
and he may not always look at the whole picture. However, it is important to bear in mind this is during
the patient's psychotic episode, and his AVL may improve as his psychosis continues to improve.

CONDITION AT TIME OF DISCHARGE Mental Status Examination: At discharge, the patient reported that he was
I'm fine, doing good today. He denied any depression or anxiety. He denied any suicidal or homicidal
ideation, intention, or plan. The patient was anxious
to be discharged, and although he had to wait several
hours later than anticipated for his ride, he was
bale to appropriately manage himself. He was cooperative and his affect was bright, and his mood was more
euthymic. The patient was denying any perceptual disturbances. His eye contact was good. He did not exhibit any psychomotor agitation or retardation at
discharge. His thought process was linear. He was
very goal directed. There was no evidence of overt
delusional elements.

DISCHARGE MEDICATION: Risperidone 1 mg tablet for a
total of 2.5 mg. q.a.m. and q.p,m,

DISCHARGE DIAGNOSES
AXIS I: Psychosis, not otherwise specified.

Rule out LSD-induced psychosis.
LSD and cannabis abuse.
AXIS II: Deferred.
AXIS III:
1. Status post Tonsillectomy.
2. History of multiple sinus infections.
AXIS IV: Moderate to severe, including family arguments, recent relationship breakup.
AXIS V: Global Assessment of Functioning current at discharge 65 to 70.

TREATMENT RECOMMENDATIONS FOR FOLLOWUP CARE
Patient's Strengths: The patient has very supportive parents. He is attending college, and appears to have a significant social and familial support system.

Barriers to Treatment: None identified at this time.

RECOMMENDATIONS FOR THERAPY OR PROGRAMS: It is recommended that Peter continue to be closely followed by a psychiatrist due to the significance of his psychosis. He would also benefit from alcohol and drug treatment, as well as individual therapy for close monitoring.

FOLLOWUP APPOINTMENTS: The patient has a followup appointment through the Cutler Health Center at the University of Maine at Orono, on Thursday, September 14, 2000, at 1 p.m. He will meet with a therapist at that time, and will be connected with mental health services, particularly a psychiatrist, after that intake evaluation. He an also obtain his medical appointments through the Cutler Health Center, as well. His safety plan was reviewed. He was provided with the 24-hour crisis response number. He was advised to restrict access to guns, and he was also instructed that he should not drive at this time, and that his ability to drive be reevaluated in 3 to 4 weeks by his outpatient psychiatrist.

THIS REPORT IS STRICTLY CONFIDENTIAL.
Redisclosure is prohibited by law.

D: 09/14/2001
T: 09/15/2011 11:49

BANGOR INTIAL EVALUATION

PT NAME: HUNT WELCH, PETER
SEX: M
ADMIT DATE: 10/18/2000
DOB: 02/28/1980
DISCH DATE:
ATT: _____
DICTATED BY: _____
DOS: 10/18/2000
SITE OF SVC:

IDENTIFYING INFORMATION: Peter Welch was referred by
Dr. _____ from the emergency room at Eastern
Maine Medical Center, as well as the client's mother,
Barbara Welch for a psychiatric evaluation at The
Acadia Hospital. The client is a 20-year-old single
white male from Hancock Point. He was accompanied by
himself today. Sources referenced for this interview
were a patient Information Form on October 16, 2000,
a discharge summary dictated by _____, date of
service September 13, 2000, and also the client himself.

CHIEF COMPLAINT/HISTORY OF PRESENT ILLNESS: Peter reports that approximately 6 weeks ago he dropped acid
with a friend then went and wrecked a store and was
taken to a hospital. After that point, Peter went to
Massachusetts, and had not slept significantly and
began to use acid in Massachusetts, as well. He
stated this went on for approximately 2 weeks. At
that point he reports becoming delusional, thinking
that he was _God, a secret agent and an android sent
to the future._ He states that he had delusions of
conspiracies and the occult and he thought that his
friend Jake was dead and that he killed him. He
states that he returned to Maine and essentially wandered around and took some odd jobs. At one point be
began to believe that he was a fish and attempted to
swim in the Atlantic Ocean, however, got too cold and

swam back to the pier. He began to experience visual
hallucinations in which everything was a _glass bowl_
and he experienced a blurred periphery. He states
that time slowed. He believes that at that point he
began to lose control and was having difficulty hiding his symptoms. He believed that it was a combination of sleep deprivation and also the acid that he
took. He presented to the Bar Harbor hospital and
quoted to them that he was doing every drug in the
book and that he believed he had killed someone. He
states that he did not stay there and that he walked
out, and that his mom picked him up and took him
home. When he got there he took 3 of her Progesterone
because _they were there._ He continued to have difficulty with sleep. He then took his mother's car and
broke into someone's truck. At that point the police
were called who took him back to the Bar Harbor hospital. He states that he also believed that he was
the living dead, and his job was to _get people to
quit smoking_. He subsequently was admitted to The
Acadia Hospital. While obtaining an EEG he evidently
eloped and stole a car from the parking lot. He
states that he was experiencing a delusion to _become
a taxi driver and to go and do good deeds._ He was
stabilized inpatient on Risperdal, however, he reports that he was _just as crazy when he left as when
he went in._ His current medications include Risperdal 1.5 mg in the morning and 2.5 mg at bedtime. His
current providers include Dr. _____ as a primary
care provider, and he does not currently have a psychiatrist.

PAST PSYCHIATRIC HISTORY: Peter reports no previous
psychiatric hospitalizations and no previous psychiatric treatment. He states that he has never been on
psychiatric medications before. He denies ever having
suicidal ideation or attempt. He denies any use of
guns. He denies any self-mutilation, any homicide attempt, and assault history. He denies any trauma history.

SUBSTANCE ABUSE HISTORY: Peter states that approximately 3 years ago he began using acid and has used it subsequently 6 times to present. His last known use was 5 to 6 weeks ago, previous to his admission here at The Acadia Hospital. He began using marijuana 3 years ago and has had bouts in which he has used it daily, and also episodes of using it sporadically. He states that 3 years ago he has also initiated mushrooms and has used those approximately 4 times to present. He states that he is an occasional drinker. Currently he states that the government is requiring that he get drug testing so he has been clean based on that. He states that he does have a probation officer.

MEDICAL HISTORY: Peter reports he has an allergy to antibiotics. However, he was unable to tell me the specific one. His current primary care provider is Dr. _____ in Ellsworth. He has one previous head injury at the age of 4 in which he hit his head on concrete and reportedly had lost consciousness. To his recollection he did not get treatment at the emergency room as he did not inform his parents that this had occurred. He denied any significant illnesses as a child. He has had his tonsils out. There are no physical barriers to treatment identified.

DEVELOPMENTAL HISTORY: He was born in San Francisco. He is currently living with his mother and brother. His brother is 16 years old. His father is living in Augusta as that is where his place of employment is.

SOCIAL HISTORY: Peter enjoys reading, writing, bike riding and tennis. He does not identify any religious denomination. He does not currently have a partner. He is currently living with his mother. He does have legal issues of stealing the car and he is due to go to court on Friday.

FAMILY HISTORY: Peter is unmarried. He does not have any children. He denies any family history of mental illness including depression, anxiety, bipolar disorder, drug use, etc.

EDUCATIONAL HISTORY: Peter most recently dropped out of college as he was stating that the medication was causing him to be mentally dulled and making it difficult for him to concentrate. At that time he had no declared major. His goal is to become a writer.

VOCATIONAL HISTORY: He is currently unemployed.

MENTAL STATUS EXAMINATION: Peter is a thin and fairly well-groomed white male. He has a long dark Army jacket on and approximately 20 to 30 beaded bracelets on each wrist. He has a goatee, his hair is blond. Peter's eye contact is intermittent throughout the interview. He is noted to be pleasant and cooperative. His posture is open and relaxed. His speech is somewhat hushed in volume but is of regular rate and rhythm. His thought process is clear, goal focused and sequential. There is no evidence of any delusional content, no grandiosity, no persecutory delusions, no auditory or visual hallucinations, and he denies all of those. There is no evidence of paranoia. His fund of knowledge appears to be good. He appears to be above-average intelligence. His thought process is clear, goal focused and sequential. His insight and judgment appears to be intact. He appears to be a reliable historian today.

PATIENT STRENGTHS: He reportedly has a supportive family. He has an insurance, and he is willing to seek outpatient treatment. Also, because of drug testing, he is abstaining from substances.

FORMULATION/SUMMARY: based on the past psychiatric history that Peter has given, it is very likely that this was drug-induced psychosis directly correlated to his acid use. It is also likely that because of the acid use he had severe sleep deprivation, which incurred delusional thinking and auditory and visual hallucinations. At that time he was believed to be a danger to himself. Peter has been stabilized on antipsychotic medication and has obtained good sleep, per his report. He is hesitant to continue utilizing this medication as he is experiencing the muscle spasms that accompany the Risperdal. He is clear that he does not want to take a medication that would reverse those side effects as he _does not like taking medications._ It is highly likely that he is feeling mentally dulled from Risperdal and we are fairly confident that this psychosis was directly related to illicit drug use.

PROGNOSIS: Fair pending that people is able to stay away from illicit drugs. The likelihood of any future psychosis is minimal based on his ability to abstain.

TREATMENT GOALS: Abstaining from illicit drugs and a return to his school environment.

BARRIERS TO TREATMENT: Intermittent substance abuse.

DIAGNOSIS:
AXIS I: Substance induced psychosis.
AXIS II: Deferred.
AXIS III: None.
AXIS IV: Psychosocial Stressors: Mild to moderate.
AXIS V: Global Assessment of Functioning: Current 65.

TREATMENT RECCOMENDATIONS: At this time we will decrease Peter's Risperdal to 2 mg at bedtime only. We are fairly confident that this was a drug-induced psychosis, therefore the likelihood of continuing need for an antipsychotic is minimal. However, we are hesitant to discontinue it abruptly for fear of any rebound symptoms. Also, because Peter is experiencing muscle spasms and is unwilling to take some Cogentin

to assist him with this, we will decrease the dose to
see if this alleviates the side effects that he is
experiencing.

It is likely that when Peter goes to court he will be
mandated to have random drug testing and also to par-
ticipate in some sort of drug treatment, and this may
be the means to have him abstain from illicit drug
use. We have provided a letter today for Peter to
take with him to court stating that he is under the
care of a psychiatrist for medication management. A
followup appointment was scheduled in 2 weeks time to
ascertain the effectiveness of intervention. Also, we
will assess for any residual or resurfacing psychotic
symptoms. If there are none, the likelihood that we
could discontinue Risperdal is good.

THIS REPORT IS STRICTLY CONFIDENTIAL.
Redisclosure is prohibited by law.

D: 10/18/2000
T: 10/22/2000 12:59

BANGOR PROGRESS NOTE

PT NAME: HUNT WELCH, PETER
SEX: M
ADMIT DATE: 10/31/2000
DOB: 02/28/1980
DISCH DATE:
ATT: _____
DICTATED BY: _____
DOS: 10/31/2000
SITE OF SVC:

CLINICIAN: _____, RNC.

ATTENDING PHYSICIAN: _____, MD.

TYPE OF SERVICE: This was a 30- minute medication management session provided by _____, RNC, and _____, MD

SUBJECTIVE: Peter reports that be decreasing the Risperdal, he did have less pain in his muscles and legs. He states that his thinking remains clear and is reporting that he is experiencing what my be a depression. He described anhedonia, anergia, hypersomnia, and apathy. He states that this may be because he is living in his parents' home and he is not currently at school in a more social environment. He did go to court and they have given him a year's probation and he is subjected to random drug testing. Because of this, he has remained sober. He has questioned the possibility of utilizing an antidepressant, as he has had depressions before; however, he is clear that he does not want to utilize Zoloft or Prozac. He has heard good things about Paxil and may consider that. We did discuss many medications options and I did provide medication education in regards to Paxil, Wellbutrin, and Celexa. Peter is receptive to the possibility of utilizing one in the future. We also discussed that he is currently seeing two psychiatrists and that is concerning to us. He had a followup appointment with his psychiatrist from the school. It may be his plan in the future that he will seek services from this individual. However, in the meantime, medication management will be done via our office, per Peter's request.

OBJECTIVE: Current medications include Risperdal 2 mg at bedtime. Peter reports to this appointment on time. He is alert and oriented x3. his speech is of regular rate, rhythm, and volume. His posture is open and relaxed. His thought process is clear, goal focused, and sequential. There is no evidence of delusions. There is no paranoia noted. His memory is intact for immediate, recent, and remote. His concentration is adequate. He denies any suicidal or homicidal ideation.

ASSESSMENT: Peter is seen in the clinic for drug-induced psychosis. It is clear that there is no psychotic symptomology seen today. It is possible that the remaining Risperdal 2 mg is causing an apathetic presentation, or in fact, we could be dealing with _____* depression. As opposed to making two different changes and not being able to recognize which is most effective, we have agreed as a team to simply the intervention process today.

PLAN: In consultation with Dr. _____, we will discontinue the Risperdal today. Per Peter's request he will come back in two weeks' time to ascertain if that was effective in alleviating his apathetic mood. If not, then we will consider utilizing either Celexa or Wellbutrin, per our educational discussion today.

THIS REPORT IS STRICTLY CONFIDENTIAL.
Redisclosure is prohibited by law.

D: 10/31/2000
T: 10/31/2000 14:34

BANGOR PROGRESS NOTE

PT NAME: HUNT WELCH, PETER
SEX: M
ADMIT DATE: 11/21/2000
DOB: 02/28/1980
DISCH DATE:
ATT: _____
DICTATED BY: _____
DOS: 11/21/2000
SITE OF SVC:

TYPE OF SERVICE: This was a 30- minute medication
management session provided by _____, RNC,
and _____, MD

SUBJECTIVE: Peter reports that he is experiencing a
level of depression. He reports that his symptoms include amotivation, anhedonia, hypersomnolence, and
anergia. He has fleeting thoughts of suicidal ideation with no plan and no intent. He states that at
times he has had episodes of depression that have
lasted for a significant period of time before re-
lenting. He has never been treated for depression via
medication. When asked by Dr. _____ for a bipolar disorder history, he does not endorse any
euphoria, any risk taking behaviors, excessive spending, gambling, hypersexuality, etc. Peter has clearly
thought out what medications we have discussed in the
past and has approached us today with initiating one
of those medications for treatment.

OBJECTIVE: Current medications: None. Peter reports
to this appointment on time. He is alert and oriented
x3. He is well groomed and dressed appropriately for
the season. His affect and mood are dysthymic. His
speech is of regular rate, rhythm, and volume. His
thought process is clear, goal focused, and sequential. He has remained sober due to probation. His attention span is adequate. His memory is intact for

immediate, recent, and remote. His insight and judgment are intact. He denies any suicidal or homicidal ideation.

ASSESSMENT: Peter is seen in this clinic for a drug induced psychosis; however, at this point we also need to rule out major depression, recurrent, based on his subjective history. We have reviewed many medications with Peter and to enhance medication compliance, we have given him two options that include Celexa and Wellbutrin. The biggest indicator for him will be the side-effect profile.

PLAN: In consultation with Dr. _____ and after a discussion with Peter, today we will initiate Wellbutrin SR 100 mg p.o. q.a.m. x7 days, then increase to b.d.d. and continue. A prescription was dispensed for #60, with one refill. A follow-up appointment was scheduled in one month with the covering doctor and myself. Instructions, risks, and benefits were described to Peter and he did consent to treatment. Also today, consents were signed for his new primary care physician, _____, MD, and also for his probation officer in Ellsworth.

THIS REPORT IS STRICTLY CONFIDENTIAL.
Redisclosure is prohibited by law.

D: 11/21/2000
T: 11/24/2000 01:31

BANGOR DISCHARGE SUMMARY

PT NAME: HUNT WELCH, PETER
SEX: M
ADMIT DATE: 01/09/2001
DOB: 02/28/1980
DISCH DATE:
ATT: _____
DICTATED BY: _____
DOS: 01/09/2001
SITE OF SVC:

TYPE OF SERVICE: this was a 30-minute medication management session/discharge summary provided by
_____, RNC and Dr. _____.

IDENTIFYING INFORMATION: Peter Welch was admitted to
the ambulatory services clinic in October 2000, after
having a significant psychotic break after utilizing
alternative substance, i.e. acid. His symptoms included delusional thinking, grandiosity, insomnia,
after utilizing acid. We saw Peter briefly in this
clinic and upon admission he was not seen to have any
significant psychotic symptomatology as he had been
stabilized on medications. He had been on the inpatient unit of 3-South from August 24, 2000. At the
time of discharge, his medications were as follows:
Risperdal 2.5 mg b.i.d. when Peter reported to this
appointment he was pretty clear that he did not wish
to continue taking medications and that he felt that
the medications were mentally dulling him. We slowly
titrated Peter's Risperdal until it was discontinued
and no psychotic symptomatology returned. On November
21, 2000, Peter reported symptoms of depression,
which included anhedonia, anergia, and iolation, and
he requested a trial of an antidepressant as we had
previously discussed medications for depression in
the past. He was in agreement to take Wellbutrin SR
100 mg b.i.d., and this was in fact ordered. He reports to this appointment stating that he did not

continue with that as he believes that it was clearly related to situations, i.e., living with his parents, not being in school, and most recently one of his friends has been in the area, and this has been mood lifting for him. Peter is going to be returning to the University of Maine in Orono in his sophomore year and will be living on the campus. We have had discussions throughout Peter's treatment as to who would be prescribing medications or following him in lieu of his attendance to the University of Maine in Orono. He has been very clear that he does not believe that he needs any medication and he will be seeking the psychiatric services at the University of Maine in Orono campus. He does have a primary care physician, Dr_____, who he will seek out if in fact he needs medications prescribed. He is clear today that he wishes to discontinue services with us.

MENTAL STATUS EXAMINATION: Peter reports to this appointment on time. He is well groomed and dressed appropriately for the season. His affect and mood are both stable. His speech is of regular rate, rhythm and volume. His thought process is clear, goal focused and sequential. His attention span is adequate. He denies any psychotic symptomatology. He has not used substances _I'm on probation and I don't want to go to jail._ He drinks on occasion. His insight and judgment are intact. He denies any suicidal ideation.

ASSESSMENT: Peter was seen in this clinic for a drug-induced psychosis, which we believe has resolved. His symptoms have been stable despite a titration and discontinuation of the atypical antipsychotic. It is possible that Peter will use substances after his probation is over. However, he has been advised of the indications that should he do that that the likelihood is there that he may again have a psychotic episode.

FORMATION/PLAN: Today in consultation with Dr
_____, we will officially discontinue Peter from
the clinic. No medications were prescribed as he is
not currently taking any, and he will seek services
through the University of Maine campus and will continue with Dr. _____ as his primary care provider. No followup appointment was scheduled. Today
his chart will be officially closed.

THIS REPORT IS STRICTLY CONFIDENTIAL.
Redisclosure is prohibited by law.

D: 09/11/2001
T: 01/11/2011 13:35

Bibliography and Further Reading

Since this is mostly a memoir, and not so much a journalistic or research endeavor, the bibliography is fairly sparse. I hit the books to get some background and alternate viewpoints on psychedelics and theories of the brain and consciousness, and to correct my assumptions about LSD in particular, since the college LSD community is an endless labyrinth of misinformation.

Some of these sources are not directly quoted or referenced in the text, but all of them had a direct influence on my understanding of the brain and consciousness before and after my swim with madness. I recommend them all to anyone who wants to be even more confused about what's going on in their heads.

Alpert, Richard, and Sidney Cohen. *LSD*. New York: New American Library, 1966.

Austin, James H. *Zen and the Brain: Toward an Understanding of Meditation and Consciousness*. Cambridge: MIT Press, 1999.

Balleine, Bernard W., Mauricio R. Delgado, and Okihide Hikosaka. "The Role of the Dorsal Striatum in Reward and Decision-Making." *Journal of Neuroscience* 27 (2007): 8161–65.

Block, Ned, Owen Flanagan, and Güven Güzeldere, eds. *The Nature of Consciousness: Philosophical Debates*. Cambridge: MIT Press, 1998.

Eco, Umberto. *Kant and the Platypus*. New York: Harvest, 2000.

Grof, Stanislav. *LSD: Doorway to the Numinous*. Rochester: Park Street, 2009.

Grugle, Nancy Lynn. "Understanding the Effects of Sleep Deprivation on Executive Awareness on Executive Function, Complex
Task Performance and Situation Awareness." PhD diss., Vir-
ginia Polytechnic Institute and State University, 2005.

Guttenplan, Samuel, ed. *A Companion to the Philosophy of Mind*.
Cambridge: Blackwell, 1996.

Hagewoud, Roelina, et al. "Coping with Sleep Deprivation: Shifts
in Regional Brain Activity and Learning Strategy." *Sleep* 33
(2010): 1465–73.

Hawkins, Jeff, with Sandra Blakeslee. *On Intelligence*. New York: St.
Martin's Griffin, 2005.

Helm, Els van der, Ninad Gujar, and Matthew P. Walker. "Sleep
Deprivation Impairs the Accurate Recognition of Human
Emotions." *Sleep* 33 (2010): 335–42.

Hintzen, Annelie, and Torsten Passie. *The Pharmacology of LSD: A
Critical Review*. New York: Oxford University Press, 2010.

Hofmann, Albert. *LSD: My Problem Child*. Santa Cruz: MAPS,
2009.

Hofstadter, Douglas. *Gödel, Escher, and Bach: An Eternal Golden
Braid*. New York: Basic, 1979.

Huxley, Aldous. *The Doors of Perception and Heaven and Hell*. New
York: Harper Perennial, 2004.

Jaynes, Julian. *The Origin of Consciousness in the Breakdown of the
Bicameral Mind*. New York: Mariner, 2000.

Larson, Molly K., Elaine F. Walker, and Michael T. Compton.
"Early Signs, Diagnosis and Therapeutics of the Prodromal
Phase of Schizophrenia and Related Psychotic Disorders." *Ex-
pert Review Neurotherapeutics* 10 (2010): 1347–59.

Leary, Timothy, Ralph Metzner, and Richard Alpert. *The Psychedelic
Experience: A Manual Based on the Tibetan Book of the Dead*.
New York: Citadel, 2007.

Lee, Martin A., and Bruce Shlain. *Acid Dreams: The Complete Social
History of LSD: The CIA, The Sixties, and Beyond*. New York:
Grove Weidenfeld, 1992.

Pinchbeck, Daniel. *Breaking Open the Head: A Psychedelic Journey
into the Heart of Contemporary Shamanism*. New York: Broad-
way, 2003.

Pinker, Steven. *How the Mind Works*. New York: W. W. Norton, 1999.

———. *The Stuff of Thought: Language as a Window into Human Nature*. New York: Penguin, 2008.

Price, Gary, et al. "Brain Pathology in First-Episode Psychosis: Magnetization Transfer Imaging Provides Additional Information to MRI Measurements of Volume Loss." *Neuroimage* 49 (2010): 185–92.

Sacks, Oliver. *The Man Who Mistook His Wife for a Hat and Other Clinical Tales*. New York: Summit, *1985*.

Schultz, Mitch, dir. *DMT: The Spirit Molecule*. Spectral Alchemy, 2010.

Shea, Robert, and Robert Anton Wilson. *The Illuminatus! Trilogy*. New York: Dell, 1984.

Taber, Katherine H., and Robin A. Hurley. "Functional Neuroanatomy of Sleep and Sleep Deprivation." *Journal of Neuropsychiatry and Clinical Neurosciences* 18 (2006): 1–5.

Tucker, Adrienne M., et al. "Effects of Sleep Deprivation on Dissociated Components of Executive Functioning." *Sleep* 33 (2010): 47–57.

Wikipedia. "Sleep Deprivation." Accessed February 8, 2012, 16:17 GMT. http://en.wikipedia.org/wiki/Sleep_deprivation.

Wolfe, Tom. *The Electric Kool-Aid Acid Test*. New York: Bantam, 1999.

Wright, Tony, and Graham Gynn. *Left in the Dark*. N.p.: Kaleidos, 2007.

. . . and, finally, if you're looking for more stories or information about drugs, go to erowid.org.

CPSIA information can be obtained at www.ICGtesting.com
Printed in the USA
BVOW07s1049160614

356493BV00005B/420/P

9 780985 318130